NATIONAL GEOGRAPHIC

TRAVELER
Beijing

NATIONAL GEOGRAPHIC

TRAVELER
Beijing

Paul Mooney
Photography by Catherine Karnow

National Geographic
Washington, D.C.

Contents

How to use this guide 6–7 About the author & photographer 8
The areas 65–236 Travelwise 237–266
Index 267–270 Credits 270–271

Page 1: Local peaches
Pages 2–3: Forbidden City
Left: Strolling along
Wangfujing

How to use this guide

See back flap for keys to text and map symbols

The *National Geographic Traveler* brings you the best of Beijing and nearby excursions in text, pictures, and maps. Divided into three main sections, the guide begins with an overview of history and culture. Following are eight area chapters with featured sites selected by the author for their particular interest and treated in depth. Each chapter opens with its own contents list for easy reference.

The regions, and sites within them, are arranged geographically. A map introduces each region, highlighting the featured sites. Walks and a bike ride, plotted on their own maps, suggest routes for discovering an area. Features and sidebars offer detail on history, culture, or contemporary life. A More Places to Visit page generally rounds off each chapter.

The final section, Travelwise, lists essential information for the traveler—pre-trip planning, getting around, communications, money matters, and emergencies—plus a selection of hotels, restaurants, shops, and entertainment.

To the best of our knowledge, site information is accurate as of the press date. However, it's always advisable to call ahead.

Color coding

116

Each region is color coded for easy reference. Find the region you want on the map on the front flap, and look for the color flash at the top of the pages of the relevant chapter. Information in **Travelwise** is also color coded to each region.

Temple of Heaven

🅰 115 B1–B2

✉ Yongdingmen Dongjie (south gate)

☎ 010/6702 8866

💲 $ (extra fee for Yuanqiu & Qinian Dian)

🚌 Bus: 2 or 35 to Tiantan Ximen; 36, 53, 120, or 122 to Tiantan Nanmen

Visitor information

for major sites is listed in the side columns (see key to symbols on back flap). The map reference gives the page and grid where the site is mapped. Other details are the address, telephone number, entrance fee ranging from $ (under $5) to $$$$$ (over $25), and the nearest metro stop or transportation options. Visitor information for smaller sites is provided within the text. Admission fees are based on the prices foreigners pay.

Hotel and restaurant prices

An explanation of the price bands used in entries is given in the Hotels & restaurants section beginning on p. 246.

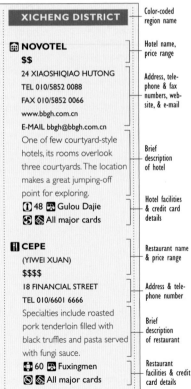

TRAVELWISE

XICHENG DISTRICT — Color-coded region name

🏨 **NOVOTEL**
$$ — Hotel name, price range

24 XIAOSHIQIAO HUTONG
TEL 010/5852 0088
FAX 010/5852 0066
www.bbgh.com.cn
E-MAIL bbgh@bbgh.com.cn — Address, telephone & fax numbers, website, & e-mail

One of few courtyard-style hotels, its rooms overlook three courtyards. The location makes a great jumping-off point for exploring. — Brief description of hotel

ℹ 48 🚇 Gulou Dajie
💳 🚫 All major cards — Hotel facilities & credit card details

🍴 **CEPE**
(YIWEI XUAN)
$$$$ — Restaurant name & price range

18 FINANCIAL STREET
TEL 010/6601 6666 — Address & telephone number

Specialties include roasted pork tenderloin filled with black truffles and pasta served with fungi sauce. — Brief description of restaurant

🍽 60 🚇 Fuxingmen
💳 🚫 All major cards — Restaurant facilities & credit card details

AREA MAPS

District name

Other point of interest

Important point of interest

- A locator map accompanies each area map and shows the location of that area in the city.

WALKING MAPS

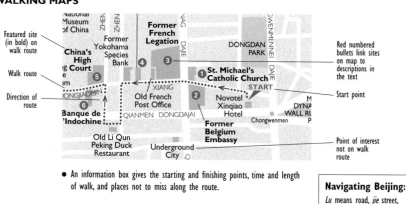

Featured site (in bold) on walk route

Walk route

Direction of route

Red numbered bullets link sites on map to descriptions in the text

Start point

Point of interest not on walk route

- An information box gives the starting and finishing points, time and length of walk, and places not to miss along the route.

Navigating Beijing:
Lu means road, *jie* street, *xiang* lane, and *hutong* alley. North is *bei*, East *dong*, south *nan*, west *xi*, and center, *zhong*. Frequently these are combined as in *donglu*. Odd or even numbers can be on either side of the street.

EXCURSION MAPS

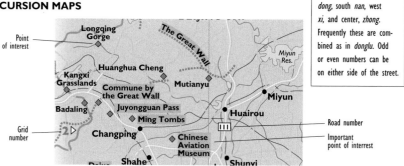

Point of interest

Grid number

Road number

Important point of interrest

- Towns and sites described in the Excursions chapters are highlighted in gray on the map. Other suggested places to visit are shown with a red diamond symbol.

NATIONAL GEOGRAPHIC

TRAVELER
Beijing

About the author & photographer

Paul Mooney, an American freelance journalist, has reported on China, Taiwan, and Hong Kong since 1985, contributing articles to leading publications around the world, including *Newsweek, Far Eastern Economic Review, International Herald Tribune, South China Morning Post, San Francisco Chronicle,* and the *Asian Wall Street Journal.* He is also the author and editor of more than a dozen travel books on Taiwan and China. Paul has been living in Beijing with his wife and two daughters since 1994.

San Francisco–based photographer **Catherine Karnow** was born and raised in Hong Kong, the daughter of an American journalist. She has photographed for the National Geographic Society and other international publications for more than 12 years, covering Australian Aborigines; Bombay film stars; Russian "Old Believers" in Alaska; Greenwich, CT, high society; and an Albanian farm family. She also gained unprecedented access to Prince Charles for her 2006 *National Geographic* feature, "Not Your Typical Radical."
  She has also participated in several Day in the Life series, *Passage to Vietnam,* and *Women in the Material World.* Catherine is known for her vibrant, emotional and sensitive style of photographing people.

Damian Harper wrote the "Beijing Today" section, and Christopher Pitts wrote the "Beijing Architecture" and "Arts & culture" sections.

History & culture

Detail of Tiananmen Square worker sculpture

Beijing today

THOUGH BEIJING IS NOT AT THE GEOGRAPHIC CENTER OF CHINA, MANY believe—especially locals—that this former imperial capital is the heart of China's past, present, and future. Shanghai may flaunt its ultramodern skyline and unmatched credentials as China's economic powerhouse, but to most Beijingers that city is nothing more than an ill-mannered upstart. Hong Kong, too, suffers in comparison. For history, culture, food, and language, all roads lead to Beijing.

Beijing was the capital of China as early as the 13th century, when imperial commands were issued from the Forbidden City and sent to the most distant outposts of the Chinese Empire. Today, China's ponderous political directives are composed in neighboring Zhangnanhai, not Beijing. But take a walk through stately Tiananmen Square and you will immediately sense the continual significance of what is arguably China's greatest city.

There's little that is ornate or showy about Beijing culture, but this is not to say that this

city lacks finesse. Beijing provides access to stunning portions of the Great Wall, superior opera companies, the most delectable roast duck, the finest palaces in China, and the world's largest public square, to name just a few of its rich historical and cultural treasures. And even though China ranges through several time zones, the whole nation—officially at least—sets its clocks to Beijing time.

Beijing folk *(Beijingren)* are dependable and forthright, with a pleasing wholesomeness and an honest appreciation of life's simple pleasures. They also carry with them wherever they go a sense of pride about the city and its long history, while their unique accent sets them apart from other Chinese. Beijingers

speak Beijinghua, the highly distinctive language spoken for centuries in the city's *hutongs* (alleys). To them, the rest of China rattles away in outlandish dialects peppered with occasional references to Putonghua (Mandarin). Mandarin—China's official language—is itself based on Beijinghua, minus much of its quirky slang.

Beijingers are notably amiable and generous, down-to-earth even. Famously bookish and well read, they talk far more about politics than their fellow countrymen. Political action these days may be theoretical at best, but Beijing's instinct for protest has frequently translated into action—from the May Fourth Movement of 1919 to the pivotal disturbances of 1989. And unlike in other Chinese cities, being an artist is more acceptable in Beijing, where a large number of galleries and small art spaces cluster in the city's celebrated 798 Art District.

Despite its modern facade, today's Beijing is a huge, arid, dusty, polluted, and flat metropolis infused with a potent sense of timelessness. Unlike Hong Kong, where Victoria Harbor divides the city, and Shanghai, its east and west parts separated by the Huangpu River, no geographical feature splits Beijing in two. If a partition does exist, then the city cleaves into old Beijing—the archaic, hutong-riddled region surrounding the Forbidden City—and new Beijing, the recently fashioned area outside the confines of the now vanished city walls. But such a division is just a mirage; large-scale construction projects and the disappearance of historic hutongs have left the city an often bewildering mix of old and new.

However stylish and worldly Beijing may look on the outside, the city is, of course, deeply Chinese. You can shop for Western groceries and goods for sure, sip Belgian beers in a Western bar, or dine on international cuisine, but this is the capital city of a land that only began reaching out to the world less than three decades ago. Pockets of modern Beijing are highly cosmopolitan, but don't let

Shoppers walk under colorful billboards on bustling Wangfujing, Dongcheng District, one of Beijing's most famous shopping streets.

that fool you; speakers of English are rare in the city, where the flavors of China are as thick as the incense wafting from the bulky braziers of roadside Buddhist temples.

NEW BEIJING

After the communists came to power in 1949, Beijing experienced its most dramatic redesign since the Ming-dynasty Emperor Yongle laid out his conception of the capital in the 15th century. In fact, the communists left not just one stamp on the city's appearance, but many. Beijing's architectural mish mash follows the lurching twists and turns of the Communist Party—from builders of a socialist utopia (the Great Hall of the People) and champions of nationalist aspirations (the China Millennium Monument) to capitalists (Oriental Plaza). The only agreement between the stylistically incompatible phases has been the gradual, and often dramatic, altering of ancient Beijing.

Under the communists, the vast city walls

and most of their splendid gates, along with numerous old temples, were the first to be destroyed and replaced with graceless socialist buildings. Along with reform in 1979 came new directives to play catch-up with the West. Narrow hutongs made way for wider roads, shopping malls, and apartment blocks; Beijing as a modern city of high-rises and shimmering towers began to take shape.

More recently, China has proven itself to be a significant player on the global

Bridges and flowering trees at the Summer Palace hark back to the city's earlier days. Built during the Jin dynasty (1115–1234) and expanded through succeeding dynasties, it is the largest and best preserved imperial garden in China.

economic stage as its economy surges to new-found heights, a fact that has fueled boundless growth in its major cities, especially Beijing. This, combined with the

city's hosting of the 2008 Summer Olympic Games, have turned Beijing's architectural narrative increasingly topsy-turvy. More than ever before, huge swaths of old hutongs and courtyard houses have been razed to make way for new housing, business complexes, hotels, and Olympic venues. Estimated to cost more than 20 billion dollars, the preparations for the Summer Games have altered the city's layout in a manner that hasn't been seen in this city since imperial times. Glassy new skyscrapers, highways, subway lines, and sidewalks paved with shiny new tiles all combine to create the look of a sophisticated modern city.

International architects have flocked to the scene, among them Paul Andreu, who designed the enormous National Grand Theater, a modernist glass dome that seems to float on a man-made lake; and Norman Foster, the creative mind

behind the new Terminal 3 at Capital International Airport, with its striking monitoring tower topped with a red roof. Both buildings are symbolic of the new Beijing, yet both are at odds—ideologically and aesthetically—with adjacent traditional buildings and even with the spirit of the city itself.

Beijing's makeover, however, has delivered massive shots of confidence to the city's residents. Riding a swelling tide of patriot-

Friends enjoy a pot of tea on Nan Luogu Xiang, a 700-year-old street in old Beijing. It's a sign of the times that some of the city's most ancient neighborhoods are being gentrified rather than razed.

ism, the 2008 Olympics have come at a time when China's international stock is on the rise at a blinding pace. Beijingers have the world's attention and are reveling in the spotlight.

OLD BEIJING

Beijing's new skyscrapers and modern hotels are electric, but they reveal little about the city's unique character. For this, it is essential to delve deeply into hoary, creaking quarters, where cyclists propel tottering piles of trash for recycling and winter sees spent coal briquettes strewn along cracked hutongs that haven't changed in 50 years.

The original Ming-dynasty conception of the city survives in part, and although its narrative is patchy and inconsistent, historic Beijing can still be found—as long as you are adventurous and willing to explore. For this is what the capital is all about, and to miss it is simply not to see the real Beijing at all.

The grounds of the former imperial capital envelop the Forbidden City, which is also surrounded by the true soul of Beijing: the city's grid of charming hutongs. Lose

yourself in these narrow old alleyways—where whole communities still thrive—and you will see Beijing at its most authentic. The low-rise, one-story Qing-dynasty courtyard houses of Xicheng and Dongcheng Districts typify old Beijing; they are modest but attractive, gracious, and delightful. Many former residents may have moved out of the hutongs into the modern housing springing up all over the suburbs, but the alleys still ring with the laughter of children and the cries of

Old and new: The Temple of the City God is the lone survivor of a newly developed piece of land in the fast-rising Financial Street.

peddlers, where old folks in *laotoushan* and *laotouxie* (white T-shirts and black cloth shoes) hunch over chess sets while cyclists weave down ancient lanes thick with the aroma of roast lamb kebabs.

The constant tussle between the old and

new has found new areas of conflict. In 2000, a branch of the popular coffeehouse chain Starbucks opened in the Forbidden City to the rear of the Hall of Preserving Harmony, but it was replaced by a local café in 2007, much to the unmistakable delight of local traditionalists. Some Beijingers are also understandably indignant at the cavorting parties that rock fragile sections of the Great Wall in summer.

Several pages of Beijing's history may have been shredded, but people everywhere are trying fitfully to glue them back together. The magnificent gate of Yongding Men has been rebuilt from scratch, but like much else in town, it's only a modern reconstruction of what was once a price-less historical treasure.

More and more recently, the city is making efforts to retain some of its proud history, declaring some hutongs protected sites, remodeling or rebuilding courtyard houses in a few areas, and collecting the bricks of the original city wall in order to rebuild a small section. A number of citizens have also banded together, forming nongovernmental organizations dedicated to the preservation of the city's past.

MODERN LIFE

Beijing increasingly rings with the sound of unfamiliar tongues as economic migrants from all over China come to the city in search of jobs. Hordes of foreigners are also suddenly everywhere to *zuo shengyi* (do business), act, teach English, or edit expat magazines. Beijing has quickly become the place to be. Even the Great Wall has its own international marathon.

Famously hardworking, Beijingers are putting in even longer hours to afford living space in a city where property prices have spiraled too high for low-income earners. In a land where material gain has replaced socialist altruism as the dominant creed, a powerful preoccupation with money has taken hold.

As China continues to muddle along with an autocratic political system, hopes that political evolution will soon accompany economic liberalization have so far been dashed. And the members of the middle-class

Chinese in Beijing, like the rest of their compatriots, keep their heads down, focused primarily on such issues as fuel prices, the cost of health care, property inflation, education, and employment. The typical topics that have galvanized the West—democracy, the war on terror, and even global warming—are of little popular interest in Beijing.

After decades of inhabiting a spiritual dead zone, many Beijingers are undergoing a religious reawakening. Christianity, perhaps surprisingly, is leading the way; if left to its own devices, the religion could transform China into a predominantly Christian nation within three decades.

The city's astonishing aridity (just how

do the trees grow from the baked dirt?) is likely to grow worse as the surrounding water table shrinks and aquifers are further drained. The population of Beijing has long endured epic dust storms that swirl into town during the spring, depositing tons of dust on the city and forcing pedestrians and cyclists to don plastic bags over their heads for protection.

A nationwide affliction, pollution is sadly an ever present irritant for the residents of Beijing. In preparation for the Olympics, the city's officials sought ways to decrease the amount of pollution and limit its effects on the games. They even drew up the draconian plan to sweep Beijing's cars from the roads in

A new bride jumps rope with some children in one of Beijing's old hutongs.

the weeks leading up to the Olympics in order to decrease sulfurous emissions.

These days, your average Beijinger may not give a foreigner a moment's thought, but a mere 15 years ago many locals would still be slack jawed and wide-eyed at the sudden appearance of *laowai* (foreigners). For historical reasons, the novelty of foreigners in Beijing has yet to fully wear off, and you will be exploring a city that has—in sum—had minimal contact with the outside world. At heart, this is what makes Beijing such a unique and remarkable destination. ∎

Food & drink

CHINESE CUISINE IS DIVERSE AND COMPLICATED, WITH EACH PROVINCE AND city boasting its own unique flavors and style of cooking. All coalesce in Beijing, which has become a pilgrimage site for Chinese food lovers. As a result, it's possible for you to do a culinary tour of China without ever leaving the confines of the city.

Chinese cuisine is divided broadly into regions. The culinary map should be taken only as a rough guide, however, since it is impossible to portray the diversity and complexity of Chinese cuisine in such a simplistic manner.

NORTHERN DISHES

Because of its harsh and cold climate, the northern region—which includes the cities of Beijing and Tianjin, as well as the areas of Shandong and Dongbei—features typically hearty fare. Most dishes rely on wheat flour, and no meal is complete without dumplings or steamed breads *(mantou)*.

Shandong cooking is the foundation of Beijing cuisine and also includes facets of Manchu (Qing imperial) cooking as well as Han Muslim dishes.

Beijing food has been influenced greatly by Chinese-speaking Muslims (Hui), whose dishes have become an integral part of the city's cuisine. Sour bean juice, boiled tripe, rinsed mutton or hotpot *(shuan yangrou),* mutton scrap soup *(yang zasui),* and door-nail meat pies are all local favorites.

While Peking duck is a hallmark of Beijing cuisine, there is a plethora of good dishes virtually unknown to outsiders, such as incredibly tasty *ma doufu,* made from the dredges of mung beans that are then stir-fried with mutton fat and accented with soy beans and pickled *xuelihong* (greens).

Equally grand is *zhajiang mian,* Beijing's signature noodle dish. Wheat flour is kneaded to the right consistency then combined with a delectable sauce that has been cooked with pork and topped with multi-colored vegetables, including bean sprouts, sliced red radish, and cucumber. A bowl makes for a wholesome and satisfying meal.

Diners enjoy their meals at a restaurant in Beijing's old Legation Quarter.

EASTERN & WESTERN REGION

The eastern (or southeastern) region of China encompasses Taiwan, as well as the provinces of Jiangsu, Zhejiang, and Fujian. Stressing fresh ingredients and a natural taste, eastern cuisine is typically light and sweet, with moderate flavors.

Sichuan, Guizhou, and Yunnan Provinces make up the western region, where food is characteristically spicy, hot,

and sour. Popular throughout China, western cuisine is chock-full of mouth-numbing spices and fiery red chilies; the liberal use of the piquant peppercorn is especially prominent in Sichuan cooking. *Yuxiang* (literally "fish fragrant") and *mala* (spicy and numbing) dishes are the highlights of Sichuan cuisine, but, plenty of nonspicy dishes—like camphor wood and tea-smoked duck (*zhangcha ya*)—are also on the menu.

CENTRAL & SOUTHERN FOOD

Hunan and Hubei, located in the center of China, are known for their country-style cooking. Cured meat and smoked bean curd are the hallmarks of Hunan Province. Hubei dishes use chilies moderately and are not as spicy as Hunan or Sichuan food.

Southern cuisine is typified by Cantonese cooking, which is known in Chinese as *yuecai*. Light and refined, food from this region often borders on bland.

MEDICINAL FOODS

Chinese have long believed that a healthy diet consists of both yin and yang—cold and hot elements. Loofah (a bitter gourd) and winter melons are considered "cold" vegetables, which are perfect for warding off summer heat, while mutton, beef, and turtle are "hot" and best eaten in the winter.

The four heavenly foods—bird's nest, sea cucumber, shark's fin, and abalone—are considered to be delicacies, which have supplementary nutritional properties. These items are consumed today as status symbols.

VEGETARIAN

Chinese have been preparing strictly vegetarian dishes for thousands of years. Perfected in the kitchens of Buddhist temples, they are often prepared to look and

A young chef prepares steamed snacks for the hungry crowds of Beijing.

taste like meat or fish, although they rely mainly on soy bean and gluten products.

Tanjia cai, or Tan family cuisine, is a little known style of cooking that was created by Tan Zongjun, a native of Guangdong Province who was a government official at the end of the 19th century. The Tan family was very fond of rare delicacies, and the many officials and friends invited to their home were impressed with the food that was served there. This unique style of cooking employs techniques from the regions of Huaiyang and Guangdong.

CULINARY REVOLUTION

In recent years, a growing number of Beijing's chefs have begun to experiment with different ingredients. Contemporary, or fusion, cuisine pairs Chinese and Western ingredients with traditional methods of cooking. The result is frequently a fantastic, palate-pleasing experience for everyone.

Beijing is undergoing a culinary revolution of the most amazing kind, and there's never been a better time to try these different cuisines. Over the past decade, restaurants specializing in dishes from around China—and the world—have sprung up across the city. And the venues, which range from chic, modern restaurants to hole-in-the-wall eateries, are a big part of the fun.

This is a long way from the early 1990s, when eating in the capital meant dining at one of the ubiquitous Cantonese or Sichuan eateries, usually drab affairs with dim fluorescent lighting and plastic garbage bag table cloths. It was not that long ago that huge heads of cabbage were piled on street corners and the roofs of houses, a reminder of the limited fare that was available.

The variety today is even more impressive when you consider that just two decades ago the city was virtually a culinary desert, the result of anticapitalist policies developed by Mao Zedong during the 1950s. The policies led many private restaurants, including *laozihao,* or old brand-name favorites, to shut their doors.

In 1980, Yuebin Fanzhuang became the first *getihu,* or private, restaurant to reopen in Beijing, ending the long hiatus and offering markedly better food and service than the primarily lethargic state-run restaurants. Thousands of simple restaurants followed, providing the capital with a variety of eateries from which to choose.

In 1999, the Red Capital Club opened in a restored courtyard house, sparking a trend that has seen courtyard restaurants springing up across the city, each offering diners the pleasant opportunity of eating outside beneath the trees and stars. Gui Gongfu, the former home of Empress Dowager Cixi, specializes in dishes prepared with oolong tea leaves. The beautifully renovated The Source offers Sichuan dishes, while The

Courtyard, once an old house next to the East Gate of the Forbidden City, is a bright space that serves fusion food. Restaurants have also been moving into the city's parks. Xihe Yaju, Xiao Wangfu, and Le Galerie are all set amid the pleasant scenery of the Sun Altar Park, and Baijia Dazhaimen is located in a sprawling garden that dates to the beginning of the Qing dynasty.

Beijing has also witnessed a wave of restaurants opened by artists. Located in the Sanlitun area of the city, Old Character (Lao Hanzi)—opened by artist Chi Nai and specializing in earthy Hakka food—was one of the first. The simple cement walls in the (1.6 km) long—is best known for its hot and mouth-numbing crayfish *(mala xiao longxia)*, spicy duck's neck, and hot-and-sour fish stew.

Most recently, a growing number of chic restaurants with ultracontemporary designs have been opening in Beijing. The avant-garde People 8 is so fashionably dark inside that you need a flashlight to make your way to what are probably the coolest toilets in the city; fortunately, you can still see the designer crockery and creative cuisine. Lan, one of the latest additions to Beijing's dining scene, was designed by Philippe Starck, the world-famous contemporary designer,

Deep-fried crickets are a popular local treat.

dining room are covered with rice paper and adorned with calligraphy. Around the same time, Fang Lijun opened South Silk Road (Chama Gudao), which features the exotic dishes of southwest China's Yunnan Province. He set his second restaurant in a minimalist factory loft in Soho New Town (Xiandaicheng), complete with a glass see-through second floor and huge walls displaying his own cynical art works.

Red lanterns line Guijie, or Ghost Street, where more than a hundred restaurants stand shoulder to shoulder. This crowded all-night dining boulevard—about 1 mile who transformed the huge space into a fairy fantasyland.

The past few years have also seen a foreign invasion as restaurants from all over the world have set up shop and changed the culinary face of the city. In addition to American, European, and Asian venues, the city now also offers Iranian, Turkish, Israeli, Tunisian, Cuban, and Greek restaurants, all run by natives of those countries.

It's difficult to imagine where the next culinary trend will take Beijing, but one thing is certain—dining out in the city will never again be a dull affair. ■

Religion & philosophy

CHINA IS A DEEPLY RELIGIOUS COUNTRY, AND BEIJING FOLLOWS THE COUN-
try's lead, with three main faiths: Buddhism, Taoism, and, to a lesser extent, Confucianism.
Confucianism is not strictly a religion but more a philosophy, while Buddhism was
imported from India, leaving Taoism as the only truly indigenous Chinese faith.

TAOISM

Taoism *(daojiao)* is essentially more mystical
than religious, although certain strains are
presided over by deities. Supposedly founded
in the seventh century B.C. by Laozi, who
wrote the *Daodejing (Classic of the Way of
Power),* Taoism aims to cultivate a philosophical awareness of life. Lacking an anthro-
pomorphic god, it seeks revelation of "the
Way"—the term used to describe the dyna-
mism of nature and the operating force
behind the universe. Taoists believe in achievement through inaction *(wu wei),* allowing
things to develop and occur of their own
accord. Those who wish to experience the Way
can peruse Laozi's classic, a book that has, as
closely as is humanly possible, captured the
feeling of the Tao. The Way is also experi-
entially revealed through the practice of *tai ji
quan,* a martial art that draws on the Taoist
precepts of softness, heightened awareness,
and avoidance of conflict.

BUDDHISM

Most temples in China are Buddhist, pointing
to the popularity of Buddhism *(fojiao)* among
the Chinese. Founded by an Indian prince
named Siddhartha Gautama (563–483 B.C.),
Buddhism migrated to China from the third
through the sixth centuries A.D. The faith seeks
to cure suffering through the neutralization of
desire. Only by following the "eight-fold path"
can a Buddhist reach nirvana, a transcendent
state of freedom.

Chinese Buddhists generally follow
Mahayana Buddhism (greater vehicle), which
differs from Theravada Buddhism (doctrine
of the elders) found in India. Mahayana
Buddhism mandates that those who have
reached nirvana and attained enlightenment
should remain on earth and help others.

**Buddhist monks clad in saffron robes pray
at the Source of Law Temple.**

CONFUCIANISM

Confucianism *(rujia sixiang),* named after the
sage Confucius, is a paternalistic philosophy of
social behavior that has given the Chinese
people their codes, rules, and norms of

conduct. Many Chinese consider genuflecting to one's elders as ordained by Confucianism a thankless task, yet the philosophy has spread through the soul of the nation. Over the centuries, Confucianism has been loaded with all the trappings of religion and even turned into a national institution, despite being a very human philosophy that offers real answers to suffering and bad governance.

ISLAM

Arab merchants leading camel caravans along the Silk Road brought Islam *(yisilan jiao)* to China. The Muslim community of Beijing speaks Chinese and is considered a group distinct from the Muslims of the Middle East. Beijing's oldest mosque dates back well over a thousand years ago.

CHRISTIANITY

The Nestorians (a Christian sect from Syria) arrived in China in the seventh century A.D., followed later by the Jesuits, who helped build the Old Summer Palace in Beijing. Today, Christianity *(jidu jiao)* is China's fastest growing faith, in part because of the links

A bride hides her face at a traditional Chinese wedding ceremony in Ritan Park (above).
A wizened Taoist monk at White Cloud Temple (right)

made between Protestantism and the spirit of capitalism; the spiritual bankruptcy at the heart of society; and the flourishing number of house churches, illegal places of worship for China's swelling number of Christians.

JUDAISM

Judaism *(youtai jiao)* in China can be traced back to the seventh or eighth century A.D. Although the Jews played an important role in the area's history, there was no Jewish community in the city until very recently.

RELIGION & POLITICS

With varying degrees of success, the Chinese Communist Party tried to replace religion with devotion to Marxism-Leninism *(makesilieningzhuyi)*. Chairman Mao Zedong attempted to purge China of superstition during the Cultural Revolution (1966–1976), but instead he turned himself into a demigod who is still idolized and worshipped today.

The current bankruptcy of communist theory has left a spiritual vacuum in China that has been filled with a medley of religions.

The Communist Party reacts with concern to any creed that offers an alternative vision to that bequeathed by Karl Marx. Recent riots involving Chinese Christians point to the growing hold that Christianity has in China and the problems the authorities have in dealing with it. Falun Gong (which means "art of the wheel of the law"), a quasi-Buddhist "cult," was banned because of fears that it challenges the primacy of the Communist Party. Despite being marshaled by middle-aged women and the elderly, Falun Gong has managed to worry the Communist Party, whose grip on power is fretful and insecure. Adherents periodically demonstrate in Tiananmen Square, only to be bundled off to prison. Banning Falun Gong has not solved the problem of spiritual emptiness in China; indeed, it may simply have exacerbated it. ∎

History of Beijing

"Possibly the greatest single work of man on the face of the earth is Peking."
—Edmond N. Bacon, *The Design of Cities*

HUMANS HAVE LIVED IN OR NEAR MODERN-DAY BEIJING FOR MORE THAN 3,000 years. Even prehistoric Peking Man made his home in the caves not far from the city. However, the city of Beijing owes its early existence not to indigenous populations but to non-Chinese tribes from northern Asia who first built the city and made it their capital.

Chinese records first mention a settlement in the area of modern Beijing during the Western Zhou dynasty (ca 1122–771 B.C.), when a walled village called Ji, or Reeds, was built in the general area of present-day Xuanwu District. Author Juliet Bredon, who was writing in the early 1900s, said that in those days a marble tablet stood near the Bell Tower on which Emperor Qianlong had written: "Here stood one of the gates of the ancient city of Ji."

In 907, the Khitans, a non-Chinese nomadic tribe, founded the Liao dynasty and set up their capital in Yanjing, today a poetic name for Beijing that's still used for things such as the popular Yanjing beer. The Khitans were the first to build a "city" on the site where Beijing now stands. The city—which was encircled by walls that were 30 feet (9 m) high—had a circumference of 12 miles (20 km) and an impressive imperial palace. From this base, the Khitans began to make inroads into the heartland of China, which was not brought under control until the Song dynasty in 960. The name Cathay for China is said to derive from the word "Khitay," another name for the Khitans.

In 1120, the Jurchen, a Manchu tribe, formed an alliance with the Song dynasty, and five years later they set up their own Jin

Gold mask from the Liao dynasty, late first millennium A.D.

(Gold) dynasty to the southwest of present-day Beijing and turned the ruins of Yanjing into a larger walled city, which they called Zhongdu, or Middle Capital. The Jurchen then expanded quickly into central China, extending their control over a large swath of land, to the dismay of the Song dynasty rulers.

The Mongol troops of Genghis Khan attacked Zhongdu in 1215 and almost completely destroyed the Jin capital. In 1267, his grandson, Kublai Khan, made the city the capital of what would become the Yuan dynasty. He called his new city Khanbalik, or City of the Great Khan, marking the first time Beijing had become the capital of all of China. In Chinese, the city was known as Dadu (Great Capital), but foreigners came to know it as Cambaluc, Marco Polo's spelling of the Mongolian word "Khanbalik." This was the city that the Venetian explorer described so intriguingly in *The Travels of Marco Polo,* where he wrote that Beijing is "altogether so vast, so rich, and so beautiful, that no man on earth could design anything superior to it." Curiously, there is no mention of Marco Polo in Chinese history books, and some contemporary scholars wonder if the Venetian actually ever walked the streets of the old capital.

GRAND CAPITAL

Dadu was a grand city, designed according to the ideals spelled out in the Confucian

bien .r. mille homnes entour lui. qui sont tut ordone. ij. et. ij. et laque
tastaor. qui vault a dire homnes qui se premnent garde. Car dire e dire
ement ca en la. sy que bien tiennent detire asser.

This miniature painting (ca 1410) from *The Book of Wonders* by Marco Polo depicts a meeting with Kublai Kahn.

classic, *The Rites of Zhou* (*Zhou Li*)—one of the earliest books on geomancy, or feng shui—which describes the principles for the construction of homes and villages. In fact, it's been said that the plan of this new city was more classically Chinese than any imperial city that had come before it within Chinese territory. Dadu was built with evenly spaced rectilinear streets and was centered on a north–south axis. The book said that the imperial city should be a square formed by four walls, each 9 li (about 2.8 miles/4.5 km) long and each divided by three gates. Nine roads should connect the whole city from east to west and from north to south. The Mongols followed these rules except that the city walls, which were made of rammed earth, were longer than 9 li on each side.

About a hundred years after establishing their dynasty, the once nomadic Mongolians, softened by city life, suffered a disas-trous defeat at the hands of rebels from the south led by Zhu Yuanzhang, an itiner-ant Chinese monk. The Yuan dynasty came tumbling down and the capital was torched, although the basic layout of the city survived.

The new Ming dynasty moved its capital south to Nanjing, near Shanghai, in 1368, and Beijing was reduced to a simple prefec-ture called Beiping Fu. But it was not to remain down for long. The dynasty's found-ing emperor gave the city to his fourth son, Zhu Di, who immediately began to change the way it looked. In 1403, Zhu Di usurped the throne from his young nephew and adopted the reign name of Yongle. He decided to move the imperial capital from Nanjing to his own power base in the north: Beiping Fu. In 1405, Emperor Yongle began to rebuild the city on the ruins of Khanbalik, but it took 200,000 corvée labor-ers 15 years to complete the massive project, which Yongle intended to inspire awe and fear in his subjects. Beijing was to remain the capital of China until 1928, when the Nationalist government moved it back to Nanjing.

Emperor Yongle, dubbed the "architect of Beijing," is also credited with building beautiful bridges, Jingshan (or Coal Hill) Park, the Rear Lakes, the Temple of Heaven, and the Altar of Earth.

Bredon writes that when the Forbidden City was built, France's Versailles was "an insignificant shooting lodge," the Kremlin in Moscow was still surrounded by a wooden palisade, and construction on Hampton Court Palace had not yet begun in London. "Had all the Mings been of the mettle of Yongle," she writes, "the whole course of Chinese history might have been changed."

MANDATE OF HEAVEN

As with previous dynasties, the Ming dynasty soon fell victim to apathetic and inefficient rulers, corruption, and natural disasters that fueled rising public dissatisfaction and rebellions. The government was already in a state of serious decline when in April 1644 a peasant rebel leader named Li Zicheng managed to take over the capital, facing little resistance. Abandoned by his aides and officials, and with the rebels at the city gates, the last Ming-dynasty emperor slit the throats of his concubines and retreated to Jingshan Park behind the palace, where he hung himself on a tree at the foot of Coal Hill, his imperial robes stained by the blood of his concubines. (The tree is long gone, but the spot is still marked by a sign.) His death brought the last Chinese-ruled dynasty to a tragic end.

While Li Zicheng's army was knocking at the gates of the imperial city, Manchu soldiers—from the same Jurchen tribe that had established the Jin dynasty earlier—were gathering strength in the north, preparing to take advantage of the chaos. Ironically, although the Great Wall had been fortified during the Ming dynasty, the invading Manchus easily slipped through an opening at Shanhaiguan, the eastern terminus of the wall, with the assistance of Wu Sangui, a disgruntled Ming general who could not bring himself to cooperate with the peasant rebel leader. According to one popular story, Wu Sangui defected to the Manchu side out of anger after his mistress was allegedly kidnapped by Li Zicheng. According to Bredon, the Manchus "owed their dynasty, under heaven, to the little singing-girl known to contemporary chroniclers as Lady Chen, the Round Faced Beauty."

MANCHURIAN RISE

The Jurchen troops poured into Beijing, pushing Li's army out of the capital, and established the Qing dynasty (1644–1911). The change in rulers took place without the kind of destruction that had typically followed changes in rule. However, the new Qing rulers, who were keen to retain their unique Manchu traits, ordered that Manchus and Chinese live separately. The northern section of Beijing—known as Tartar City—was maintained as a garrison for the Banner Men (Qi Ren), Manchu troops responsible for defending the capital. The Han were relegated to the southern part of the city. Anxious to project a sense of continuity, the rulers of the Qing dynasty did not destroy the capital but instead built on the legacy established during the Ming dynasty. The government carried out a far-reaching expansion of the Forbidden City, constructed magnificent garden retreats in the western suburbs, and built a number of wonderful mansions.

Emperor Qianlong ascended the throne in 1736 and remained in control for six decades, a period considered by many to have been Beijing's golden era. The emperor added military forces, while at the same time promoted literature and the arts. Qianlong was also interested in Tibetan Buddhism, and he supported the construction of lamaseries in the capital. While he forbade Chinese from converting to Roman Catholicism (Jesuit Matteo Ricci was the first Catholic priest to arrive in the capital in 1603), he welcomed the skills of foreign priests in the service of the court. Qianlong also left his mark on the city by building

Portrait of Qianlong, the emperor who presided over Beijing's golden era

China's dynasties

Xia ca 2000–1600 B.C.

Shang ca 1600–1045 B.C.

Zhou ca 1045–221 B.C.
Spring & Autumn ca 722-481 B.C.
Waring States ca 450–221 B.C.

Qin 221–206 B.C.

Han
Western 206 B.C.–A.D. 8
Xin (Wang Mang) A.D. 8–23
Eastern A.D. 25–220

Three Kingdoms period 220–265

Jin
Western Jin 265–316
Eastern Jin 317–420

Northern
Northern Wei 386–534
Eastern Wei 534–550
Western Wei 535–557
Northern Qi 550–577
Northern Zhou 557–581

Southern
Song 420–479
Qi 479–502
Liang 502–557
Chen 557–589

Sui 581–618

Tang 618–907

Five Dynasties
Later Liao 907–923
Later Tang 923–936
Later Jin 936–947
Later Han 947–950
Later Zhou 951–960

Song
Northern 960–1127
Southern 1127–1279

Yuan 1279–1368

Ming 1368–1644

Qing 1644–1912

Republic of China
1912–1949 (maintained in Taiwan)

People's Republic of China
1949–present

new sites, many of which still exist today.

It's said that Emperor Qianlong would sometimes sneak out of the palace in order to make incognito visits to the restaurants, temples, and shops located just outside the gates of the Forbidden City. According to one popular story, it was Chinese New Year's Eve in 1752, and all the shops in the normally bustling Dashilan area of Beijing were closed as shop owners busily settled their annual accounts. The still burning lanterns at one small wine shop attracted three well-dressed patrons. Wang Ruifu, the owner, politely ushered the visitors upstairs and personally served them his best dishes and wine. When one of the guests asked the name of the shop, Wang answered, "I don't have a name." One of the men gratefully said to the owner, "At this hour, you are probably the only shop still open. Why not call it 'Du Yi Chu'?" Du Yi Chu is Chinese for "the only place."

Wang soon forgot the incident and was surprised days later when eunuchs from the imperial city showed up to present him with a wooden plaque emblazoned with three characters: Du Yi Chu. It was only then that he realized that one of the guests dining at his store that night was none other than Emperor Qianlong. Wang fell on his knees, kowtowing to show his gratitude. Today, the sign bearing Qianlong's calligraphy sits in a glass case in the restaurant, proof that Du Yi Chu is one of Beijing's oldest eateries, dating back some two and a half centuries.

FOREIGNERS AT THE GATES

The imperial court proved unwilling to modernize and was unable to match the military prowess of the foreign powers of the day, resulting in a series of humiliating defeats, each of which brought new demands for concessions and unequal treaties. Toward the end of the 19th century, the government had no choice but to cave to foreign demands for a permanent presence in Beijing. Soon the foreign Legation Quarter sprang up just to the southeast of the Forbidden City, ushering irrevocable changes and a new style of Western architecture into the capital. Previously, no one had been permitted to climb the ramps of the city walls to look down into the palaces, but in 1860, Prince Gong, in an attempt to propitiate foreigners in the city, allowed them to walk on the walls for the first time.

By the mid-1890s, the Harmonious Fists (Yihequan), a secret martial society known in English as the Boxers (see pp. 36–37), had emerged. The Boxers, who claimed magical powers that enabled them to withstand blows by swords and bullets, adopted a strongly anti-foreign attitude and began to attack for-eign missionaries and Chinese converts to Christianity. In 1900, the group laid siege to the Legation Quarter, home to much of the foreign com-munity in Beijing.

The siege ended after a multinational force, made up of troops from eight allied nations, marched into Beijing, sending the Boxers scattering and the imperial court fleeing to the safety of Xi'an in Shaanxi Province. The foreign troops remained in Beijing and the surrounding area for a year, harassing Chinese citizens and looting cultural arti-facts. The ancient capital would never be the same again.

Because the foreign powers held them responsible for the rebellion of the Boxers, the Qing-dynasty rulers were forced to agree to an indemnity, payable over several decades to the nations that had helped quell the disturbance. After the foreign troops withdrew, the emperor and empress quietly returned to the capital. The incident had shocked the imperial court and resulted in a last-minute attempt to carry out reforms, but it was too late.

The Qing failure to deal with foreign encroachment fueled growing public resent-ment against the Manchu court, which was already reeling from an array of internal problems. Peasant rebellions sprang up around the country—a clear sign that the Mandate of Heaven was about to fall from the hands of the Qing-dynasty emper-or. Emperor Guangxu, who had been placed under house arrest in the Hall of Jade Ripples in the Summer Palace after he tried to implement radical reforms in 1898, died in 1908, one day before the Empress Dowager died. Rumor has it that Cixi had him poi-soned. In October 1911, a revolution brought the imperial system to an end, and the Manchus readily agreed to abdicate, ending 267 years of Qing rule.

WARLORDS & REPUBLICANS

On February 12, 1912, Prince Chun, on behalf of the boy emperor Puyi, issued an offi-cial degree acknowledging that imperial rule had come to an end. Under an agree-ment with the new Republican government-headed by its first president Yuan Shikai, a former powerful general in the Manchu army, the court was permitted to remain within the Forbidden City, the Summer Palace, and the Imperial Resort (Bishu Shanzhuang) in Chengde.

In 1915, President Yuan attempted to revive the imperial system, with himself as the new Son of Heaven. He even ordered new custom-made imperial robes and chi-naware marking his new reign. Yuan's plan

Yuan Shikai (1859–1916), first president of the Republic of China

Chiang Kai-shek (right) with his personal adviser, American Owen Lattimore

met with fierce opposition, and he had to postpone his enthronement. The frustrated former general died the following year, his dream unfulfilled.

Puyi made a brief comeback in 1917 when Zhang Xun—an imperial loyalist known as the Pigtail General because he made his soldiers retain their Manchu braids—attempted to restore the monarchy. The farcical attempt failed within just a few days after another warlord counter-attacked, hand-dropping bombs from an airplane into the Forbidden City below. Puyi's sad story was told—with a bit of cinematic license—in the 1987 Bertolucci classic, *The Last Emperor*. In 1924, Feng Yuxiang, a warlord better known to the world as the Christian General (so called because he made his soldiers read the Bible and baptized them with a garden hose), forced the emperor to vacate the Forbidden City.

A victim of a succession of rulers, the grand old capital didn't fare well during the next few decades. However, it was also a period of excitement. Students marched to Tiananmen Square in May 1919 to protest the Versailles Conference, which ceded Germany's territories in China to the Japanese. Leading intellectuals, scholars, and artists flocked to Beijing, where they passionately debated China's sad state of affairs. The most outspoken shouted out "Down with the Confucian shop!" and called for Mr. Science and Mr. Democracy to take the place of the Great Sage, Confucius. There was also a movement away from the highly stylized, classical tradition to a vernacular and more accessible form of written Chinese. It was at this time that a Hunanese farm boy named Mao Zedong began work as an assistant librarian at Peking University, which was then just a bit to the northeast of the Forbidden City.

In 1921, a group of intellectuals, influenced by the Russian Revolution, met in Shanghai to establish the Communist Party of China. From these small beginnings, the

Communist movement began to gradually take hold among people throughout the country. After Sun Yat-sen died in 1925, Commander Chiang Kai-shek emerged as the new leader of the Republic of China, and he soon launched a purge of the Communists in the Kuomintang (KMT), or Nationalist Party.

In 1928, the KMT government moved the capital of China back to Nanjing and changed the name of Beijing (Northern Capital) to Beiping (literally Northern Peace). During this period, the city suffered greatly from both neglect and vandalism.

In 1937, Japan used the pretense of a Chinese attack against Japanese troops to justify opening fire on nationalist troops on the Marco Polo Bridge (Lugou Qiao) in southwest Beijing. The event, known as the Marco Polo Bridge Incident, was the beginning of a brutal eight-year occupation of the city, which was once again named Beijing. The nationalists were forced by the presence of the Japanese to move their government inland to Chongqing in Sichuan Province and to form a temporary alliance with the Red Army to fight the Japanese. The Japanese surrender in 1945 was followed by bitter civil war between the declining KMT forces and the resurgent Red Army that dragged on for another four years until the communist victory.

NEW CHINA

The Red Army marched into Beijing on January 31, 1949, after a prolonged battle with nationalist forces, who fled across the Formosa Strait to the island of Taiwan, taking with them truckloads of valuable pieces of art pieces from the Forbidden City and setting them up in the National Palace Museum in Taipei. Beijing became the capital of New China on October 1, 1949, when Chairman Mao Zedong stood on the rostrum of the Gate of Heavenly Peace and declared to millions of cheering Chinese that "The Chinese people have stood up!"

But there was one problem. The Communist Party leadership was made up of (continued on p. 38)

Mao Zedong, Chairman of the Chinese Communist Party, speaks at a ceremony marking the establishment of the People's Republic of China on October 1, 1949.

Boxer Rebellion

In 1898, a small group of martial artists began to gather strength in the northwest corner of Shandong Province. They called themselves the Society for Harmonious Fists, but they were better known in the rest of the world as the Boxers. Their name and style of fighting came from secret societies and other martial arts groups that were spreading throughout the southern part of the province for several years already and who were opposed to the growing influence of Western Christian missionaries.

The Boxers, who believed that they had magical powers that made them invulnerable to bullets and swords, successfully attracted a wide number of farmers and laborers who had been adversely affected by recent flooding. They were ready for a good fight, especially if it was with the detested Christian missionaries and Chinese converts. As early as 1899, the Boxers began to take credit for the murder of numerous Chinese converts. When more murders began occurring on the Hebei border, foreigners in China began to get nervous and

French soldiers man a barricade in Tianjin during the Boxer Rebellion (ca 1900).

started urging the Qing-dynasty rulers to put an end to the movement.

The Boxers' slogan, "Revive the Qing, destroy the foreign," appealed to many Chinese. According to one popular jingle that appeared on walls around the city:

> Their men are all immoral;
> Their women truly vile.
> For the Devils it's mother-son sex
> That serves as the breeding style.
> No rain comes from heaven,
> The earth is parched and dry.
> And all because the churches
> Have bottled up the sky.

By spring 1900, the movement had begun to pick up steam, mainly among poor young peasants, who accounted for 70 percent of the Boxers—the remainder was a mix of disaffected itinerant sellers, rickshaw pullers, boatmen, and artisans, all of whom were down and out at the time, and so prime candidates to take part in a revolution.

The most famous group of female Boxers was called the Red Lanterns Shining. Made up of young girls just 12 to 18 years old, the group alleged to have powers that would counteract the "pollution" of the Chinese Christian women and their power to weaken the strength of Boxer men. Another colorful group was the Cooking Pan Lantern, which allegedly cooked meals for the Boxer soldiers using pots that were said to somehow refill themselves magically after each meal.

Leaderless Boxers began to wander into Beijing and Tianjin on their own in early June 1900. They walked the streets of the cities, dressed in colorful but strange outfits, white charms dangling from their wrists. A Christian or possibly any Chinese in possession of a foreign good was a likely target.

The Qing government wavered about what to do, caught between urgent pleas from increasingly nervous Westerners living in the Legation Quarter and the secret hope that the Boxers might just have some sort of magic power that could rid the country of troublesome foreigners once and for all.

Tensions heightened on June 19, 1900, when the German minister was shot dead in the street and Boxer forces organized a siege against the Legation Quarter. The Empress Dowager, apparently believing the Boxers' claims of being invincible, or possibly duped, summoned up the courage on June 21 to issue a declaration of war against the foreign powers: "The foreigners have been aggressive towards us, infringed upon our territorial integrity, trampled our people under their feet…. They oppress our people and blaspheme our gods. The common people suffer greatly at their hands, and each one of them is vengeful. Thus it is that the brave followers of the Boxers have been burning churches and killing Christians."

Enjoying the support of the Manchu court, the Boxers began to carry out vicious attacks against international complexes and foreign residents, who sought refuge in the Legation Quarter where they built makeshift barricades using furniture, mattresses, and sandbags. Fortunately, for those living inside, the Boxers were not well organized, and the Manchu soldiers in the end declined to take part in the attack on the foreign enclave.

On August 4, an expeditionary army made up of troops from eight countries marched on Beijing. The Boxer soldiers crumbled in the face of the superior Western and Japanese military force; just ten days later the siege was lifted. As the foreign troops marched on the city, the Empress Dowager and her nephew Guangxu made a quick escape to the safety of western China. The Boxer protocol placed all sorts of restrictions and humiliating demands on the Chinese. These included building monuments to the memory of the incident in cities where atrocities against foreigners had taken place, the execution of the Boxer leaders, and an indemnity for a whopping 333 million dollars, although some of this money was returned as a fund to build schools.

In January, the Empress Dowager and her nephew/emperor quietly returned to their capital, and apparently she had had a lot of time to think while she was away. She introduced a series of reforms and began holding receptions in the Forbidden City for foreign diplomats and their wives.

But it was too late. The once imposing Manchu court had been seriously discredited by the foreign invasion, and the Mandate of Heaven was about ready to fall. ∎

(continued from p. 35)

outsiders, who had no attachment to the city. The party was also bitterly anti-urban, and it had no love for what it termed "consumer cities," which were full of people living bourgeois lives and consuming a lot of limited agricultural products while at the same time producing few consumer goods.

And so the party leaders soon set about turning their new capital from a consumer city into an industrial one. In other words, if Beijing wanted to eat, it would have to work for it. The Soviet Union was far more advanced than China, and so more than a thousand Soviet technicians flooded into China in order to organize and run many of the new ministries. Not surprisingly, the same experts who had helped to dismantle Moscow years earlier were now on hand to help design the urban plan for Beijing.

Factories went up all over the city, and gradually Beijing seemed less and less like a traditional city. People were organized into small, self-dependent *danwei*, or work units, while each factory became a walled compound, where the workers worked, lived, and took part in party functions. For the average Beijinger, there was little need to step out of one's own work unit.

DESTRUCTION OF CITY WALLS

No doubt the most traumatic part of the Communist Party's renewal of Beijing was the dismantling of the one thing that was symbolic of the ancient capital—its city walls, which came down to make way for a subway system and highways ringing the city. In 2001, Anthony Tung, an urban preservation expert, observed in *Preserving the World's Great Cities:* "In themselves, like the great pyramids at Giza and Teotihuacan, the walls of Beijing were an extraordinary monument of world civilization. As an integrated component of a vast urban composition, they were unparalleled."

Historians and older residents of Beijing still speak with sadness of the decision made in the late 1950s and early 1960s to tear down Beijing's historic city walls. Liang Sicheng, an architect trained at the University of Pennsylvania who was also comfortable with traditional Chinese architecture,

drew up a master plan to save the walls. Liang's design has since become a classic, enjoying the reputation among Chinese urban planners that Le Corbusier's 1925 Voisin Plan for Paris had in the West, although the two plans are diametrically opposed. Le Corbusier wanted to erase the historic center of Paris and construct a modernist city of high-rises and superhighways. Liang, on the other hand, called for wrapping old Beijing safely within the city walls as a living museum. The path on top of the walls would be converted into an elevated park. Meanwhile, a modern city would rise outside the city walls.

The municipal government overwhelmingly opted for a Soviet design instead, which envisioned the new industrial city as

a potent symbol of the socialist state. "We'll see a forest of chimneys from here," Mao Zedong reportedly pronounced with glee from atop the city walls, spreading his arms in front of him toward the horizon. Liang was heartbroken.

In 1953, the "Draft on Reconstructing and Expanding Beijing Municipality" called for Beijing to become a socialist city, the center of the national government, and a major industrial hub. It added the warning that the "major danger is an extreme respect for old architecture, such that it constricts our perspective of development."

Over the next few decades, the city underwent wrenching changes. Ancient structures made way for bland, Soviet-style architecture and boxlike urban factories.

Students gather in Tiananmen Square in April 1989 to mourn the death of popular Communist Party leader Hu Yaobang.

The city walls were torn down—except for the odd gate or tower—to make way for a new highway, a subway, and a massive underground bomb shelter. During the Cultural Revolution (1966–1976), Red Guards damaged temples and historic sites, anxious to destroy "the four olds": old customs, old habits, old culture, and old thinking. The residents of the city's magnificent old courtyard homes were pushed out to make room for additional families, and their beautiful old homes, which were built to house one family, now held several. The building were further damaged when the

Beijing or Peking?

If you've done a bit of reading about Beijing, you're likely to feel a little confused. Is the name of the city Beijing or Peking? Indeed you could be forgiven for thinking Peking and Beijing are two different places.

China's capital city has existed on its present site for hundreds of years, and its name has changed many times over the centuries. At one time or another it has been known as Ji, Dadu, Zhongdu, Shuntian, and Beiping (Northern Peace). The name of the city was changed to Beijing, or Northern Capital, after the Ming-dynasty court moved the seat of government back to the north in the 14th century. The communists referred to the capital as Peking before adopting Beijing during the late 1970s. Peking is simply the old transliteration of the Chinese pronunciation; Beijing is the officially sanctioned Pinyin spelling, based on the Mandarin (Putonghua) dialect.

With the government's adoption of Beijing as the capital city's official name—which has now been accepted by pretty much the rest of the world—the historical confusion has, for the most part, been laid to rest, except in old books about China. ∎

new tenants started building small structures inside the yards.

The half of historic Beijing that has survived is "a wonder beyond compare," said Anthony Tung. "The half of Beijing that was destroyed in the three decades from 1950 to 1980," he added, "constituted one of the single greatest losses of urban architectural culture in the twentieth century."

Belgian Sinologist Simon Leys visited Beijing in 1972 and was shocked when he went off to look for the city's famous gates and found them destroyed. "Peking now appears to be a murdered town," he wrote. "The body is still there, the soul has gone."

CAPITALISM WITH CHINESE CHARACTERISTICS

Three years after the death of Chairman Mao Zedong in 1976, Deng Xiaoping, China's new leader, called for the modernization of agriculture, industry, defense, and science and technology. The new economy —an intriguing mix of capitalist practices and party regulations—sparked profound change throughout China and especially in Beijing.

The city began to encourage large-scale investment, while businesses formerly run by the state ceded ownership to private local companies. International hotels, filled

Throughout Beijing, old neighborhoods are being reduced to rubble to make way for the construction of high-rise buildings.

with foreign tourists, popped up all over the city during the early 1980s. By 1988, Beijing was a sea of new buildings, many of which had been designed and built by international companies.

The population of Beijing also grew during the 1980s, as migrants from rural areas arrived in search of jobs. Aiming to improve the quantity and quality of available housing, Beijing's leadership fostered the rapid construction of residential high-rises and luxury apartments. By the end of the decade, Beijing, with its new subway stations and highways, had modernized.

But economic growth bred popular dissatisfaction. In the summer of 1989, thousands of Chinese students—with the hearty support of the people of Beijing—occupied Tiananmen Square to express their frustration with runaway corruption and spiraling inflation. The People's Liberation Army forcefully cleared the square, and the government launched a crackdown against dissent that brought the short-lived open period to a crashing halt.

Beijing rebounded in the 1990s, however, and started to fulfill its promise of becoming an international economic leader. Private ownership and investment exploded, while the city's consumer economy thrived. Along with the boom came a newfound confidence, culminating in Beijing's success-

Like Beijing, much of Tianjin's early history is gone, but the Astor Hotel remains.

ful bid in 2001 to host the 2008 Summer Olympic Games.

DYNAMIC BEIJING

The city remains a hodgepodge of changing cultures, tottering on the brink of past and future, as if uncertain in which direction it should move.

Every morning, people crowd Beijing's parks to do their morning exercises: *tai ji quan,* martial arts, badminton, and ballroom and disco dancing. Elderly Beijing men play cricket, fly their kites, or admire their birds hanging in ornate cages from tree branches. Some pass the time by playing a game of Chinese chess, surrounded by a dozen friends all craning their necks to see what's happening on the board.

The city's streets are packed with a steady stream of cars—from the locally made Geely to Audi, Mercedes Benz, and even the occasional Mini Cooper or Hummer—all competing for space with bicycles, still the preferred means of transportation for many Beijingers (although flashy mountain bikes have taken the place of the once coveted Flying Pigeons).

Walk around just about any part of the city and you'll find a bevy of shops, from small mom-and-pop ventures selling traditional Beijing snacks and daily necessities to glitzy malls showcasing the best designer products the world has to offer. Take your pick of old and new, from cotton-padded shoes and roasted sweet potatoes to Tiffany jewelry, Prada bags, Bentley automobiles, and the latest skateboarding gear from Quicksilver. At meal times, local Chinese and foreign expatriates rub elbows at the city's countless eateries, from little holes in the wall selling exotic southern foods to chic fusion restaurants in new high-rises.

Today's Beijingers are showing a renewed interest in their colorful past. Photographers and artists race around the city, anxious to record Beijing's old hutongs, courtyard houses, and traditional way of life before they completely disappear. *Laozihao,* the famous old brand-name shops and restaurants, are sprucing up their images and attracting a growing number of customers nostalgic for the good old days. The city has also seen an increase in the number of restaurants offering old Beijing specialties, dishes that were, until recently, on the verge of extinction. The once deserted theaters are again packed with laughing audiences eager to see performances of traditional Beijing storytelling and comedy dialogues. And classic plays about old Beijing, such as Lao She's *Teahouse* or Cao Yu's *Peking Man,* are being staged for young, enthusiastic audiences.

In a wonderful essay entitled "City without Walls," Beijing author Zha Jianying tells of a friend well known for his graceful, nostalgic stories about the city. "Modern Beijing," she quotes him as saying, "is a city where it's impossible to find a spot to hang up one's birdcage."

To understand what he means, says Zha, you have to know about an older image of Beijing: "A gentleman with his tamed birds in a bamboo cage hanging on a branch in a quiet park or in a merry teahouse, or simply in his own courtyard. It is the quintessential image of leisure and a certain type of cultivation. The birdcage is a symbol whose disappearance would mean that a certain lifestyle and a whole set of values had gone with it."

As Beijing transforms itself into a global metropolis of the 21st century, there is increasing hope that the city will find a reasonable balance between past and present.

A century ago, Juliet Bredon lamented the changes that had taken place in the city in words that could very well have been spoken today: "Peking, like China, stands at the cross roads where 'the old and the new meet and mingle.' Will it not be possible some day—when the transitional period is over—to combine the best Chinese traditions with the necessary modifications or west civilisation? May not the metamorphosis take place without giving century-old grey brick walls for new red brick barracks, graceful silk garments for vulgar semi-foreign clothes, poetic legend for marketable facts, and quaint harmonies of splintered tones for blaring jazz music?" ∎

A man pedals a cart loaded with birdcages through the streets of modern Beijing.

Beijing architecture

IN THE SPACE OF LITTLE MORE THAN 15 YEARS, BEIJING HAS CATAPULTED itself into the 21st century, going from traditional single-story gray-brick courtyard houses to Rem Koolhaas's contortionist 755-foot (230 m) CCTV Tower in one fell swoop. As the Chinese say, *"Jiu de bu qu, xin de bu lai*—If the old doesn't go, the new won't come," an idiom that has come to define an era when China's leaders are reaching enthusiastically toward a future filled with prosperity. With big budgets, relaxed zoning regulations, and a cheap labor force, China is unquestionably the place to be for the world's leading architectural firms. But such a vision does not come without its costs, and many question whether the character and soul of the city will survive the transformation.

Although Chinese authorities began dismantling old Beijing about 50 years ago (the city walls, built during the Ming dynasty, were pulled down in 1958), the original city plan laid out by the Mongols in the 13th century is still evident. The basics of Chinese town planning—an orderly rectangular grid arranged on a north–south axis and enclosed by walls with a palace at the center—are even older, having served as a model for more than 2,000 years. Beijing was actually composed of two rectangles. The first, the Inner City, surrounded the Forbidden City and contained government buildings, granaries, and residential areas. The second, the larger Outer City, was located to the south and consisted of the entertainment and commercial districts, as well as the residences of commoners. Today, you can trace the outline of the Inner City walls along the Circle Line, where the former nine city gates have been commemorated as modern subway stations.

THE COURTYARD HOUSE & HUTONG ALLEYWAYS

Three main styles of traditional architecture can be found in Beijing: imperial, residential, and religious. But look closely and you'll see that all are different adaptations of one and the same thing—the one-story courtyard house, or *siheyuan*. The siheyuan is most important because of what it evokes: the harmonious, interconnected relationship of an entire complex rather than one individual building.

During their break time, some workers play shuttlecock in the Financial District.

Like the city layout, Beijing's siheyuans follow a strict geometric order that adheres to the tenets of feng shui (see sidebar p. 46). All are symmetrically aligned on a north–

south axis, with the entrance—a red door flanked by stone lions—always located in the southeast corner. In its most basic form, a siheyuan consists of a main courtyard surrounded by buildings on each side. The northern building was the main hall; the eastern and western wings were of lesser importance; while the southern building was used as a kitchen and space for entertaining guests. As an owner's wealth increased, new courtyards were added, always using the same form.

The courtyards themselves often served as gardens planted with trees, which gave Beijing the impression, when viewed from the surrounding hills, of being "a forest walled in by many miles of ramparts." Thus these traditional dwellings, whose outer walls usually consisted of simple gray brick (unlike the elaborate facades of European homes), provided residents with a surprising degree of privacy and tranquility.

Siheyuans were the fundamental units of Beijing life, and they came together to form neighborhood communities along narrow east–west alleyways known as *hutongs*. Still the heart of the city, hutongs today offer glimpses of old Beijing, from the tofu and soy sauce peddlers wheeling their carts along the tiled lanes to the public chess matches held in front of open doors. The hutongs themselves were joined together by north–south alleyways, the result being a labyrinth-like series of passages.

Feng shui

Feng shui translates literally as "wind water." A popular practice with just about everyone in China, feng shui offers a clear set of guidelines to help people live in harmony with the environment and flow of energy (qi). Historically, it has been most commonly used to locate burial sites and provide guidance for the construction of new buildings. Although generally regarded as superstition, many of its teachings are nevertheless rooted in practicality, and it has exerted massive influence on all aspects of traditional Chinese architecture: The entirety of Beijing is laid out in accordance with the principles of feng shui! Thus, the city and all its old buildings face the south, the source of positive yang energy (and sunlight). To the north of the city are mountains, which protect Beijing from negative yin forces (and invading nomadic tribes).

Closely related to feng shui is numerology. Like many early civilizations that benefited greatly from mathematical advances, the Chinese have long been fascinated with numbers. Hence, everywhere you look in China, you'll see references to numerology: Nine is the magic figure in imperial Beijing (nine city gates, eighty-one knobs on imperial doors), though lately this has been supplanted by the number eight—which sounds like the Chinese word for prosperity. The Olympics, for example, are scheduled to begin on August 8, 2008, at exactly 8:08 p.m. ∎

The layout of the siheyuan was also applied to imperial and religious architecture. The Forbidden City, for example, comprises a series of enclosed courtyards with the most important buildings situated in the north. Aside from the obvious grandeur, imperial architecture distinguished itself with a complex interplay of symbolism, numerology, and color.

Temples in China also follow a similar layout (see pp. 224–225). Although Confucian, Taoist, and Buddhist structures all vary slightly, they reveal their differences in the gods and deities found within their halls; or, in the case of Confucian temples, the total absence of statues.

MODERN TRANSFORMATION

Beijing's architectural future is fraught with controversy. Many traditional residences still lack basic facilities (like sewage pipes), and one-story courtyard homes do not appear to provide an effective solution to the pressing problems of urban migration, high population density, and escalating traffic gridlock. Something clearly needs to be done, though many have criticized the way in which the government has approached the matter.

To date, between 40 and 60 percent of the original 3,000-plus hutongs have been demolished to pave the way for modern towers and thousands of residents have been relocated—willingly or not—to apartment buildings on the outskirts of the city. Although some of the older hutongs have been marked for preservation, Beijing has no doubt set its sights on a skyline like Hong Kong's, and the traditional remnants of the city are not going to stand in the way.

The 2008 Olympic Games have been the one catalyst in the modernizing effort; the Olympic village and new hotels compose most of the city's new high-profile edifices. Topping the list is the National Stadium, designed by the Swiss firm Herzog & de Meuron and Chinese artist Ai Weiwei. Dubbed the "bird's nest," the stadium is a visionary weave of steel ribbons enclosing an otherwise open and environmentally minded structure. Adjacent to this venue is the shimmering National Aquatics Center.

Other well-known architects, designers, and developers working in Beijing today include: Rem Koolhaas, whose firm OMA has designed both the CCTV Tower and its partner, the Television Cultural Center; Paul Andreu, who designed the titanium-domed National Grand Theater near the Forbidden City; Norman Foster, whose Terminal 3 at Capital International Airport is the world's largest; Handel Lee, the developer behind the renovation of the Legation Quarter in Beijing; and Philippe Starck, who oversaw the interior of the LAN Club. ∎

The Poly Plaza, designed by a San Francisco firm, was completed in 2007.

Arts & culture

BEIJING HAS LONG BEEN CHINA'S CULTURAL WELLSPRING. THE COUNTRY'S most innovative minds, in the past drawn by government positions and serious patronage, and in modern times by top universities and a thriving intellectual community, have conferred a pedigree upon the capital that Beijingers are anxious to uphold. Not that they need worry: The city is currently the nexus of the hottest art scene in Asia, and startling quantities of money and international recognition continue to pour in. But while most artists—from writers and actors to painters and musicians—agree that Beijing is the place to be, no one is really sure of the direction that Chinese art is going to take. Will Beijing's artists successfully recast their rich cultural tradition to depict the mix of angst and excitement that many feel in the face of an increasingly global future?

LITERATURE

Writing (*wen*) lies at the heart of Chinese culture (*wenhua*, change brought about by writing) and civilization (*wenming*, the brightness of writing). The source of learning and knowledge, writing—and by extension, literature—was what positioned the Middle Kingdom at the center of the world and elevated it a step above its neighbors.

Although Confucius himself was no poet, his emphasis on education and his legendary status as the compiler of *The Book of Songs* (ca 600 B.C.), China's first anthology of poetry, undoubtedly paved the way for

Artist Zhang Xiaogang and his "Big Family" series

the enormous influence of literature on Chinese society. Formal poetry was the style of choice for over a millennium, and once the bureaucratic examination system was introduced in the seventh century, composing verse became an essential component in securing a government position.

In terms of artistic achievement, poetry lost its edge to drama during the 13th century, and drama was in turn succeeded by fiction in the 14th century. Nevertheless, despite this rich tradition, up until a century ago, literature in China had one major drawback—it was written in classical Chinese and thus could only be read by a relatively select few. This changed with the reform-minded May Fourth Movement (1919). A handful of writers—notably Lu Xun, Mao Dun, Guo Moruo, and Bing Xin—set out to make literature vastly more accessible by writing in *baihua*, or common speech.

A bust of the writer Lu Xun stands outside the Lu Xun Museum.

Widely regarded as the founder of contemporary Chinese literature, Lu Xun (1881–1936) wrote fiction, essays, and criticism, in addition to translating French and Russian literature. Born in southeastern China, he was awarded a government scholarship to study medicine in Japan. However, while still in school he came to the conclusion that medicine was of little use—it was only capable of treating individuals and could not cure the pervasive spiritual malaise and apathy that, he believed, afflicted most of his countrymen. He abruptly switched his focus to literature, seeing writing as the most effective means to raise public consciousness and instigate change. After taking up a teaching position in Beijing, he

published his first short story, the satire "A Madman's Diary," in 1918. A number of other stories followed, including "Kong Yiji" and "The True Story of Ah Q," all of which were finally published in the seminal collection *Call to Arms* (1922). Although much of his writing is harshly critical of Chinese society, he nevertheless evokes a certain tenderness in the portrayal of his characters, and he remains one of the most influential cultural figures of the 20th century.

The writer with the deepest attachment to Beijing is Lao She (1899–1966), another May Fourth writer. Of Manchurian descent, Lao She grew up penniless in Beijing and worked his way through school, while supporting his mother, before moving to London for several years to work at the School of Oriental and African Studies. After returning to China, he published his first and most famous novel, *Rickshaw Boy* (1936), which describes the life of a peasant who comes to Beijing to work as a rickshaw driver, tracing a tragic arc of physical exhaustion and poverty that culminates in a solitary death. Lao She is also famous for the play *Teahouse* (1957), which follows the events in a Beijing teahouse over a 50-year period. He was heavily criticized during the Cultural Revolution, and he eventually died, perhaps by suicide.

Communist rule understandably did little to encourage individual creativity, and until the 1980s there was little real literary output. One of the first voices to break the silence was Wang Meng, a Beijing native born in 1934. Like many writers of his generation, Wang wrote stories, such as "The Butterfly" (1983), that deal with the lives of those who were reeducated by the party and sent to work on communal farms. (Wang himself was sent to the northwestern province of Xinjiang for seven years.) He served briefly as the minister of culture before resigning after the Tiananmen Square protests in 1989. He was nominated for the Nobel Prize for literature in 2003.

Zhang Jie paved the way for female authors with her novels *Love Must Not Be Forgotten* (1979) and *Leaden Wings* (1980), which challenged social mores and the traditional roles of women within marriage.

Despite a mere 25-year gap, Zhang's idealism and quiet provocation seem to be centuries removed from today's sensationalist voices of Chun Sue, who vividly describes the rock-and-roll lifestyle of Beijing's youth culture in *Beijing Doll* (2004), and Annie

the younger generation an outlet for publishing their own thoughts and stories.

Other major writers who previously studied or lived in Beijing include Su Tong (*Raise the Red Lantern, Rice*) and the "spiritually polluted" (i.e., dissident) voices of

The titles of the many poems, books, and essays of Lu Xun (1881–1936)—written in calligraphy—adorn a wall of the Lu Xun Museum.

Wang, who mixes sex with gender politics in *The People's Republic of Desire* (2006).

Sex and drugs notwithstanding, Beijing's most famous contemporary author remains Wang Shuo, a prolific novelist who tackles urban slackers, political satire, and the murder-mystery genre all at once. Only two of his many books have been translated into English: *Playing for Thrills* (1998) and *Please Don't Call Me Human* (2000).

Although the capital is home to most major book publishers, one of the main obstacles for Chinese authors remains censorship. Consequently, many writers are only able to publish complete editions of their works in Taiwan. More recently, the rise of the Internet and blogging has given

Gao Xingjian (*Soul Mountain*) and Ma Jian (*Red Dust, The Noodle Maker*). Gao, a resident of France since 1987, won the Nobel Prize for literature in 2000. His work has been banned in China since 1989.

CALLIGRAPHY & INK PAINTING

It should come as no surprise that in China's literary culture, calligraphy—the practice of instilling writing with beauty—stands at the root of the country's visual arts. Calligraphy has given a particularly unique character to Chinese aesthetics: the art of the line.

It is the dual nature of Chinese characters, which are both conceptual (as a word) and visual (as a stylized image), that lends calligraphy its particular form of expression. The leap from simply writing a character as a word to wanting to endow it with aesthetic qualities seems only natural. Yet this leap wasn't instantaneous—Chinese writing dates back to at least the Shang dynasty (1600–1045 B.C.), but it wasn't until the Spring and Autumn period (770–476 B.C.) that calligraphy began its long evolution as an art form. Despite the various styles that have developed over the centuries, the main emphasis has remained consistently on the brush strokes that make up each character. These lines are what convey personal feeling. As Lu Fengzi wrote in *A Study of Chinese Calligraphy:* "Lines that express happiness are continuous and flowing, with no pauses or breaks, and no sharp turnings. Lines that express unpleasant feelings usually have stops in them, suggesting difficulty or impediment. When there are too many stops, it is a sign of grief and anxiety."

The most common form of art in China, calligraphy appears everywhere: above entrances to temples, adorning the doorways and walls of homes and restaurants, as decoration on teapots and paintings, and inscribed on stone steles at important monuments. In Beijing, it's not unusual to come across men practicing water calligraphy on the ground in public places.

There are five main calligraphic styles, each developed during a different era: seal script (Zhuan Shu), clerical script (Li Shu),

semicursive script (Xing Shu), cursive script (Cao Shu), and standard script (Kai Shu). The "chops" or seals dipped in red ink and used as personal signatures are traditionally in the seal script, the oldest and most complex form of Chinese characters.

Traditional painting

Traditional painting, which uses the same media—brush, ink, and paper or silk—is inseparable from both poetry and calligraphy. Artists trained in calligraphy from an early age, and this training provided the basis for many of the brush techniques they developed. There are deep connections between the three arts—paintings generally contain at least one line of poetry written by

the owner, artist, or master calligrapher—but painting conveys a different realm of concepts and emotions.

One of the fundamental artistic principles of ink painting is qi. In most contexts, qi is translated as "energy." In painting, however, qi has a more figurative meaning. It is the inner spirit or underlying essence of whatever is depicted, animate and inanimate objects alike. Chinese artists weren't nearly as concerned with capturing the exact likeness of something as they were with expressing its qi or underlying reality.

Early artists painted aristocratic portraits and religious parables or figures; the most unique style of Chinese painting, landscape painting, developed later. This genre, which shifted the focus of visual art from human activities to the natural world, began in the fifth century and gained importance with the works of the eighth-century poet and intellectual Wang Wei (699–761). Heavily influenced by the philosophies of Taoism and Chan (Zen) Buddhism, landscape painting reached full maturity during the Song and Yuan dynasties. The most sophisticated works portrayed visual representations of the tao, or underlying force of the universe.

One of the unique characteristics of landscape painting is its temporal dimension. Such paintings weren't meant simply to be viewed; they were intended to be experienced. Mounted on scrolls, landscape paintings were often unrolled from right to left, which added an element of time: seasons changed, rivers flowed, voyages were made. Ideally, landscape painting was a spiritual experience that used the imagination to convey otherwise inexpressible ideas.

Sadly, many of China's priceless artistic masterpieces were looted by foreign powers in the early 20th century, shipped to Taiwan by nationalist forces a few decades later, or destroyed during the Cultural Revolution of the 1960s and 1970s. Today the best place to see traditional Chinese artworks in Beijing is the Capital Museum.

Using water, an artist expresses his thoughts in Beihai Park—"Dragon dancing, Phoenix Flying."

The audience is treated to a stunning acrobatic performance at the Lao She Teahouse.

BEIJING OPERA

No other art form so clearly marks the differences between Chinese and Western cultural tastes than opera. Other traditional arts might be just as abstruse, but even the untrained eye and ear can pick up on elements of pure aesthetic beauty. A Beijing opera, on the other hand, transports viewers into a world that is utterly foreign. In a way, this is one of the best means of visiting an ancient China that has otherwise disappeared. The elaborate costumes, expressive makeup, shrill falsetto, and whirling acrobatics come together to form the country's most sophisticated and popular form of entertainment.

The exact origins of Chinese opera—a convergence of folk tales with traditional music and dance—are debatable, but most scholars agree that by the Yuan dynasty it had become a recognized art form. Traveling opera troupes staged performances in outdoor settings such as teahouses, markets, and temple complexes, which is generally thought to account for the piercing style of music—a natural means of amplification.

As dynasties rose and fell, hundreds of local opera variations slowly spread throughout the empire; Beijing opera is actually a relative newcomer to the stage. In 1790, several troupes from southeastern China performed for the court of Emperor Qianlong. A tremendous success, the actors (men only) stayed on and over time developed Beijing opera, which became the most popular form of opera in the country.

Known as *jingxi,* or opera of the capital, in Chinese, Beijing opera incorporates elements of Chinese opera from the Anhui and Hubei Provinces and is sung in Mandarin. Since stage props are kept simple, most actions in Chinese opera are suggestive and rely on the audience's imagination. Opening a door and holding a battle are easy enough to grasp, but other actions, such as going on a journey (indicated by walking in a circle) will take more guesswork. Likewise, emotions and character traits are also depicted through symbolic gestures and makeup. A red face stands for loyalty and bravery, while a white face indicates cunning; a sleeve raised in front of an actor's mouth means embarrassment, while trembling hands indicates anger. These stylized gestures are considered to be a focal point, and the ability to execute them with grace is how performers are generally judged.

Though it's virtually impossible for foreigners to follow the plot (common themes are mythical stories, battles, and love stories driven by ethical conflicts), it is at least possible to keep track of the characters. The four main roles in Chinese operas are the male (Sheng), the female (Dan), the "painted face" (Jing, usually a god or warrior), and the clown (Chou). Colors also distinguish the characters: The imperial family appears in yellow, high-ranking officials in purple, virtuous characters in red, servants and students in blue, and common folk in black.

Musicians are another integral part of the performance. Operas use a standard

A female opera performer receives the final touches to her makeup before a show at the Lao She Teahouse.

(and comparatively small) repertoire of instruments. Melodies are played on the *huqin* or *erhu,* two-stringed violins, and accompanied by the *ruan* or *yueqin* (a plucked four-string lute). The person who plays the *ban* (a wood block or clapper) directs the orchestra and gives the actors their cues. The 1993 film *Farewell My Concubine* by Chen Kaige offers an intriguing behind-the-scenes look at Beijing opera.

MUSIC

Music is a particularly popular form of entertainment and expression in Beijing. The disenfranchised youth have rallied around hard rock and punk groups since the 1980s, setting themselves apart from the sappy pop stars of Hong Kong and Taiwan. At the other end of the spectrum, China's most brilliant musicians are pursuing classical Western music with unanticipated enthusiasm and talent at the Central Conservatory of Music. Chinese virtuosos have already begun dazzling the West, and some believe that the future of classical music will, to a certain extent, be determined by Chinese talent.

In the wake of all this development, traditional folk and classical music have unfortunately lost a great deal of their popularity in Beijing. Two of the best places to hear classical music concerts include the Lao She Teahouse and the Sanwei Bookstore. There is an enormous variety of Chinese instruments; the most common include: the *guqin* and *guzheng* (zithers), erhu and huqin (two-stringed violins), *pipa* (lute), *yangqin* (hammer dulcimer), and *dizi* and *sheng* (flutes). Northern Chinese processions (typical of weddings and funerals) feature the *suona*, a type of high-pitched clarinet—you'll know it when you hear it.

CINEMA

Following its establishment in 1949, the Beijing Film Studio (Beijing Dianying Zhipianchang) was immediately made into the production center for government propaganda, fulfilling the vision of Mao Zedong and other CCP leaders of creating art that glorified the masses. Its counterparts, the Beijing Film Academy (Beijing Dianying Xueyuan) and Central Drama Academy (Zhongyang Xiju Xueyuan), were both founded in 1950 and served as the training ground for waves of proletarian heroes and capitalist villains. And such was cinema in China for a good three decades. Following the relative loosening of censorship in the 1980s, the unique and lavish imagery of Chinese cinema suddenly began to make headlines at international festivals. The "fifth generation" directors—the first crop of students to graduate from the Beijing Film Academy following the Cultural Revolution —led the charge. Directors Zhang Yimou *(Red Sorghum, Ju Dou, Raise the Red Lantern, To Live)*, Chen Kaige *(Yellow Earth,*

Farewell My Concubine, Temptress Moon), and Tian Zhuangzhuang *(The Horse Thief, The Blue Kite, Springtime in a Small Town)*, along with the iconic actress Gong Li (a graduate of the Central Drama Academy), have produced some of China's most widely acclaimed movies. Many of these earlier films, due to their controversial nature, were produced in Xi'an in lieu of the more conservative Beijing Film Studio.

As both Zhang and Chen gradually moved away from politically provocative themes toward more commercial ventures *(Hero, House of Flying Daggers, and The Promise)*, a new group of independently minded graduates from the Beijing Film Academy and the Central Drama Academy —the sixth generation—sprung up in their stead. The films of Wang Xiaoshuai *(Beijing Bicycle)*, Zhang Yuan *(East Palace West Palace)*, and Jia Zhangke *(Xiao Wu, Still Life) a*re generally low budget and offer an unglamorous yet compelling vision of life in contemporary China.

Aside from being the location of China's top two film schools, Beijing is also frequently used as a setting for many movies, both local and foreign. *Shower* (1999), by Zhang Yang, is a touching drama revolving around a strained father-son relationship that captures the tension between tradition and modernity that tugs at the hearts of many in Beijing. *Beijing Bicycle* (2001) also portrays a type of social tension common to Beijing, that of the migrant and the local, in its story (a nod to *The Bicycle Thief*) of two teenagers who both lay claim to the same stolen bicycle. Foreign films shot on location include Bernardo Bertolucci's *The Last Emperor* (1987), the first Western production filmed in the Forbidden City. More recently, foreign directors have also started shooting pictures at the Beijing Film Studio, including Ang Lee *(Crouching Tiger, Hidden Dragon)* and Quentin Tarantino *(Kill Bill)*.

CONTEMPORARY ART

Today Beijing's art scene bubbles over with creative fervor and excitement. In the blink of an eye, Chinese artists have begun fetching six-figure sums for their work, and more and more collectors are traveling to China

Award-winning actress Gong Li (above) has starred in some of China's most famous movies. Stunning images shimmer across the screen in *House of Flying Daggers* (below), Zhang Yimou's beautifully filmed martial arts romance of 2004.

specifically to invest in contemporary art. While some critics have likened the situation to an economic bubble driven by speculation, others claim that the contemporary art market is only in its nascent stages—local Chinese collectors have just begun to take interest, and their presence is sure to increase in the coming decades.

Of course, economic success is hardly indicative of artistic merit—it's only one factor among many that have helped fuel the community's growth. The city's artistic movement has been in the making since Chairman Mao's death, slowly growing from a handful of subversive figures to the trendy galleries and exhibition spaces scattered around the capital today. Even if there wasn't such a sudden demand for Chinese

art, the massive social upheavals of 21st-century Beijing have given artists plenty of material to work with. The constantly looming threat of political repression and the excitement of working with media previously unknown in China—video installations, abstract oil painting, performance pieces—have given Beijing the edge and creativity to propel the city to the forefront of modern art in East Asia.

When it all began back in the 1980s, life as an artist was a precarious existence. Some of the luckier figures, such as Ai Weiwei (who founded the influential avant-garde group The Stars in 1979), managed to move abroad and work in freedom. In 1989, Beijing's first exhibition of Chinese contemporary art was immediately shut down after

two artists fired guns at their works. The student protests at Tiananmen Square followed later that year, and the Chinese art world took a decisive turn, ushering in the movement known as cynical realism. Two of the most prominent names in Chinese art, Fang Lijun and Yue Minjun, developed their styles during this time. Cynical realism was succeeded by pop art, a response to growing consumerism and Western influence on Chinese culture and industry.

Independent galleries

The international community began paying attention in the 1990s, though intense political control remained the norm and exhibitions were often underground events. It wasn't until the turn of the millennium that things really exploded in Beijing. Perhaps sensing that art had an economic value, authorities eased up on restrictions, and suddenly independent galleries, both foreign- and locally owned, were everywhere.

For now, these independent galleries remain the best places to experience Beijing's unique energy. The 798 Art District (Dashanzi), founded in 2001, is a renovated industrial zone that has flourished as a subculture in its own right, with cafés, bars, bookshops, and more than a hundred art galleries. Although the 798 Art District originally served as a live-work space for artists, high rents have forced most of the artists to seek new studios. Some of the top galleries here include White Space Beijing, Red Gate Gallery, and the 798 Art Space, an enormous warehouse.

Caochangdi Village, founded by Ai Weiwei in 2000, is a 30-minute ride from central Beijing and, perhaps because of this remoteness, draws more of a cutting-edge crowd. In addition to the artist's own gallery, The China Art Archives and Warehouse, the enclave is home to the curator Pi Li's gallery, Universal Studios Beijing (no relation to the one in California), the F2 Gallery, and Shanghai's ShanghART.

Established artists who have become big names in international circles include: Fang Lijun, who depicts disillusionment and angst among China's youth; Zhang Xiaogang, who paints surrealist, family-style portraits; Wu Guanzhong, who mixes traditional styles with European impressionism; Liu Xiaodong, a haunting figurative painter who also collaborates with the independent film movement; Liu Wei, who works primarily with installations, sculpture, and painting; Zhang Peili, a video installation artist; Zhu Wei, who marries modernism with traditional ink paintings; and Huang Rui, an abstract painter.

The high points of the year take place in May during the 798 International Art Festival, and October, the month of both the China International Gallery Exposition and the Beijing Biennale (2009). ■

A woman examines a piece of sculpture at the 798 Art Space in Dashanzi.

Bright Chinese flags adorn Beijing during the weeklong National Day festival.

Festivals

CHINA, LIKE MUCH OF EAST ASIA, FOLLOWS TWIN CALENDRICAL SYSTEMS when it comes to marking and celebrating festivals. Traditional Chinese holidays and indigenous religious festivals follow the Chinese lunar calendar, while modern secular holidays and imported Christian religious holidays follow the Gregorian calendar. Notable festivals and holidays are divided below into traditional/indigenous and secular, then listed in chronological order.

TRADITIONAL FESTIVALS

Chinese New Year/Spring Festival
This traditional holiday, beginning on the first day of the first lunar month (usually January or February), is the most important date on the Chinese calendar. Millions flock to Beijing for the food and crafts at the temple fairs and to view the magnificent parades and displays of color, light, and culture. In Beijing and the rest of northern China, families eat *jiao zi* (dumplings), a symbol of renewal, the festival's philosophy.

Lantern Festival
Celebrated on the 15th day of the first lunar month, the Lantern Festival (known as Yuanxiao Jie) marks the official end of winter and the coming of a new spring. A colorful time to visit Beijing, crowds of people walk the streets at night carrying candlelit red lanterns, while other lanterns hang from lampposts throughout the city.

Birthday of the Goddess of Mercy
Known as Guanshiyin Shengri, or the Birthday of Guanyin, goddess of mercy, this little celebration is held on the 19th day of the second lunar month (generally in late March or early April). It is a perfect time to visit Beijing's Buddhist temples, many of which contain beautiful halls dedicated to the goddess.

Tomb-Sweeping Festival of Qingming
A day dedicated to the respect and memory of deceased relatives, Qingming occurs in early April. Families ritually cleanse their loved ones' gravesites and give offerings of food, wine, and flowers. "Ghost money" is burned at the graves and is meant to be used by the deceased in the afterlife.

Dragon Boat Festival

Generally held each May or June, this festival (Duan Wu) brings to life the compelling sport of Chinese dragon-boat racing. The festival, meant to commemorate the death of Qu Yuan, a third-century-B.C. poet-official, involves competing teams racing in traditional long, narrow, rowing boats. The sport is more than 2,000 years old, but it has recently become recognized worldwide, and this is still one of the most popular celebrations in Beijing.

Mid-Autumn Festival

This family-oriented festival falls on the 15th day of the eighth lunar month (generally September or October), when the moon is full. The shape of the moon represents reunion. During the festivals families get together, forgive old grudges, watch fireworks displays, and eat moon cakes, which in Beijing typically have a thin crust and are filled with beans and jujube pastes.

Birthday of Confucius

Held annually on the 27th day of the eighth lunar month, typically October, this festival celebrates the life of this renowned philosopher at the numerous Confucian temples throughout the city and country.

SECULAR FESTIVALS

Beijing International Kite Festival

Given that China is the "home of the kite," it is understandable that its capital city would hold one of the bigger festivals in honor of the "toy." Held annually in April at the Mentougou Sports Center, the festival is more about kite information than kite demonstrations. Attendees can fly both traditional and modern kites, as well as learn about flying techniques and kite history.

Dashanzi International Art Festival

A relative newcomer to Beijing festivals, this event occurs from late April to late May. Put

The Midi Music Festival attracts tens of thousands of rock fans each spring.

together by 798 Factory, the annual arts extravaganza of Dashanzi offers music, dance, art openings, theater performances, lectures, and gallery receptions. The 798 Art District of Beijing is one of the most cosmopolitan and bohemian areas of the city and is often compared to SoHo or Greenwich Village in New York City.

Midi Music Festival

Held annually in early May, this festival, which was inaugurated in 1997, pays tribute to Beijing's burgeoning rock scene. Drawing musicians from around the world to Haidian Park in the city, it is China's largest rock festival with more than 30,000 attendees and 50 bands. Hosted by the prestigious Beijing Midi School of Music, the three-day event has an environmentally conscious philosophy (in particular toward China's rivers) and is full of great people-watching opportunities.

Youth Day

Held on May 4, this festival (Qingnian Jie) commemorates the student demonstrations which occurred in Tiananmen Square on the same day in 1919. The demonstrations gave rise to an upsurge of Chinese nationalism, and today Chinese youths are encouraged by elders to contribute their wisdom to the continued building of the country. Particular to Beijing is the May Fourth Medal, which is awarded to the top Chinese youths of the year.

May Day

Beijing bursts with tourists during the May Day Holiday, which represents the International Labor Day, and according to a city-wide ordinance, all parks, gardens, aquariums, and natural resorts are elaborately decorated. During the seven-day festival, marked as Golden Week, transportation is heavily crowded with people and the capital's streets are rarely empty.

Beijing Flower Festival

Occurring in major parks and historic sites throughout the capital each spring, this festival brings magnificent floral displays to the public's eye.

Beijing International Beer Festival

Taking place annually during midsummer, this festival is held in various tourist hotels throughout the city. World-class breweries offer an international array of quality beer to sample and drink competitively, and a number of artistic performances coincide with certain brewery or hotel promotions.

Beijing Jazz Festival

The first and largest jazz event held in China, the Beijing Jazz Festival originated in Beijing in 1993. It suffered a seven-year hiatus from 1999 to 2006 but returned in 2007, promising a revival of the annual September celebration. Three days of outdoor concerts —including artists from both China and abroad—mark the festival, which takes place in Haidian District, located in the northwestern portion of Beijing. American performers from previous years include the likes of Grammy-winning trumpet player Wynton Marsalis and pianist Jon Jang.

National Day

Marking the creation of the People's Republic of China on October 1, 1949, this holiday is China's most important national festival. Beijing in particular is ornately beautified with flowers, flags, and buntings lining the streets, red lanterns dangling from shops and official buildings, and in the evening elaborate lights illuminate the city. While a variety of operas and shows are performed at all theaters in the capital, the main congregating takes place at the Great Hall of the People, where the official festival reception is held. During every fifth and tenth year, a grand parade takes place in Tiananmen Square.

Christmas

Celebrated by both Christians and Chinese traditionalists, Christmas in many cities has recently become a secular infatuation. Images of Santa Claus and Christmas trees fill Beijing's streets during the holiday as the religious symbols of Jesus and Mary take a back seat. In Beijing, the celebration is taken as a lighthearted time to give gifts, especially to children, and enjoy the abounding colorful displays presented by the capital city. ■

With many historic sights dating back to imperial times, Dongcheng, or the East District, is the heart of "Old Peking." A visit to its imperial traces or a walk through its idyllic *hutongs,* or alleyways, will provide rich glimpses of Beijing's proud past.

Dongcheng District

Soldiers stand at attention in Tiananmen Square.

Modern Wangfujing, home to century-old shops, is still a busy shopping district.

Dongcheng District

DONGCHENG, OR THE EAST DISTRICT, WAS FORMALLY ESTABLISHED IN 1958, but humans have lived here since ancient times. During the Yuan, Ming, and Qing dynasties, Beijing was the imperial capital, and this area flourished as the political, economic, and cultural heart of the city.

The concentric city walls erected here during the Yuan dynasty were expanded in the Ming dynasty, when Emperor Yongle moved the capital from Nanjing to Beijing in 1417. Dubbed the architect of Beijing, Yongle laid the foundations for a modern capital, placing the Forbidden City, and all the accoutrements that make up an imperial city, in the center. Today many of the grand homes built by the aristocrats and high-ranking government officials of the Ming and Qing dynasties can still be found scattered around the district.

Beijing runs on an invisible north–south axis that cuts right through the spine of the city, from the Temple of Heaven in Chongwen District in the south, through Tiananmen Square, the Forbidden City, and Jingshan Park, all the way up to the Drum Tower and Bell Tower in the north. Other worthwhile sights in Dongcheng include the Lama Temple and the Confucius Temple, as well as the city's colorful alleyways known as *hutongs*.

The area also boasts some of Beijing's best restaurants, from romantic old courtyard venues serving traditional Chinese foods to sleek high-end venues, where the emphasis is on fusion and nouveau cuisine.

It's also home to Wangfujing, one of the city's oldest and busiest shopping districts, where upscale shops mix comfortably with Starbucks, a modern movie theater, and even a handful of *laozihao*, or old brand-name shops, some dating back a century.

Because of all there is to see and do, you'll need at least two or three days to properly visit the major sights in Dongcheng District. ∎

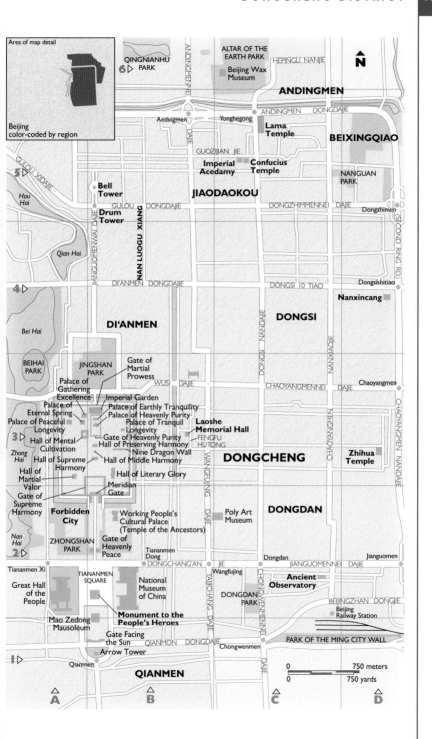

Area of map detail

Beijing
color-coded by region

N

QINGNIANHU PARK
6 ▷

ALTAR OF THE EARTH PARK

HEPINGLI NANJIE

Beijing Wax Museum

ANDINGMEN

Andingmen   Yonghegong

ANDINGMEN   DONGDAJIE

Lama Temple

BEIXINGQIAO

GUOZIJIAN JIE

Imperial Acedamy   Confucius Temple

NANGUAN PARK

GULOU XIDAJIE

Bell Tower

JIAODAOKOU

Hou Hai

GULOU   DONGDAJIE

DONGZHIMENNEI DAJIE   Dongzhimen

Drum Tower

JIANGUOMENWAI DAJIE   NAN LUOGU XIANG

Qian Hai

DI'ANMEN DONGDAJIE

DONGSI 10 TIAO   Dongsishitiao

(SECOND RING RD)

4 ▷

DONGSI NANDAJIE

DONGSI

Nanxincang

DI'ANMEN

5 ▷

Bei Hai

NANXIAOJIE

BEIHAI PARK

JINGSHAN PARK

Gate of Martial Prowess

WUSI   DAJIE

CHAOYANGMENNEI   DAJIE   Chaoyangmen

Palace of Gathering Excellence

Imperial Garden

Palace of Eternal Spring

Palace of Earthly Tranquility

Palace of Heavenly Purity

Palace of Peaceful Longevity

Palace of Tranquil Longevity

Laoshe Memorial Hall

CHAOYANGMEN

Hall of Mental Cultivation

Gate of Heavenly Purity

FENGFU HUTONG

Zhong Hai

Hall of Supreme Harmony

Hall of Preserving Harmony

Hall of Middle Harmony

DONGCHENG

Zhihua Temple

3 ▷

Hall of Martial Valor

Hall of Literary Glory

WANGFUJING DAJIE

Gate of Supreme Harmony

Meridian Gate

DONGDAN

Nan Hai

Forbidden City

Working People's Cultural Palace (Temple of the Ancestors)

Poly Art Museum

2 ▷

ZHONGSHAN PARK

Gate of Heavenly Peace

Tiananmen Dong

Dongdan   JIANGUOMENNEI DAJIE   Jianguomen

CHONGWENMENNEI

DONGCHANG'AN   JIE

Wangfujing

Tiananmen Xi

TIANANMEN SQUARE

National Museum of China

Ancient Observatory

Great Hall of the People

DONGDAN PARK

BEIJINGZHAN DONGJIE

Mao Zedong Mausoleum

Monument to the People's Heroes

Beijing Railway Station

1 ▷

Gate Facing the Sun

QIANMON   DONGDAJIE

PARK OF THE MING CITY WALL

Arrow Tower

Chongwenmen

Qianmen

0   750 meters

0   750 yards

QIANMEN

A   B   C   D

Looking north toward the Drum Tower from the top of Coal Hill

Forbidden City

FROM ITS COMPLETION IN 1421, THE FORBIDDEN CITY (Zijin Cheng) was a 78-acre (32 ha) pied-à-terre for emperors of the Ming and Qing dynasties. One of the most alluring and magnificent treasures in China, it was nevertheless a place of little happiness for the 24 emperors who lived here until 1924, when the famed Last Emperor, Puyi, was forced to vacate. "If ever there was a palace that deserved the name prison," said Reginald Johnson, Puyi's English tutor, "it is the palace in the Forbidden City of Peking."

Forbidden City
www.dpm.org.cn
🅰 65 B3
✉ 4 Jingshan Qianjie
☎ 010/6513 2255
💲 $$; Treasure Gallery & Clock Gallery add'l $
🚇 Metro: Tiananmen Xi/Tiananmen Dong; Bus: 1, 4, 52, or 57 to Tiananmen

When Emperor Yongle moved the capital from Nanjing to Beijing in the 15th century, he built the walled Forbidden City on what was the site of the palace used by the Yuan-dynasty emperors. One million la-borers and 100,000 artisans worked together to build this new city. The palace has been described as a "box within a box within a box" because it was placed in the center of the imperial wall, which was in turn

(most of the buildings you see today were built during and after the 18th century), the Forbidden City signified the distant and unapproachable emperor. It is also the finest existing example of imperial architecture in China.

The Forbidden City reflects the Ming practice of dividing Beijing into walled sections. This is the heart of China, the nucleus of the Middle Kingdom—a receptacle for the Mandate of Heaven and the source from which imperial dictates were issued to even the most far-flung of the country's provinces. The complex is not one stately building as was the Western practice (for example, at Versailles or Buckingham Palace), but rather a series of halls and buildings separated by passages, like a small city. Legend has it that 9,999.5 rooms are in the complex.

Because the palace was constructed primarily of wood, fire was a constant hazard and it regularly burned down. The Manchus (who swept down from Manchuria to install the Qing dynasty) put the palace to the torch in the 17th century. The Japanese ransacked it, as did the Kuomintang (the Chinese nationalists who fled to Taiwan in 1949). The whole labyrinthine complex was almost torn apart during the intoxication of the Cultural Revolution, but it was saved from destruction by the intervention of Premier Zhou Enlai, who interceded more than once to save the national treasure from destruction.

Since traditional Chinese architecture extends horizontally rather than vertically, the buildings in the Forbidden City are not tall, but the space around them is breathtaking.

APPROACHING THE PALACE

It is ideal to approach the site of the Forbidden City from the south,

confined within the city walls. Much of what remains today is Qing-era reconstruction—there are few traces left of the Ming dynasty.

The lackluster name of Gugong Bowuyuan, or Palace Museum, refers to an area closed to the general population. The Chinese name, which translates literally as Purple Forbidden City, is not an allusion to the color of the walls—said by some to resemble dried blood—but to two imperial symbols: the Polar Star, located at the center of the celestial world, and purple, a color associated with royalty.

Considerably restored and embellished since the Ming dynasty

The winding dragon is a symbol for the Son of Heaven.

which gives you the chance to admire the huge port-red walls that thrust out from either side of the **Meridian Gate** (Wu Men). You can enter from the northern gate early in the morning and escape the throngs coming from the south, but the cassette tour guides you from the south. The major halls and palaces are set out along a line bisecting the complex, running south to north. In fact, all Chinese temples are built along this same axis.

The entrance to the Forbidden City is north of **Tiananmen Square,** accessible via the under-ground walkway that runs under Chang'an Dajie. The **Gate of Heavenly Peace** (Tiananmen), the entrance to the Forbidden City, is marked by the monumental portrait of the late Chairman Mao Zedong. The painting was defaced during the democracy protests in 1989, when three workers from Hunan (Mao's home province) flung eggs filled with paint at it—extra copies of the painting are on standby for just such an event. The last of the three protesters was not released from prison until 2006.

The white characters on the red background to the left of the portrait signify the official mantra of China's

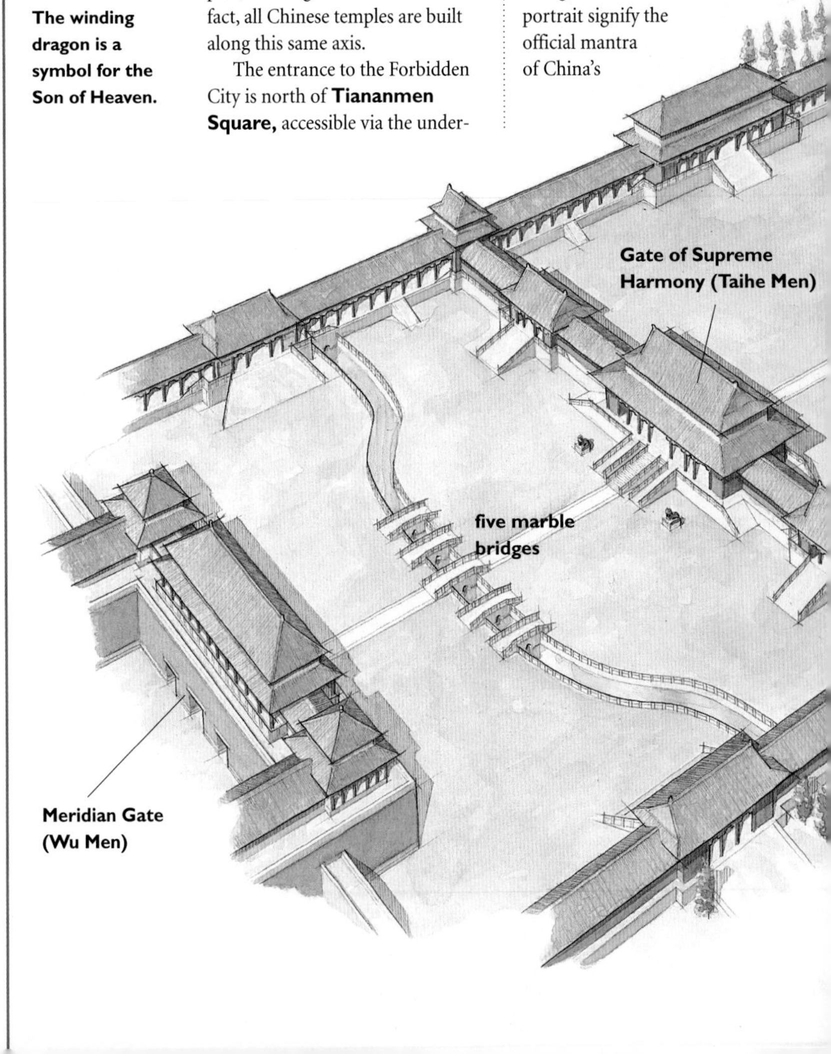

Gate of Supreme Harmony (Taihe Men)

five marble bridges

Meridian Gate (Wu Men)

government, "Long Live the People's Republic of China." To the right the characters proclaim: "Long Live the United People of the World." It was from atop this gate that Mao Zedong authoritatively announced the founding of New China on October 1, 1949, when he proclaimed, "The Chinese people have stood up." For a fee, you can climb up an inner staircase through the gate for views over the square.

It was at the ceremonial Gate of Heavenly Peace that imperial edicts were proclaimed to citizens via a scroll, which was lowered from the

Hall of Supreme Harmony (Taihe Dian)

Hall of Preserving Harmony (Baohe Dian)

Gate of Heavenly Purity (Qianqing Men)

Hall of Middle Harmony (Zhonghe Dian)

Pairs of stone lions typically guard imperial buildings and temples.

high tower by a sash pulled through the beak of a gilded phoenix.

Walking through the gate brings you into a large courtyard lined by souvenir stalls and restaurants. West of the courtyard is the attractive **Zhongshan Park** (Zhongshan Gongyuan), where the emperor used to make sacrifices in spring and autumn to ensure a fruitful harvest. To the east is the **Working People's Culture Palace** (Laodong Renmin Wenhuagong), the former site of the Temple of the Ancestors (Tai Miao), the most sacred temple after the Temple of Heaven during the Qing dynasty.

ENTRANCE

Passing through the next gate leads you to the fortress-like Meridian Gate (Wu Men), which marks the actual entrance into the Forbidden City. The gate was reserved for the sole use of the emperor, with drums and bells sounding his passage as he approached the Hall of Supreme Harmony. Special ceremonies were also held here when generals were sent out on expeditions. The 170-foot-wide (52 m) moat begins its circuit here, where the walls, standing a massive 28 feet (8.5 m) wide at the base, create colossal silhouettes at twilight. Obtain your ticket (and tour guide cassette) from the booths to the left and right.

Through the Meridian Gate you will enter a huge paved courtyard with five marble bridges straddling a central strip of water. Beyond lies the **Gate of Supreme Harmony** (Taihe Men), its ceiling a blaze of emerald green and gold. This gate was built in 1420, destroyed by fire in 1888, and rebuilt the following year. As you walk through the gate, you will see to the east the **Hall of Literary Glory** (Wenhua Dian), which contained the Imperial Library; to the west is the **Hall of Martial Valor** (Wuying Dian).

HARMONY HALLS

Ahead of you stand the three Harmony Halls, each of which had a designated ritual use. Grand audiences, New Year's celebrations, the emperor's birthday, and enthronements were all held in the imposing **Hall of Supreme Harmony** (Taihe Dian). Built at the beginning of the 15th century, the hall was the first and largest of the three Harmony Halls. However, fire destroyed it twice during the Ming dynasty and once during the Qing. The structure that stands today dates from 1695, but it has been renovated many times in the years since it was erected.

Raised on a three-tier carved marble platform, the hall was for many years the tallest building in Beijing, and a law forbade commoners to construct anything higher. No one should look down upon this most sacred of imperial buildings. Twin sets of stairs ascend to the hall, divided by a decorated stone slab over which the emperor's sedan chair would have been conveyed. Inside sits the imperial throne, as well as a sun dial and grain measure, reminders of the emperor's responsibility to make an accurate assessment of the passage of time and also to determine the correct time of year for sowing and reaping. The large bronze and iron vats outside supplied water for fighting fires. In the winter, eunuchs would wrap them in cotton and kept charcoal braziers burning underneath to keep the contents from freezing over.

Tucked behind the Hall of Supreme Harmony is the **Hall of Middle Harmony** (Zhonghe Dian), the smallest of the three halls. Each spring the new agricultural year was celebrated here with a ritual examination of plows and seeds. This is also where ministers from the Ministry of Rites were re-

ceived and where the emperor would get ready for rituals held in the Hall of Supreme Harmony.

The rectangular **Hall of Preserving Harmony** (Baohe Dian) is where the emperor oversaw the final stages of the civil service examinations. It is also where the imperial court received foreign envoys and where Ming-dynasty emperors changed their clothing before and after taking part in ceremonies in other parts of the palace.

The **Gate of Heavenly Purity** (Qianqing Men) divided the Outer Court, which includes the Meridian Gate and three Harmony Halls, from the Inner Court. The carving on the huge marble slab accompanying the stairs shows a dragon flying through the clouds.

THE INNER COURT

The courtyard behind the Gate of Heavenly Purity marks the entrance to the heart of the Forbidden City, access to which was only allowed to eunuchs and maids, as well as the emperor's own relatives.

The Gate of Heavenly Purity leads to what were essentially the imperial residential quarters of the Forbidden City. The first building, the **Palace of Heavenly Purity** (Qianqing Gong), served as the emperor's bedchambers during the Ming and early Qing dynasties. In 1542, one of Emperor Jiaqing's concubines guided a group of some dozen other concubines into the hall, determined to strangle the sleeping emperor. Their plan failed, and the women had their throats cut in public and their flesh sliced off. Yongzheng was the last emperor to live here; later emperors moved to the **Hall of Mental Cultivation** (Yangxin Dian).

Behind the palace is the smaller **Hall of Union** (Jiaotai Dian),

Members of the People's Armed Police march through the Forbidden City.

Puyi

There is probably no more tragic figure in 20th-century Chinese history than Puyi, China's famed Last Emperor, who was a victim throughout his life.

Puyi was born in 1906, and he assumed the throne two years and ten months later upon the death of his cousin, who was likely poisoned by their aunt, the Empress Dowager Cixi. Cixi had appointed the young boy emperor while she was on her deathbed. Eunuchs pulled the small Puyi away from his family kicking and screaming, and they placed the toddler in the Forbidden City, where he was kept under the care of eunuchs and consorts.

His reign was a short one. The boy emperor was forced to abdicate in 1912 following the revolution, but the new Republican government allowed him to hold on to his imperial title and to continue to be treated as a foreign monarch. Nevertheless, his life was somewhat of a cruel comedy.

Six years after abdicating, a Qing loyalist general, Zhang Xun, known as the Pigtail General because he ordered his men to retain their Qing-dynasty braids, attempted to restore Puyi to the throne. The move sent men scurrying to find fake braids to replace the ones they'd cut off in 1912. But the restoration lasted just days until another warlord dropped bombs by hand from an airplane flying over the Forbidden City. In 1924, Puyi was forced to vacate the palace by Feng Yuxiang, dubbed the Christian General because he baptized his men with a fire hose.

After his expulsion from the palace, Puyi moved to the Japanese concession in Tianjin, but in 1932 his Japanese benefactors moved him to the northeast and crowned him reluctant emperor of a puppet state called Manchukuo, a former Manchu territory to the north.

Puyi was captured at the end of World War II and held by the Soviets. He pleaded with Stalin not to send him back to China. At the urging of the Soviets, he testified against the Japanese at the Tokyo war crimes trial, but that didn't save him. In 1950, Stalin sent him back to China, where he spent a decade in a reeducation camp before Mao Zedong declared him reformed. When the Cultural Revolution rolled around, Puyi became a target of rampaging Red Guards who saw him as a symbol of feudalism. Puyi died of natural causes in 1967. ■

where the empresses slept during the Ming dynasty. This hall is also where Qing-dynasty empresses received high-ranking civil and military officials on their birthdays. Twenty-five imperial seals have been kept here since the reign of Emperor Qianlong.

North of the Hall of Union lies the **Palace of Earthly Tranquility** (Kunning Gong), where Manchu shamen once held sacred rituals. A number of Qing-dynasty emperors and empresses slept in the heated chamber connected to the east side of the hall while on their three-day honeymoon. This is also where the last emperor, Puyi, was married in 1922. In the southeast of the Forbidden City a temple known as the Tang Temple, or the Shaman Temple, once stood; its services were later transferred to the Palace of Earthly Tranquility. Immediately behind is the **Gate of Earthly Tranquility** (Kunning Men), which leads to the **Imperial Garden** (Yuhua Yuan), some portions of which date as far back as the Ming dynasty. Enjoy the garden's delightful collection of green pines, exotic flowers, rare stones, pavilions, and small houses.

If you wish, you can leave the Forbidden City through the **Gate of Martial Prowess** (Shenwu Men), which opens to a bridge over the moat that rings the walled city. This is the gate from which Empress Dowager Cixi and Emperor Guangxu fled for Xi'an in August 1900, as foreign powers descended on Beijing.

the **Palace of Eternal Spring** (Changchun Gong), once the living quarters for imperial concubines. The palace houses the theater where Cixi, who was an opera fanatic, often enjoyed performances of Peking opera.

The most important building in this part of the Forbidden City lies to the southeast: the **Hall of Mental Cultivation** (Yangxin Dian). This was the living area for Qing-dynasty emperors beginning with the reign of Yongzheng in the 1730s. This was also the place

If you're eager to see more, and you're not too tired, you can proceed to the two corridors flanking the Forbidden City. First head down the corridor to the west of the **Palace of Heavenly Purity.**

In 1861, the Empress Dowager Cixi gave birth in the **Palace of Concentrated Beauty** (Chuxiu Gong) to the boy who was eventually to become Emperor Tongzhi. (Tongzhi's dynasty was restored on Cixi's 50th birthday and lasted until 1875.) Just to the southwest stands

where emperors dealt with important state affairs and where Puyi abdicated his throne in 1912.

The hall's courtyard has two sections: The south part was used for ceremonies and the north part as the living area. The emperors Tongzhi and Guangxiu held meetings in the hall itself. Because the Empress Dowager Cixi ruled China from "behind a screen" (a term for a regency supervised by a woman), she also attended meetings in the hall, sitting to one side

A worker walks through the Imperial Garden.

Beijingers stop to admire the view of the moat surrounding the Forbidden City.

and separated from the public area by a large curtain. Guangxiu died here in 1908, just one day before Cixi passed away, and it's rumored that the notorious Empress Dowager had him poisoned.

The imperial bedroom was located in the heated chamber in the east of the hall. Here the emperor frolicked with his concubines, who are said to have been carried into the room rolled inside rugs. As the Son of Heaven engaged in sex, imperial eunuchs stood just steps away, offering warnings to the emperor to be careful.

To the south of the Hall of Mental Cultivation is the **Imperial Kitchen** (Yushanfang), which had more than a hundred stoves, each operated by three chefs. One chef selected and washed the ingredients before displaying them for inspection by a member of the imperial household. Another chopped, sliced, shredded, and marinated, while the third cooked the food once palace eunuchs had given the order. All the cooking was watched over by a representative of the imperial household. The kitchen dished out elaborate meals twice a day, at 6:30 a.m. and 12:30 p.m., and simpler meals in the afternoon and evening. The imperial chefs would prepare more than one hundred dishes for each formal meal, with the leftovers turned over to courtiers and servants, or smuggled out to restaurants just outside the Forbidden City.

From here, walk to the northeast side of the Forbidden City, cross in front of the **Gate of Heavenly**

which will bring you to the **Hall of Imperial Supremacy** (Huangji Dian). Cixi's coffin was kept here for a year after her death. Here you will find the **Treasure Gallery** (Zhenbao Guan), which has an impressive and large collection of nicely displayed ceremonial and religious objects.

The **Pavilion of Pleasant Sounds** (Changyin Ge) is in a courtyard to the northeast of the Palace of Tranquil Longevity. This palace has a three-tier opera stage, and Cixi would sit in the building to the north to watch performances. It has a good array of Peking opera props and costumes. Cut across the courtyard to the **Garden of the Palace of Tranquil Longevity** (Ningshou Gong Huayuan), a traditional Suzhou garden, and continue to the **Qianlong Garden** (Qianlong Huayuan). Just north of the garden stand three halls, the **Hall of Nourishing Heavenly Nature** (Yangxing Dian), the **Hall of Joyful Longevity** (Leshou Tang), and the **Pavilion of Peace and Harmony in Old Age** (Yihe Xuan).

Finish your walking tour of the Forbidden City on a somber note at the **Well of the Pearl Concubine** (Zhenfei Jing), which is tucked away in the northeast corner of the Forbidden City. It's said that Zhenfei, Guangxu's favorite concubine and a force behind the emperor during the Reform Movement of 1898, was stuffed down the well by a eunuch after she had angered the Empress Dowager.

To exit the Forbidden City, walk west to the **Gate of Martial Prowess,** which is the north gate. This part of the Forbidden City was reconstructed in 2007; tours of the gate's tower can be arranged for an extra fee. Cross the road to **Jingshan Park**, climb the hill, and marvel at the Forbidden City stretched out below you. ■

Purity, and continue on to the **Hall of Worshipping Ancestors** (Fengxian Dian), which housed the spirit tables of dead emperors and empresses. Continue west where the next corridor leads to the **Palace of Tranquil Longevity** (Ningshou Gong), which served as the home of the emperor's parents. This building has an excellent collection of paintings, stone rubbings, and personal effects of the Qing royal family. The Empress Dowager made this her retirement home in 1889. Directly to the south is the **Nine Dragon Screen** (Jiulong Bi), which is similar to one of the same name in Beihai Park (see p. 110).

Turning back to the north from Nine Dragon Screen you will pass through the **Gate of Imperial Supremacy** (Huangji Men),

Tiananmen Square

Tiananmen Square

🅰 65 B1

☎ 010/6522 9384

$ $ for Arrow Tower

🚇 Metro: Qianmen

Mao Zedong Mausoleum

🅰 65 B1

☎ 010/6513 1130

🕐 Closed Mon.

THE SWEEPING SQUARE OF THE GATE OF HEAVENLY PEACE— Tiananmen Square—is the symbol of China. This vast expanse of paving stones, scene of the 1989 student demonstrations and their gory climax, is an ordered microcosm of the communist universe and a colossal statement of state power. Chairman Mao is interred here, and the monolithic Chinese Parliament overlooks the square.

Tiananmen Square (Tiananmen Guangchang) was the riotous scene of exultation at the launch of the Cultural Revolution in 1966. Today, it is one of the favorite destinations of the hordes of both local and foreign tourists, who crowd just about every inch of the square on a daily basis, eager to soak up its history.

Despite the authoritarian design, the square has become a battleground in the lopsided tussle between government and disaffected groups. In May 1919, disgruntled Chinese university students and intellectuals marched here to protest the unequal Versailles Treaty, which stipulated that China cede territories to Japan. On April 4, 1976, hundreds of thousands of Beijing residents gathered to mourn the death of Premier Zhou Enlai. Wreaths laid to commemorate his passing vanished, leading to a massive riot (the Tiananmen Incident), which was branded a counterrevolutionary plot by some.

Democracy protests in the spring of 1989 were similarly molded from public grief (on this occasion, the death of reformer Hu Yaobang). Sadness again smoldered to anger when the authorities rebuffed the people. Bizarrely, the government sent tanks against unarmed workers and students, rather than riot police and tear gas.

More recently, middle-aged followers of a banned spiritual exercise system, the Falun Gong, frequently assembled in the square, only to be arrested and bundled

into waiting vans of the Public Security Bureau. The square has become a tempting forum for dissent and is perennially patrolled by plainclothes police. October 1 is China's National Day, and half of Beijing descends on the square to commemorate the event.

THE SQUARE

The square, said to be the largest public square in the world, is also a huge park, where couples stroll languidly hand in hand, children play, and elderly men enthusiastically fly their colorful kites. At twilight on a clear day the view here can be astonishing. In the early evening, soldiers of the PLA march out to lower the Chinese flag, attracting an assembly of wide-eyed Chinese.

A motley assortment of historical buildings, garish, Soviet-style monuments, and huge museums flank the square. To the north is Tiananmen and its huge portrait of Chairman Mao Zedong. In the center of the square stands the **Monument to the People's Heroes** (Renmin Yingxiong Jinianbei). Erected in 1958, the monument is dedicated to the memory of the martyrs who gave their lives for the communist revolution.

To the south is the **Mao Zedong Mausoleum** (Mao Zhuxi Jinian Tang), where the waxen-faced Great Helmsman lies in state. The hall was completed in 1977, one year after Mao's death. Today long lines of people still file through to pay their respects to the

Opposite: A sculpted page from China's revolutionary history stands in Tiananmen Square.

A guard stands at attention in front of the Gate of Heavenly Peace.

former chairman, who lies on a slab of black granite from Taishan, one of the five sacred Taoist mountains. Each night, his crystal coffin is returned to its refrigerated resting place beneath the hall. Many rumors about the state of Mao's body still circulate. Mao's personal physician, Dr. Li Zhisui, offers gory details on the bungled embalming in his book, *The Private Life of Chairman Mao.* (Visitors to the mausoleum must store their bags and cameras at special booths on the east side of the building.)

South of the mausoleum stand socialist realist statues that depict scenes of China's revolutionary past. They are a mixture of angry-looking students, fierce workers, and determined peasants. A tangible reminder of China's past, the statues offer an interesting contrast with the free-market capitalism that is sweeping across China today.

The venerable **Zhengyang Gate** (or Qianmen), and the **Arrow Tower** (Jian Lou), sit in the very south and are two of the few remaining gates of the old wall

of Beijing, originally constructed in the early 15th century. The two gates, which were once connected to each other via a semicircular enceinte wall, underwent a major renovation in 2006. The Zhengyang Gate has a photo exhibition of the old gates of Beijing on the first floor, an exhibition of Jin-dynasty bronze mirrors with dragon patterns on the second floor, and souvenirs for sale on the third floor.

The west side of the square is dominated by the **Great Hall of the People** (Renmin Dahui Tang), where China's rubber-stamping parliament meets on a regular basis. You can enter the building when the annual session of the National People's Congress (NPC) is not in session *(usually March).*

Opposite is the hulking **National Museum of China** (Guojia Bowuguan), once home to the dusty China History Museum and the Museum of the Chinese Revolution. The building was closed in February 2007 for major renovations. The new, larger museum will reopen in 2010. ∎

Drum & Bell Towers

SOUNDING OUT THE HOURS TO REGULATE THE FUNCTIONS of daily life and official ceremonies, drum and bell towers have been an integral part of urban life throughout modern Chinese history.

According to the old Chinese system, the night was divided into five *gengs,* each representing two hours. After the watch had been "set" at 7 p.m. with 13 drum beats, each subsequent geng was marked by one drum beat. Civil and military officials organized their lives around these signals. At the sounding of the third watch (1 a.m.), officials attending the morning court audience climbed out of their beds, and at the fourth (3 a.m.), they gathered outside the Meridian Gate (Wu Men) of the Forbidden City. At the fifth watch (5 a.m.), they marched into the Imperial Palace and knelt on the Sea of Flagstones in front of the Hall of Supreme Harmony to wait for orders from the emperor. Only one of the original drums survives. Today 24 new drums are beaten every half hour, from 9 a.m. to 11:30 a.m. and from 1:30 p.m. to 5 p.m.

Just across the square to the north stands the 108-foot-tall (33 m) Bell Tower. The original tower burned down and was rebuilt in stone by Qianlong in 1747; a stele from the Qianlong period stands at the entrance to mark the occasion. The massive bronze bell—which is audible more than 12 miles (20 km) away—was rung every evening at 7 p.m. until 1924, when Puyi, the Last Emperor, was forced to leave the Forbidden City. When you exit the Bell Tower, walk around to the rear yard where you'll find a collection of turn-of-the-20th-century steles. They have been damaged, but some still bear the carved name of Qianlong. Others are covered in red paint, indicating that they may have been the victims of rampaging Red Guards.

The tops of the towers provide wonderful vistas of the hutongs and courtyard houses below. However, the climb up is steep, so don't attempt it if you have bad knees. When you're finished, stop by the rustic **Drum & Bell Café** (*41 Zhonglouwan Hutong, tel 010/8403 3600*) for a drink or a snack. If the weather is nice, head up to the terrace, which has nice views of the Drum and Bell Towers. ■

Drum Tower

🅰 65 B5

✉ 3 Zhonglouwan Linzi (N end of Di'anmen Dajie)

☎ 010/6404 1710

💲 $

🚇 Metro: Gulou Dajie

Bell Tower

🅰 65 B5

✉ 9 Zhonglouwan Linzi (N end of Di'anmen Dajie)

☎ 010/6404 1710

💲 $

🚇 Metro: Gulou Dajie

Performers reenact an old tradition by beating the drums at the Drum Tower.

Hutongs

There is probably nothing more representative of Old Beijing than its charming—but ever fading—hutongs lined with courtyard houses. "To a certain extent, the hutongs and lanes are the soul of Beijing," wrote Liang Bingkun, a well-known Beijing writer, in a book on hutongs.

No one knows how many of these alleyways there are, but according to an old Beijing saying, "There are as many as the number of hairs on an ox," or more than one can count. The Beijing urban planning committee says there were 3,000 hutongs when the Communist Party came to power in 1949, but that only 1,559 still existed in 2003, and hundreds more have disappeared since.

The word hutong is said to come from the Mongolian *hong tong,* which means water well. And they date back more than seven centuries to the Yuan dynasty (1271–1368), when Kublai Khan built his capital, Dadu, where modern-day Beijing stands.

During imperial days, the names of the hutongs were only passed on orally. It was not until the fall of the Qing dynasty that street signs were hung up on the walls. Many of these names come from the trades that once gathered on these streets. Thus, we have Cotton Hutong, Rice Hutong, Scissors Hutong, Tea Leaf Hutong, and Great Li's Hat Hutong.

ARCHITECTURAL NOTES

The smallest hutong in the city stretches just 1.3 feet (0.4 m) wide at its narrow end, which means only one bicycle can head down it at one time. The shortest hutong is no more than 82 feet (25 m) in length, the longest 1.8 miles (3 km).

Architectural details still visible today reveal a great deal about the former inhabitants of these houses. In imperial days, there was a strict hierarchy that dictated style and design. Places with elaborate Chinese gates were the residences of imperial officials or prosperous businessmen; the commoners had basic square-topped gates, known as "eagle will not alight" gates.

There are two to four lintels, usually decorated with auspicious Chinese characters, above each doorway. Common families would have two lintels, wealthy ones four. A typical phrase on the lintels includes the characters *ru yi,* or as you wish. Others say "revolution." Wealthy homes also had decorative door clasps, cymbal-shaped door knockers, and protective brass wrappings often in the shape of a pomegranate—popular because of its many seeds, a wish for many offspring.

When walking through a hutong, note the beautiful carved *mendun*—doorstone. The purpose of which is to provide a brace for the door axle. These stones tell us about the status of the early residents. The bigger the doorstone, the more important the person inside.

The round doorstones represent drums and indicate that the owner has some sort of government tie; rectangular ones graced the homes of scholar-officials, usually found in houses built in the last century. The tops of the stones seat small lions, while the front, right and left sides are usually carved with flowers and auspicious things, such as magpies, plum blossoms, and gourds.

Normally facing south, the houses are made up of one or more quadrangles, depending on the family's wealth. Five courtyards were the limit because of the streets on the house's two sides. The exception, of course, was for members of the royal family. Ronald Knapp, an expert on traditional Chinese architecture, notes that the quadrangle complexes "echo on a small scale the plan of the imperial palaces."

The open central courtyard accounts for some 40 percent of the total area, making it bigger than all the combined structures. Narrow verandas provide a covered space to walk around the complex. The surrounding walls and gates offer seclusion so sitting in a courtyard house, even in a bustling area, allows one to feel miles away.

One good way to explore the insides of these houses is by visiting one of the restored homes, which have been transformed into museums. The house of opera

Top: Young girls play jump rope in an alley. Above: A pair of traditional brass door knockers decorate the entrance to a courtyard house. Right: Beijing's fast disappearing hutongs

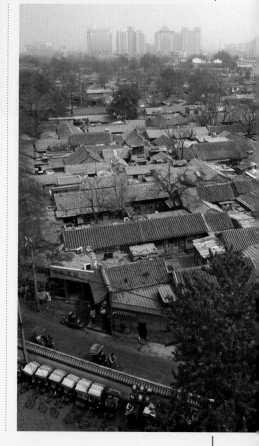

legend Mei Lanfang (see p. 106) is an excellent example open to the public.

Over the years, Beijing's old hutongs and their courtyard houses have inspired hundreds of the city's artists and writers. Well-known authors such as Lu Xun, Lao She, and Mao Dun all lived in Beijing courtyard houses. "Without the hutongs, modern Chinese literature in China would only have been half as significant as it is," opines one writer. The same can be said of Chinese art, as famous painters such as Qi Baishi and Xu Beihong also thrived in the old city's beautiful courtyard houses. ∎

Walk among the Hutongs

This walk will take you through some of the rapidly fading hutongs of Beijing. You'll also have a chance to experience some of the old traditions of the city, passing by shops selling traditional goods and snacks and the occasional itinerant peddlers carrying the tools of their trade on their bicycles. Fortunately, many of the streets along this walk have their names written in pinyin, which should keep you on track.

A poster of Mao Zedong decorates the wall of a small hutong restaurant.

Start at the **China National Museum of Fine Arts** (1 Wusi Dajie, $). Turn left after exiting the museum, and walk to the small **park** on the corner. In the morning you'll find locals practicing *tai ji quan,* dancing, or spinning a *diabolo*—a top-like device that dates back some 2,000 years.

Walk north through the small park and you'll come to a **siheyuan,** a large courtyard house said to have been a gift from the Empress Dowager to her niece. Like many in Beijing, this house has been added to by the families who moved in during the Cultural Revolution. Two wood carvings of a lotus flower—a symbol of purity and happiness—hang from the door. The two lions on either side of the door, as well as the four lintels *(mendang),* indicate that this house once belonged to a high official. If the door is open, you'll notice two large stone screen holders inside, each covered with intri-

cate drawings; unfortunately the screens are long gone.

Leaving the gate turn to your left (east) walk a short distance and make a left at the corner of Meishuguan Dongjie. Cross the street where it veers to your left and continue north down the smaller street on your right. **Dafosi Dongjie** ❶ is lined with food shops. **No. 24-2** sells snacks like *youtiao,* a Chinese-style cruller, and *huoshao,* a round roll with a filling made of sesame paste and brown sugar. The shop next door sells handmade noodles. At the next corner, you'll come to another shop, that sells all kinds of nuts, plus sunflower and watermelon seeds.

The street bears left at the next corner. Walk past the big red gate with the Chinese roof. The **second house** has two large square stones on either side of the door for mounting horses, a relic of the days when horses were still quite common in this part of the city. If the door is open, you might notice the small screen wall, or *yingbi,* just inside. Turn your back to the door and you'll see a similar screen *(zhaobi)* across the street. The Chinese once believed the screens could prevent evil from entering the house.

SHIJIN HUAYUAN & GANGCHA HUTONGS

Retrace your steps back to Dafosi Dongjie. Turn left into the narrow hutong, then bear right on to **Shijin Huayuan Hutong ➋**. Just follow the winding street—there's only one way to go. At the first building on your right is a semicircular millstone used to grind corn. The brass plaque on the next corner explains the history of the hutong.

Turn left at the plaque on to **Gangcha Hutong**. Take the first right. The first house on the left has four lintels, another symbol of high rank. At **No. 1** on this street you'll see a pigeon coop on the roof and 13 electric meters at the entrance, which indicates that there are 13 families living in this compound that was built for one. Unfortunately, the beautiful mendun are

hidden behind a pile of trash and bicycles.

At the next corner, turn left onto **Nanjianzi Xiang ➌**, or South Scissors Street. Notice the new courtyard house on your right. At **No. 78** *(also on right)* you'll see the *pushou,* or son of the dragon, door handles, with huge rings in their mouths, which are good for protecting the home. **No. 72** is a Republican-era structure with a European look. The wooden window over the door is decorated with peaches and a bat.

At some point during the walk, you may

> 🅐 See area map p. 65
> ▶ China National Museum of Fine Arts
> ↔ 4 miles
> 🕐 2 hours
> ▶ Nan Luogu Xiang

NOT TO BE MISSED
- Archway, No. 15 Dong Mianhua Hutong
- Nan Luogu Xiang

A group of men pass the time playing a game of *xiangqi,* or Chinese chess.

hear the loud whistling made by pigeons, with bamboo whistles tied to their tails, that have just been released from a nearby pigeon coop.

WANG ZHIMA HUTONG
After you pass **No. 33** (a round red door and brass door rings) turn right down **Wang Zhima Hutong** ❹. This street has small courtyard houses. The roof tiles on **No. 59** have been decorated with the symbol for double happiness, as well as the characters *xinxiang shicheng,* meaning "whatever you wish will come true." **No. 56** has two small mendun, and the door, like most courtyard houses, has a brass plate to protect it. The

shape of the plate and the order of the nails resemble an auspicious motif. **No. 49** has one of the few doors that is painted green, and the mendun are carved with gourds with a lion sitting on top. The beam over **No. 39** has magpies, which symbolizes double happiness coming to your doorstep *(shuangxi linmen).*

No. 28 has two nicely carved horse-mounting stones—one carved with a reverse swastika and a bat, a symbol for long life. The second has an ancient coin motif, indicating the owner was a merchant. The second door of this complex is the **Huadu Hotel.** On two sides of the doors are stone carvings of baskets and grapes. In addition, there are two large red lanterns. Finally, notice the rare communist-looking stars on the lintel at **No. 15.**

DONGSI BATIAO

At the end of the street you'll come to Dongsi Bei Dajie. Cross it and plunge into **Dongsi Batiao ⑤**, the lane opposite. **No. 70** has two cylindrical millstones beside the door, which means that this must have been a grinding shop. A local old women says that the house belonged to a *lao dizhu,* or old landlord. "It used to be quite nice," she says.

Enter the small yard that leads to **No. 111** and you'll see two storage places to your right —one for cabbage, one for coal. Enter the next door and turn right. The windows are Republican era with wooden shutters. Walk to the end and enter the covered walkway for a peek at the colorful Western-style floor tiles. There's a stone carving over the door, and the mendun is carved with a bat and coin, both symbolizing the wish to achieve prosperity.

Retrace your steps back to Dongsi Batiao and turn left. Notice the roof tiles on **No. 109,** which have the infinity knot on them and mendun designed with Buddhist symbols. There's a swastika over the door and a plaque decorated with chrysanthemums.

A sign at **No. 89** indicates that it's a Muslim eatery with bean-curd custard, flat breads, lamb, and intestines with sesame sauce specialties. The stone squares flanking the door at **No. 71,** a historically protected house, feature nicely carved lions, their heads stolen long ago.

With two stone lions guarding **No. 67,** it's clear that this was once the home of an official. The lintels have four beams, each with a Chinese character for a popular flower or plant: plum, orchid, bamboo, and chrysanthemum. **No. 61** has two large stones for mounting horses and good mendun.

At **No. 43** you'll see a wooden door unlike many of the doors remaining in China. The characters are carved in the standard style, which indicates that the writing probably pre-dates liberation in 1949, before the party officially switched to simplified characters.

MENLOU HUTONG

When you reach the end of Dongsi Batiao, turn left on Chaoyangmen Bei Xiaojie. Cross the intersection and walk down to Dongsishitiao (*marked by a big street sign*). The large, gray, modern complex on your right is the former site of the Haiyuncang Imperial Granary. Walk to **Menlou Hutong ⑥,** the third alley on your left— marked by a red sign—and turn left. The big gray building on your right is identified as the site of the old pawnshop. There used to be a guard tower on the corner here.

The redbrick building on your left is an example of 1950s urban-socialist housing— there is no central heating (coal briquettes are burned for heat and cooking) and the bathrooms on each floor are shared. At the corner of **No. 55,** you will see another millstone planted on the corner to protect the building.

At the intersection, the name of the street changes to **Xinsi Hutong ⑦.** Formerly a nunnery, **No. 35** on the right is home to several families today. Bear left here, and then turn right onto Dongsi Bei Dajie.

FUXUE HUTONG & DONG MIANHUA HUTONG

Cross Dongsi Bei Dajie and walk about 55 yards (50 m) to **Fuxue Hutong ⑧.** There's not much to see at first, but you'll discover several geomancy, or feng shui, masters. Several neighboring shops have hung mirrors to repel any evil emanating from the feng shui shops. On the right is the **Wen Tianxiang Temple,** built in the Ming dynasty. **No. 65** is a school.

Cross Jiaodaokou Nan Dajie and enter **Dong Mianhua Hutong ⑨,** or East Cotton. At **No. 15** notice the plaque that marks the home as a protected site. Walk inside the gate and continue to the carved brick archway. The former residence of a Qing-dynasty general, this archway combines Chinese and Western architectural styles with carved flowers, animals, and other auspicious symbols.

After exiting the hutong, turn right and continue walking west. This street houses part of the **Beijing Central Academy of Drama,** so the streets are filled with students. A few blocks ahead is **Nan Luogu Xiang** (see p. 92), the end of your walk and a wonderful place to stop for a drink or a meal. Afterward explore the boutiques or head up and down the neighboring hutongs, which are rich in history and architectural detail. ∎

A commemorative arch marks the entrance to the Imperial Academy.

Confucius Temple & the Imperial Academy

ONCE DUSTY AND NEGLECTED, THE CONFUCIUS TEMPLE is enjoying newfound popularity. In preparation for the 2008 Olympics, and with the Great Sage once again revered around China (see pp. 88–89), this formerly run-down temple underwent a much needed renovation in 2007.

Confucius Temple & the Imperial Academy

🅰 65 C5
✉ 13–15 Guozijian Jie
☎ 010/8402 7224
💲 $
🚇 Metro: Yonghegong

You can reach the temple, first built in 1306, heading north and west from the Lama Temple to Guozijian Jie. On the way, you'll pass a stone table that says: "Military Officials must dismount from their horses here, and civil officials must descend from their sedan chairs."

Enter the temple through the **Gate of the First Teacher** (Xianshi Men). In the first courtyard, you'll find 198 stone steles carved with the names and towns of 51,624 successful candidates in the civil

service examination during the Yuan, Ming, and Qing dynasties. While most names have faded with time, many can still be identified.

Continue north to the **Gate of Perfection** (Dacheng Men), where a set of ancient white stone drums are carved with poems about hunting, a popular Manchu pastime.

To the left is the well-named **Pool of Water for Inkstones** (Yanshui Hu). It was said that anyone who drank water from this well would pass the imperial civil service exam with flying colors. Although the well has long dried up, recently it has been attracting numerous high school students each year before the very competitive national university entrance exam.

The annual sacrifice to Confucius was made in the **Hall of Perfection** (Dacheng Dian), the temple's main structure. The spirit tablets of Confucius were placed on the altar in the middle of the hall during the rituals, with the spirit tablets of his disciples placed to the side. Reproductions of ancient ritual implements and musical instruments are on display.

In a corridor to the west of the Hall of Perfection is a set of 189 stone tablets, on which the texts of 13 Confucian classics have been meticulously carved.

On the west side of the Confucius Temple is the site of the former **Guozi Xue,** a school set up in 1306 to educate the Mongol sons of the Yuan rulers. After the fall of the dynasty, the Ming rulers turned it into an institution of higher education, today known as the **Imperial Academy** (Guozi Jian).

In the second courtyard you'll find a **drum** and **bell tower** on each side. In the center is an impressive glaze-tiled **pai-lou,** or commemorative arch, with a line from the *Analects* by Confucius. In front of the arch is **Biyong,** a hall built in 1784 and where the emperor would give a speech each year during the spring. Walk around the **River of Crescents** (Pan Chi), which has four marble bridges breaking the pool into four arcs. ■

Examination hell

Passing the imperial examinations was an essential step up the imperial civil service ladder. Candidates came to Beijing from the provinces every three years to take the exam, which tested their ability to remember huge portions of the Confucian classics. They spent three days and two nights in solitary confinement in tiny cells, their only comforts a board for a seat and another that served as a small table. Before entering their cells, examinees had to change clothes to prevent cheating. The corridors between the cells were patrolled by vigilant overseers. To further prevent cheating, once the cell doors were shut and sealed by the Imperial Commissioners, they could not be opened again until the exam was over. This was true even in the case of death, when a hole would be cut in the wall and the body removed, which the sources tell us sometimes happened.

These extraordinary efforts to prevent cheating were apparently not enough. We have evidence that many of the men who took the exam resorted to all sorts of tricks to help them, including the smuggling in of mini-books and cheat sheets the size of a fingernail. Some of them purchased essays in advance or bribed the judges for good marks. An exhibition dedicated to cheating, in Beijing's old Imperial College, displays the shirt of one cheater covered with Chinese characters.

The system of imperial exams came to an end after 1900, when the Empress Dowager Cixi finally realized that the civil service system was the main obstacle to reform and tossed the system aside, substituting modern education for the classics. ■

Confucius:
The comeback kid

Once banned, works by Confucius—who is the country's most influential and inspiring philosopher—are again being studied and celebrated throughout China.

Inside a classroom on the campus of Tsinghua University, Tang Wenming is having an animated discussion with ten doctoral students about the differences between the Greek and Confucian concepts of virtue. The blackboard behind Mr. Tang is nearly covered with Chinese characters—heaven and

The once reviled philosopher Confucius is now basking in newfound popularity.

earth, morality, virtue—and a smattering of English words.

He pauses to take a drink of water, jumps into the differences between Taoism and Confucianism, and then continues on to other classical Chinese concepts: the I Ching, yin

and yang. The students tap away on their laptops or scribble in notebooks. The three-hour class, which began at 8 a.m., should have been over 25 minutes ago, but the students continue to ask questions, and Mr. Tang, an associate professor of philosophy, shows no sign of breaking away.

His course, "The Ethics of Qin Confucianism," is just one of many manifestations of the Confucian fever that is currently sweeping across China. Scholars and students are dusting off classics once banned from the classroom, while the general public is snapping up books and attending university lectures on this formerly taboo topic.

For more than 2,500 years, China was guided by Confucian thought, which advocates a state guided by highly ethical scholarbureaucrats and a society ruled by morality with a strong emphasis on hierarchical relationships. But by the end of the 19th century, the Chinese state, powerless to fight off foreign encroachment and growing public dissatisfaction, was teetering on the brink of collapse.

Leading intellectuals pointed an accusing finger at Kong Fuzi (551–479 B.C.), better known outside China as Confucius. During the May Fourth Movement of 1919, intellectuals frustrated by China's failures shouted "Down with the Confucian store!" and called for science and democracy to take the seat of the Great Sage.

Confucius was even more harshly attacked when the communists came to power in 1949. During the Cultural Revolution, Confucian temples throughout China were damaged by rampaging young Red Guards, and Confucian scholars were frightened—and often beaten—into silence.

Now, almost a century after Confucianism first came under attack as an obstacle to development, it is being heralded as a solution to the many political, economic, and ethical problems China faces.

In addition to impressive economic gains over the past 30 years, China has experienced a growing gap between rich and poor and a rise in corruption, crime, and divorce. Academics say few people still believe in Marxism or communism, but nothing has risen yet to take their place, leaving an ideological vacuum. Nevertheless, many Chinese find Confucianism an appealing alternative to both free-market economics and hard-line communism.

Confucian scholars are basking in a new-found popularity that none could have imagined just a decade ago. Books and DVDs on

A man reads an inscription carved on a stone slab in the Confucius Temple.

Confucianism are selling well, and some 18 universities around the country offer courses on Confucianism or have set up Confucian institutes. Academic conferences on the philosophy have become regular events, so that even the most dedicated Confucianists find it difficult to keep up with the pace of events.

China's national fascination with the topic was made evident in the fall of 2006 when Yu Dan, a 41-year-old media professor at Beijing Normal University, appeared on "Lecture Room," a popular television program. For seven nights, millions of people around the country watched Professor Yu as she put the *Analects* of Confucius into simple words. A book based on the lectures sold three million copies over the next four months.

Even children are caught up in Confucian fever. On a Saturday morning at Beijing's Confucius Temple, a five-year-old girl recites from the Confucian classic, *Discipline of Students*. Her mother confesses that she's not even sure her child, who has not yet learned to read, understands her lines, but she insists, "My daughter has become much more polite since she started attending classes here."

Located in a quiet area about 1.5 hours outside Beijing, the Saint Tao Experimental School was founded in 1998 by some of China's leading intellectuals who were concerned about the lack of traditional education in Chinese schools. St. Tao, which has a total of 56 students from all over China, provides students with the core curriculum offered in other state schools but it also adds a heavy dose of classical studies.

In a third-grade classroom, ten students sit up straight in their chairs, hands behind their backs. For twenty minutes they recite from memory—effortlessly it seems—lines from some of China's most famous classics. Students also receive training in traditional music and art and Chinese martial arts, as well as computer science and English.

Jiang Qing, a retired humanities professor who is now a guest lecturer at Shenzhen University and a conservative Confucianist, applauds Professor Yu's effort to simplify Confucianism. "Chinese who once felt Confucianism had no value have now found that it is very valuable," he says. "That's incredible."

Mr. Jiang is probably the most extreme example of the love affair with Confucianism. In many of his articles he argues that only a Confucian revival can save China. *Political Confucianism*, a 462-page work, calls for a legislature made up of elected officials, the successful candidates of a rigorous examination based on Confucian texts, and elites charged with ensuring cultural continuity. The latter would be proven descendants of Confucius.

Mr. Jiang says further that he'd like to see required college courses on Marxism replaced by courses on Confucianism. "Confucian principles teach one how to be an upright person and the right way to do things," he says. "No matter what you do, you need to know this."

Confucianism survived the attacks of the influential May Fourth generation and more than three decades of harsh persecution by the communists. The 2,500-year tradition permeates Chinese society and culture in ways that many may not even realize. No matter what form this revival takes, it's not likely that Confucianism will disappear anytime soon. ■

Lama Temple

THE LAMA TEMPLE, OR YONGHE GONG IN CHINESE, WAS originally a mansion, built by Kangxi in 1694 for his fourth son, Prince Yong, better known to the world by the name Yongzheng. After Yongzheng ascended the throne in 1723, some of the buildings in the large complex were converted into a Lama temple, and the roof tiles were changed to yellow, a royal color. Yongzheng died in 1735, and his son, Qianlong, made the complex a lamasery, inviting hundreds of lamas from Mongolia to stay permanently. Lamaism is the main religion of Tibet, Mongolia, Sikkim, and Bhutan.

Lama Temple

- 🗺 65 C5
- ✉ 12 Yonghegong Dajie
- ☎ 010/6404 4499
- 💲 $
- 🚇 Metro: Yonghegong

A long path runs north and south along the center of the entrance to the temple. Thousands of monks once lived on the east side of this path. After passing under the first gate, you'll come to the first courtyard, which is flanked by the traditional drum and bell towers that are found in many temples. The two stone tablets, each with its own pavilion, are engraved with Qianlong's essay "On Yonghegong," written in Chinese and Manchu in the eastern pavilion and Mongolian and Tibetan in the western.

The first building you'll come to is the **Hall of Heavenly Kings**

(Tianwang Dian. Today, the ebullient Future Buddha, in his guise as the **Laughing Buddha** and accompanied by the Four Heavenly Kings on either side, greets all. Above him is written: "If the heart is bright, the wonderful will appear." Behind him is the trusty **Weituo,** the defender of the faith, holding his scepter, a symbol of strength for fighting evil spirits. The stone tablet in the courtyard behind is engraved with Qianlong's essay "On Lamaism."

In the next courtyard is the **Yonghe Palace** (Yonghe Dian), the main hall of the temple. It houses statues of the 18 luohan, or arhats (see p. 140), and three golden, robed Buddhas: the Last Buddha, the Historical Buddha, and the Future Buddha. In front of the three Buddhas are the eight magic weapons of Tibetan Buddhism: the wheel of the law, the umbrella, the infinity knot, the conch shell, the lotus, the vase, the pair of fish, and the canopy. And don't forget to look up; the decorated ceiling is startlingly beautiful.

Next is the **Hall of Eternal Divine Protection** (Yongyou long rows of cushions in the hall. The roof is an interesting mixture of Chinese and Tibetan architectural styles; piles of Tibetan scriptures printed from woodblocks lie against the walls.

The **Wanfu Pavilion** (Wanfu Ge), or Pavilion of Ten Thousand Happinesses, is built around a colossal statue of the Maitreya Buddha. Carved from a single block of sandalwood, the statue stands 86 feet (26 m) high, with one-third of its body below ground to steady it in case of an earthquake.

Dian), once the home of Prince Yong. When Yongzheng passed away in 1735, his sarcophagus was placed here before it was buried in the Western Tombs of Qing along with other Qing-dynasty emperors.

On the altar of the **Hall of the Wheel of the Law** (Falun Dian)—which was built during the Qing dynasty—stands a statue of Tsong Khapa, the founder of the Yellow Hat sect of Lamaism. The lamas who live here visit five times a day to take part in religious activities, during which they sit on the In the northwestern part of the temple is a display of Qing-dynasty articles from Tibet and an exhibition on Tibetan Buddhism and the Lama Temple. The collection includes dharma wheels, scepter-like *dorjes,* bells, effigies of Buddha, and a multiarmed statue of Guanyin, goddess of mercy.

After you finish touring the main structures of the Lama Temple, wander around the corridors on either side in order to take in some of the smaller halls of this important temple. ∎

Religion is making a resurgence in China as more and more people flock to temples.

More places to visit in Dongcheng District

ALTAR OF THE EARTH PARK (DITAN GONGYUAN)

Built in 1530 for the worship of the earth, the Altar of the Earth was the second most important imperial altar after the Temple of Heaven (see pp. 116–120), which stands at the opposite end of the city's north– south axis. Emperor Yongle dedicated the Temple of Heaven to the worship of both heaven and earth, but later, court astrologers advised Emperor Jiajing to build a separate sacred space for the latter. Every summer solstice, the emperor, dressed in yellow robes, would offer sacrifices at the altar, and officials would report here on special occasions. The altar consists of two square terraces of marble (symbols of the earth). South of the altar is the **House of the Imperial Gods** (Huangqi Shi), which houses the spirit tablets for the earth, mountains, seas, and rivers, as well as some imperial ancestor tablets. A temple fair is held here during Chinese New Year. The **One Moon Gallery** is located in a beautifully restored Ming-dynasty building near the south gate.

🅰 65 C6 ✉ Andingmenwai Dajie ☎ 010/6421 4657 💲 $; extra fee for Altar & Huangqi Shi 🚇 Metro: Yonghe Gong (East Gate) /Andingmen (West Gate)

ANCIENT OBSERVATORY

Construction on the Ancient Observatory (Guanxiang Tai)—which was built on the remains of the old city wall—began in 1437. Dedicated to astronomy, astrology, and seafaring navigation, it was operated by Muslims and later Jesuits. The observatory museum is dedicated to Chinese astronomy. Displayed on the roof are pieces designed by the Jesuits in 1674 on the orders of Emperor Kangxi.

🅰 65 C2 ✉ Jianguomenwai Dajie 💲 $ 🚇 Metro: Jianguomen

LAO SHE MEMORIAL HALL

Lao She, one of China's most talented writers, was the author of *Rickshaw Boy (Luotuo Xiangzi)*, a novel published in 1936 that tells the tragicomic tale of a rickshaw puller's life in an uncaring society, and *Teahouse,* a bittersweet play from 1957 that describes the changes in China from the overthrow of the

Qing dynasty in 1911 to the nationalist period.

The son of a Manchu soldier, Lao She was born in Beijing in 1899. He moved to London in 1924, where he taught at the School of Oriental and African Studies. In 1946, Lao She moved to New York, where he taught Chinese literature at Columbia University. He returned home at the urging of Premier Zhou Enlai in December 1949, after the communists came to power, and moved into this traditional courtyard house. The living room and adjoining bedrooms remain much as they appeared when his family lived here in the 1960s. Two other rooms house his personal effects and books. The calendar on Lao She's desk remains open to Wednesday, August 24, 1966, the day his body was found floating in a Beijing lake. It's unclear whether he committed suicide or was murdered.

🅰 65 C6 ✉ 19 Fengfu Hutong, just off Dengshikou Xijie ☎ 010/6514 2612 💲 $ 🚍 Bus: 103, 104, or 108 to Dengshikou

NAN LUOGU XIANG

This narrow street, which dates back some 700 years, is flanked by eight hutongs to its east and west, and is said to resemble a giant centipede. In recent years it has taken on new life with a string of artsy restaurants, coffee shops, bars, and boutiques established in cozy old Beijing houses. Check out **Wenyu Nailao** (*No. 49, tel 010/6405 7621*) for delicious Chinese custard; **Plastered 8** (*No. 61*), a shop offering T-shirts with amusing Beijing motifs; and the **Jindian Consignment Shop** (*No. 43*) for nostalgic items. What really makes the neighborhood interesting, however, is that it's right in the middle of a traditional Beijing neighborhood. The hutongs and courtyard houses on surrounding streets are some of the most colorful in the city. Head out in any direction and wander.

🅰 65 B3 ✉ Bet. Di'anmen Dong Dajie & Gulou Dong Dajie

NANXINCANG

Beginning with the Ming dynasty, the beautiful old structures at Nanxincang stored grain

The newly renovated Ming-dynasty granaries at Nanxincang

Astronomical instruments erected by Jesuits remain atop the Ancient Observatory.

for the imperial family and court officials. Now this historic site is home to three art galleries, shops, a teahouse, bars, and restaurants. The structures at Nanxincang—just ten years younger than the Forbidden City—were among the more than 300 granaries that existed during imperial days. The granaries were all built according to conventionalized standards, and the floors were paved with thick bricks and covered with wooden boards resting on brick shoulders to insulate the grain from the moisture of the earth. An elevated opening placed in the center of the roof, which can still be seen today, was enclosed with woven bamboo strips to prevent birds from entering, while providing sufficient ventilation. The 5-foot-thick (1.5 m) walls stabilized the room temperature and prevented the grain from getting moldy. Grains shipped north along the 3,000-mile-long (4,828 km) Grand Canal fed the various granaries. Sadly, Nanxincang is the only one to survive.

🗺 65 C2 ✉ SW of Dongsi Shitiao Qiao, one block W of the 2nd Ring Road 🚇 Metro: Dongsi Shitiao

POLY ART MUSEUM

This very impressive museum, located in the New Poly Plaza, a beautiful glass office tower, was originally established in 1998 to prevent Chinese artwork from falling into the hands of foreign collectors. The Poly Art has made a number of high-value overseas acquisitions of ancient bronzes, sculptures, and paintings. The museum is divided into two galleries: one for the display of early Chinese bronzes, and the other for Buddhist scriptures carved in stone. Also on display here are four bronze animal heads that were once stolen from the Old Summer Palace.

🗺 65 C2 ✉ 9 New Poly Plaza Tower, 1 Chaoyangmen Bei Dajie ☎ 010/6500 8117 💲 $$ 🚇 Metro: Dongsi Shitiao

ZHIHUA TEMPLE

Zhihua Temple was built in 1444 by a wealthy Ming-dynasty eunuch, Wang Zhen, as a place where he hoped monks would carry out ancestral rites in his memory. It's said that the eunuch was put to death a couple of years after the temple was completed. A wooden statue of him stood here for some 200 years. The complex, an excellent example of Buddhist architecture in the Ming dynasty, has three courtyards. **Rulai Hall,** in the rear, houses a 29.5-foot-high (9 m) copper seated Maitreya Buddha of the Future accompanied by two attendants. Niches in the wall are filled with an army of small Buddhas that number more than 9,000. The ceilings, which have been removed from the temple, are now housed in the Philadelphia Museum of Art and the Nelson-Atkins Gallery in Cleveland.

🗺 65 D3 ✉ 5 Lumicang Hutong ☎ 010/6525 0072 💲 $ 🚇 Metro: Jianguomen ■

Xicheng District (Xicheng Qu) is an eclectic hodgepodge of old *hutongs*, courtyard houses, idyllic lakes, and quaint old homes dating back to imperial days.

Xicheng District

Prayers written on small wooden plaques hang from trees in Beihai Park.

Residents do their morning exercises alongside the lake in Beihai Park.

Xicheng District

XICHENG, OR THE WEST DISTRICT, IS A ROMANTIC LAKE AREA THAT INCLUDES Beihai Park (the former romping ground of the Manchu royal family), temples, and a series of lakes ringed by willow trees and *hutong*-lined courtyards. Located between the university area to the northwest and the Forbidden City to the southeast, this area provides a quiet respite from the hustle and bustle of the city center.

Six connected lakes, their waters originating in the northwestern section of Beijing, pierce the eastern edge of Xicheng District. Farthest north are the three Rear Lakes: Xi Hai, Hou Hai, and Qian Hai. In the middle is popular Bei Hai, located just north and west of the Forbidden City. Zhong Hai and Nan Hai are situated to the south, with the walled fortress known as Zhongnanhai (or Central and South Seas) standing between them. Not open to tourists, Zhongnanhai has served as headquarters and home to senior Communist and central government officials since the party came to power in 1949.

All of the rulers who made Beijing their home used the lakes and the beautiful grounds around them as their imperial playground. The earliest mention of the lakes dates back nearly 2,000 years to the Jin dynasty, whose rulers built the hill in the middle of Bei Hai that is known today as Hortensia Isle. Later the 13th-century Mongol rulers of the Yuan dynasty created an imperial garden here, while the areas around Bei Hai, Zhong Hai, and Nan Hai were the pleasure gardens of the imperial court during the Ming and Qing dynasties.

The Republic of China, which was established in 1911 after the fall of the Qing dynasty, had its presidential office on the shores of Nan Hai until 1925, when the capital was moved to Nanjing. In 1949, after much debate, the party took up residence in Zhongnanhai, making this the center of politics in China. Party officials contemplated a move to the Forbidden City but opted for Xicheng District, fearing that the old imperial city reeked too much of feudalism.

A number of notable figures in Chinese history called Xicheng home, including Princes Gong and Chun, Song Qing-ling (the wife of Sun Yat-sen), and opera star Mei Lanfang. A bike ride through the area provides an excellent opportunity to explore their former residences. ■

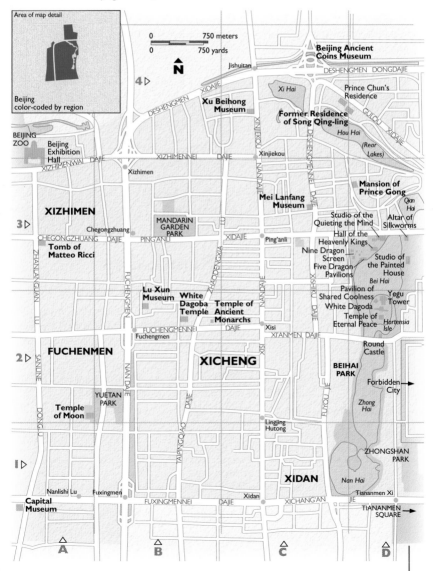

Rear Lakes

THE REAR LAKES IS ACTUALLY A SINGLE, CRESCENT-SHAPED lake divided into three sections: Xi Hai to the north and west, Hou Hai in the center, and Qian Hai to the south and east. This busy, sometimes noisy area is nevertheless a great place for a quick taste of Old Beijing.

A paddleboat slowly makes its way south on a rainy day in the Rear Lakes.

Rear Lakes
- 97 C1–D4
- Ping'an Da Dao
- $
- Bus: 111, 107, or 108 to Beihai Houmen (rear gate of Beihai Park)

A lake was first formed here during the Wei dynasty (ca 250 B.C.), when water was brought to the area from the western suburbs as part of a conservation project. In the 12th century, Jin-dynasty leaders adopted the area as their imperial playgrounds, and the lake was incorporated within the new city wall under the Mongols. Gradually Manchus built elaborate homes facing the lakes and in the narrow surrounding hutongs.

H. Y. Lowe observed in his 1992 book, *The Adventures of Wu*, that, "With few exceptions, all the princes had their mansions in that neighborhood, a quiet and picturesque district conveniently near their 'jobs' at the Forbidden City—like Beverly Hills is to the movie studios of Hollywood."

many old courtyard homes. One of the worst affronts came in recent years, however, when aggressive entrepreneurs rented much of the property facing the once idyllic lakes and turned the area into a bustling bar area that echoes with loud music and is crowded with cars and rickshaws.

Nevertheless, the Rear Lakes is a popular place to pick up some traditional treats like candied hawthorn berries and roasted sweet potatoes. A number of small restaurants in the area offer other old favorites, such as tripe and sour bean juice (an acquired taste).

You can also still visit many of the historic mansions scattered around the area, such as the **Mansion of Prince Gong** (see p. 107) and the **former residence of Song Qing-ling** (see p. 100). You can also visit the old courtyard **home of Chinese opera legend Mei Lanfang** (see p. 106), as well as the **home of Prince Chun** (see p. 104). Many of these places are included in the bicycle tour (see pp. 102–105).

A LITTLE WALK AROUND THE LAKES

A leisurely walk around both Qian Hai and Hou Hai takes about an hour. Start on the west side of Qian Hai and go north to the **Silver Ingot Bridge** (Yinding Qiao). Turn right for a walk down **Yandai Xiejie**, which has a lot of small gift shops and boutiques. Return to the bridge and proceed north along Hou Hai with the water on your left. When you reach the northern end of the lake, turn left and continue south to the other side of the bridge. Walk along Qian Hai until you come to an archway on your left. This is **Lotus Market** (Hehua Shichang), a pleasant place to stop. ■

During the 19th century, the Empress Dowager Cixi would visit the Rear Lakes in winter to be pulled around in a sled on the frozen water. You can still ice-skate or rent small "ice carts" for the kids. There are even bicycles available with running blades so you can peddle around the lakes. And every winter afternoon, members of Beijing's version of the Polar Bear Club enjoy a cool dip in an area where the ice has been cut.

During the Republican period official neglect and excessive rice cultivation reduced the size of the lakes. The area suffered even more after 1949, when the new government dredged some areas in order to erect buildings and tore down

The former home of Madame Song Qing-ling, wife of Sun Yat-sen

Former residence of Song Qing-ling

Madame Song Qing-ling was the wife of Sun Yat-sen, the father of the Republic of China. Sun died in 1926, but Song, who was some 30 years younger, lived more than five decades longer. She spent her last years in this spacious and well-manicured garden compound, enjoying special status in the People's Republic until her death in 1981.

Song Qing-ling was one of the three famous Song (aka Soong) sisters. It is said that one of the sisters married for love (Qing-ling), one married for power (Mei-ling), and one married for money (Ai-ling). Song Mei-ling married Nationalist strongman Chiang Kai-shek and retreated with the KMT government to Taiwan in 1949. There she remained a fierce anticommunist, which estranged her from her older sister Qing-ling, who had thrown her lot in with the communists. Song Ai-ling married financier Kong Xiangxi and after the communist victory fled with him to the United States, where they spent their remaining years together.

Walk around the beautiful grounds and look at Madame Song's personal possessions and black-and-white photos. ■

Xu Beihong Museum

Known as the father of modern Chinese art, Xu Beihong (1895–1953) was one of China's most famous artists. He is best known for his realistic portrayal of galloping horses.

Xu was deeply influenced by the famous reformer Kang Youwei, who believed that European painting could help China's artists reform Chinese painting, which he feared to be on the brink of extinction. In order to advance his education as a painter, Xu traveled to France and Berlin, where he developed skills missing in the Chinese context such as realistic representation. His aim was to create a new Chinese art by blending East and West.

The museum has seven exhibition halls displaying Xu's oil paintings, color ink paintings, and sketches from throughout his career. Copies of his works can be purchased in the museum. ■

Beijing Ancient Coins Museum

LOCATED WITHIN THE DESHENG GATE, THE BEIJING Ancient Coins Museum (Gudai Qianbi Zhanlan'guan) comprises just two small halls, but they have on display more than a thousand examples of ancient coins and paper money from the past 2,500 years.

Beijing Ancient Coins Museum

🅰 97 C4
✉ 9 Deshengmen Dong
☎ 010/6201 8073
🕐 Closed Mon.
💲 $
🚇 Metro: Deshengmen

Metal coins in China date back to the Spring and Autumn period (770–476 B.C.), when commerce first developed. Different types of coins were in use in different parts of China and at different times. In the north, the design of coins was based on agricultural implements, such as the spade. In the south, coins shaped like a knife were used. The first emperor of Qin, Qin Shihuang, believed that the sky was square and the Earth was round, so round coins with a square hole were used during the Qin dynasty. The museum's collection includes some Han-dynasty "folklore" coins, which feature phoenixes and dragons. These coins were not used as legal tender, but as gifts or for collecting. There is also an interesting display on the ancient technology used to cast coins, with an explanation in English.

Within the grounds of the Desheng Gate is a small market that sells copies of ancient coins and other touristy knickknacks. ∎

Old coins are for sale in the small market behind the Beijing Ancient Coins Museum.

Rebuilt in the late 1800s, the Northern Cathedral is Beijing's largest Catholic church.

Bicycle tour around the Forbidden City

Flat as a Peking duck pancake, Beijing's wide avenues and vast distances are awash with a sea of cyclists. Bicycles have their own broad lanes on many streets, where cyclists jockey for position and lobby for control at junctions. It looks terrifying, but this is one of the best ways to bring this huge city to heel. Go with the flow.

HEADING NORTH

Set out on Chang'an Jie, cycling west between the **Forbidden City** and **Tiananmen Square.** Turn right (north) on Nanchang Jie, the tree-lined road with quaint courtyard houses that runs north just to the west of the Forbidden City. As you go, you will see **Zhongnanhai** on your left. Named for the two lakes Zhong Hai (Middle Sea) and Nan Hai (South Sea), Zhongnanhai is the political nerve center of Beijing. For decades, Beijing's leaders controlled the destiny of the land from here, hidden away behind the tall, well-guarded, red walls.

Turn left at Wenjin Jie, which is just before **Beihai Park 1** (see pp. 108–110), the stomping ground of the emperors and the other members of the imperial court. Go west along Wenjin Jie until you reach Xishiku Dajie. At this intersection you'll find two popular eateries that are a good stopping place for a quick bite. Jude Huatian Xiaochi specializes in Muslim snacks, and Qingfeng Baozi Pu is known for its stuffed buns.

Turn right at Xishiku Dajie toward the imposing twin spires of the Gothic-style **Northern Cathedral 2** (Bei Tang), the largest Catholic church in Beijing. Today the church is part of the communist-controlled Catholic Patriotic Association of China, but it has had a long and sometimes dangerous history. The church was originally built on the west side of Zhongnanhai in the late 17th century. Forced to move due to an expansion

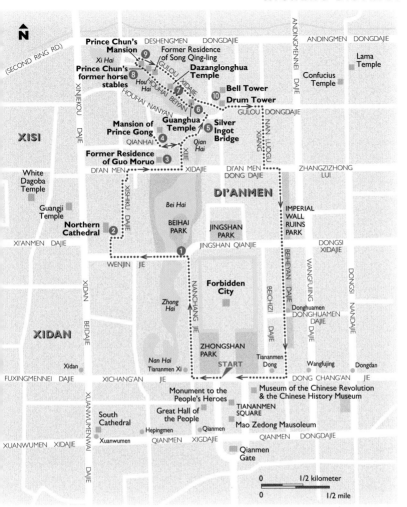

See area map p. 97
► Forbidden City
⟷ 5 miles
⏱ 3 hours
► Grand Hotel

NOT TO BE MISSED
- Beihai Park
- Mansion of Prince Gong
- Residence of Song Qing-ling

of the imperial city, the church was rebuilt in its present location in 1887 by French missionaries with funds provided by Emperor Xianfeng. The church was badly damaged when it was besieged by the Boxers in a gripping chapter of the 1900 uprising (see pp. 36–37), and it was shut down in 1958, after Beijing broke relations with the Vatican and sent the majority of Catholics scurrying underground. It served as a school during the Cultural Revolution and later as a warehouse.

Like most of the other Christian churches in Beijing, the Northern Cathedral was rehabilitated, renovated, and reopened in 1985, when the government declared it a cultural relic. With its impressive new stained-glass windows, the church is once again crowded with worshippers on Sunday mornings. Two large steles in the front of the church were erected at the order of Guangxu, in the 14th year of his reign.

Exit the church and turn right at the next intersection, then turn left. Head north up to Di'anmen Xidajie and then turn right. At the second traffic light, turn left and continue north along Qianhai Xijie to the **former residence of Guo Moruo** ❸ *(18 Qianhai Xijie, tel 010/6612 5392, $, closed Mon.)*, one of China's most famous contemporary poets, who lived here between 1963 and his death in 1978. His residence is an excellent example of a traditional courtyard house. Guo and his wife planted the peonies and ginkgo trees in the courtyard.

Continue north and turn left at the corner. Follow the gray walls on your right, bearing right at the end of the block onto Liuyin Jie, where you'll come to the marvelous **Mansion of Prince Gong** ❹ (Gong Wang Fu; see p. 107), home of the last Qing emperor's father. The extensive mansion consists of a series of elegant courtyards enclosed by rocky arrangements and walls and gardens threaded with restful walks.

Upon exiting the mansion backtrack to the crossroads. Turn east, left, along Qianhai Xijie to Houhai Nanyan on the fringes of Shichahai, passing the entrance to **Lotus Lane** (Hehua Shichang) on your right. This is a great place to stop for a meal or to enjoy a drink sitting beside the lake.

ALONG THE LAKE

After resting leave Lotus Lane at the same point where you entered, and continue along Qian Hai Beiyan to the arched **Silver Ingot Bridge** ❺ (Yinding Qiao), just a minute to the north, which crosses the lake at its most narrow point. Cross the bridge and follow the road that runs along the lake on your left.

When you reach the large opening on the right-hand side of Houhai Beiyan, turn and follow the road to **Guanghua Temple** ❻ *(31 Year Hutong, Houhai)* which was constructed during the Yuan dynasty. Zhang Zhidong, a proponent of self-strengthening during the late Qing dynasty, built the Jingshi Library here in 1908. The temple is also the headquarters of the Beijing Buddhist Association. Entry is free. When

you enter the courtyard, you'll see huge incense sticks burning in an urn and a bell and drum tower on either side. In the main hall, a large golden Maitreya Buddha, or Milefo in Chinese, is watched over by guards.

RETURNING TO THE WALL RUINS

Retrace your steps back to the road along the lake, and go north until you reach the **Dazanglonghua Temple** ❼ *(23 Houhai Beiyan)*. Now a nursery school, the temple was built in 1467 and rebuilt in 1719. Later it became the ancestral temple of Prince Chun (Zaifeng). Continue on to the **former horse stable of Prince Chun's Mansion** *(43 Houhai Beiyan)*, now the No. 2 Deaf & Mute School of Beijing. At 44 Houhai Beiyang is **Prince Chun's**

Mansion ⑧ (Chun Qinwangfu).

From here, proceed to the **former residence of Song Qing-ling** ⑨ (see p. 100), the sprawling garden mansion that was the final home of Song Qing-ling, the wife of Chinese reformer Sun Yat-sen.

Exit the complex and head south again. Turn left at the first alley on your left, and follow it until you reach a T-intersection. Turn left onto Gulou Xidajie, then turn right and ride to the **Bell Tower** and **Drum Tower** ⑩ (Zhong Lou) (see p. 79). This area is an older part of town, and the towers afford an interesting view of the hutongs below. After climbing the steep steps to the top enjoy a relaxing break.

Then cycle south to Gulou Dong Dajie, and then head east to **Nan Luogu Xiang** (see p.

Chinese seem to be able to carry almost any load on the simply bicycle.

92). This is a wonderful place to explore some excellent courtyard houses. Numerous shops, restaurants, and boutiques line this old street.

Head south on Nan Luogu Xiang to Di'an Men Dong Dajie. Turn left and ride to the first intersection. This is the terminus of the **Imperial Wall Ruins Park,** which stretches 2 miles (3 km) to Chang'an Dajie. Follow this tree-shaded street to Donghua Men, pausing anywhere that catches your eye. Perhaps at Donghua Men, where you can descend stairs and examine the original foundation of the old city wall. A few blocks beyond at Dong Chang'an Jie turn right to reach your starting point. ■

Mei Lanfang Museum

Mei Lanfang Museum

 97 C3

✉ 9 Huguosi Jie

☎ 010/6618 0351

🕐 Closed Mon.

💲 $

🚇 Metro: Changqiao;
Bus: 13, 22, 42, 55, 107, or 111

THE FAME OF LEGENDARY PEKING OPERA PERFORMER MEI Lanfang (1891–1961) stretched as far as Europe and the United States. In Peking opera, all female roles are played by men, and Mei excelled in the role of the *huadan*, a spirited young woman. He visited the United States in 1930, performing in front of enthusiastic audiences, and received glowing reviews in *New York World*, which said he was one of the most extraordinary actors ever seen in the city. He made an even bigger splash in Europe, where his performance in Berlin made a deep impression on dramatist Bertolt Brecht.

Bust of Peking Opera star Mei Lanfang

Mei's home, an excellent example of the courtyard style of architecture, is alone worth the visit. At the end of the 19th century, it was part of a much larger mansion that belonged to an imperial prince. The house had become quite run down over the years, but it was renovated for Mei and fitted with Chinese and Western furniture and fixtures.

During the Cultural Revolution in 1966, Red Guards plastered the outer walls with posters attacking the actor's "bourgeois life." His family abandoned the house, which remained closed until 1986 when it was reopened as a museum.

By boosting the status of actors, Mei made a major contribution to Chinese theater. More important, he went against contemporary practice and invited women to perform. The museum features wonderful black-and-white photos from Mei's many performances. An interesting poster hanging in one of the back rooms features pictures of his hand in dozens of traditional Peking opera poses. ■

Brightly colored lanterns light up the theater at the Mansion of Prince Gong (left). A visitor walks through a moon gate in the mansion's sprawling gardens (below).

Mansion of Prince Gong

THE MANSION OF PRINCE GONG (GONG WANG FU) IS ONE of the best preserved prince's mansions in Beijing. Prince Gong was the younger brother of the Emperor Xianfeng, whose reign lasted just ten years (1851–1861). When Xianfeng died and the young Emperor Tongzhi assumed the dragon throne at the age of five, Prince Gong served as his regent along with Xianfeng's main concubine and Tongzhi's mother, the infamous Empress Dowager Cixi.

Prince Gong was the most notable Manchu to emerge as a reformer during the Tongzhi Restoration period. In his youth, he was strongly antiforeign, but he gradually shifted to a position of patient wariness and eventually to open respect for the West.

The mansion is divided into three parts. First there is the **residence,** which has a large hall that is used for shows. Opera and acrobatic performances are staged in the **theater,** but separate tickets are required. The sprawling **garden** has several artificial hills made of Taihu Lake stones.

This mansion was once the home of He Shen (1750–1799), said to be the richest and most corrupt official of the Qing dynasty, who was executed after the death of his patron Qianlong. Scholars have suggested that it may have been the model for the Prospect Garden (Daguanyuan), described in the 18th-century novel *The Dream of the Red Chamber.* ∎

Mansion of Prince Gong
www.pgm.org.cn
⓶ 97 D4
✉ 17 Qianhai Xijie
☎ 010/6618 0573
$ $$
🚌 Bus: 111, 107, or 108 to Beihai Houmen (rear gate of Beihai Park) and N along Qianhai Xijie

Beihai Park

LOCATED TO THE NORTHWEST OF THE FORBIDDEN CITY, Beihai Park (Beihai Gongyuan) is a pleasant place to relish in the atmosphere of Beijing. The park's many historic and cultural sites—not to mention its idyllic setting—draw families, the faithful, and tourists, all eager to relax, have fun, or find a little peace.

Begin your visit to Beihai Park at the **Round Castle** (Tuancheng), just inside the South Gate entrance. The castle's main feature is the **Hall of Received Brilliance** (Chengguang Dian), where the emperors would change their outfits or rest. The structure was erected during the reign of Qianlong and now houses a large jade Buddha. It was in this hall that Yuan Shikai, the first president of China, had himself crowned emperor in 1915, to much public opposition. He died less than three months later. The Jade Wine Pot, which sits in a glass-enclosed pavilion in front of the hall, is said to date back to the days of Kublai Khan, who used it on Hortensia Isle, just to the north.

HORTENSIA ISLE

After leaving the Round Castle, walk north across the white marble bridge—with archways known as pailous at each end—to Hortensia Isle. Climb the hill to the **Temple of Eternal Peace** (Yong'an Si), a Lamaist temple built by Shunzhi, the first emperor of the Qing dynasty. After this, you will come to the **Hall of the Wheel of the Law** (Falun Dian).

Continue up to the **Hall of Universal Peace** (Pu'an Dian) and the **Hall of True Enlightenment** (Zhengjue Dian), a double complex. A statue of Zongkaba, the founder of the Yellow Hat sect of Tibetan Buddhism, sits in the former. Climb the staircase on either side, which will bring you to the

base of an observation tower. The building to the left is the **Hall of Joyful Hearts** (Yuexin Dian), where Qing-dynasty emperors held meetings with senior officials. The **White Dagoba**, which crowns this hill and offers great views of Beijing, is a Tibetan structure that was built in 1651 to mark the visit of the first Dalai Lama to Beijing. It was completely restored after the

Tangshan earthquake in 1976. The **Hall for Cultivating Good Deeds** (Shanyin Dian) is sealed but was once home to a gilded bronze image of Yamantaka, a Tibetan deity. Unfortunately, the image was destroyed by Red Guards during the Cultural Revolution. Shaman rituals were held here during the Qing period.

Behind the dagoba, paths head down the hill. Walk east at the bottom of the hill (with the lake on your left side) until you come to a tower called the **Pavilion of Shared Coolness** (Fenliang Ge). This is the beginning of a two-story veranda that winds along the north shore of the island. Soon you will come to the **Fangshan**

Restaurant, which is easy to find because of its huge red door attended by young women dressed in colorful Chinese outfits. The restaurant, which specializes in imperial cuisine, was originally opened on the north shore of the lake by former imperial chefs in 1926, two years after Puyi was forced to vacate the Forbidden City. It moved to its current location on the island in 1959. The restaurant is moderately expensive but a nice place to stop for lunch or dinner.

NORTH END OF BEI HAI

From this area you can take a boat for the short ride across the lake to the **Five Dragon Pavilions** (Wulong Ting) on the north side.

The White Dagoba looms above the trees of Hortensia Isle.

Otherwise, head east and pass through the **Tower Leaning toward the Blue Sky** (Yiqing Lou). The Nirvana Pai-lou is in front of the bridge. Walk across the bridge, then turn left and walk north, with the lake to your left, until you reach the **Haopu Water Pavilions** (Haopu Jian), which were built in 1757, and one of the many inner gardens inside the

A man touches one of the 455 glazed-tile bodhisattvas lining the walls of Shanyin Hall.

park. This small garden has roofed corridors and a nice pond.

Return to the main lakeside road and continue heading north. The next building on your right— opposite the teahouse—is the **Studio of the Painted House,** where the emperor once presided over archery contests held by Manchu princes and noblemen.

Next on the right is the **Altar of Silkworms** (Can Tan), which is now a nursery school and closed to the public. In the past, a ceremony was held here by the empress in honor of the mythological goddess of silkworms, wife of the also mythical Yellow Emperor.

Continue walking until you reach the bridge that will take you to the North Gate of the park. Cross the bridge and bear east, left, until you reach the **Studio of Quieting the Mind** (Jingxin Zhai), a garden built in 1758 that was used as a school for Manchu princes during the Qing dynasty.

Turn right after you exit and walk southwest along the lake's shore until you come to the **Hall of the Heavenly Kings** (Tianwang Dian), a Ming-dynasty workshop. To the northeast is the **Nine Dragon Screen** (Jiulong Bi), one of three such walls in China.

Farther south along the western shore is the **Five Dragon Pavilion** (Wulong Ting), whose west hall is said to have been a summer retreat for empresses and high-ranking concubines during the Qing dynasty. Just past the pavilion is a small **botanical garden,** formerly the location of the Temple of Praying Happiness (Chanfu Si). The Eight Allied Armies robbed the temple in 1900, and in 1919 it burned down; part of the temple has been rebuilt in recent years. In the northwest corner of the garden is a pagoda with 16 stone portraits of arhats that were carved during the Qing dynasty.

The final structure is a large square pagoda called **Little Western Heaven** (Xiao Xi Tian), a shrine built in honor of Guanyin Bodhisattva, the mercy Buddha, in 1770. The pagoda is circled by a moat, with four guard towers and four pailous.

If you want to visit the **Rear Lakes** (see pp. 98–99), turn around and retrace your steps to the park's North Gate exit. Or exit the park though the West or South Gate. ■

More places to visit in Xicheng District

CAPITAL MUSEUM

Formerly located in the Confucius Temple, the imposing Capital Museum (Shoudu Bowuguan) moved to its new home in 2006. The museum offers seven floors of exhibit space focusing on the history and culture of Beijing, although the logic of the arrangement may be hard to figure out. If you are patient, your visit will be rewarding. The display on the **second floor** includes imperial robes, military outfits, ancient horse fittings, and religious items related to the Buddhists and Christian Nestorians in China. There are also life-size reproductions, such as the Jishuitan Port. The **third floor** focuses on urban construction in the ancient capital, with nice models of prominent old structures and a display of city gates, as well as models of wooden bracketed roofs. A slide presentation projects an outline of the old capital that changes slowly to show the evolving shape of the city during the Yuan, Ming, and Qing dynasties. The **fourth floor** has exhibits on Peking opera, with a real opera stage and musical instruments. There's also a display about traditional weddings, hutongs, and courtyard architecture, as well as a room exhibiting items related to children.
🅰 97 A1 ✉ 16 Fuxingmenwai Dajie ☎ 010/6337 0491, www.capitalmuseum.org.cn 💲 $
🚇 Metro: Nan Lishi Lu; Bus: Muxidi

LU XUN MUSEUM

The Lu Xun Museum (Beijing Luxun Bowuguan) commemorates one of China's most outstanding modern writers, Lu Xun (1881–1936). Lu Xun moved to Japan in 1902 to study and later enrolled at Sendai Medical School. He soon decided that the pen could do more good for China than the scalpel, so turned to literature. His short stories, which have been widely translated into many languages, include "The Diary of a Madman" (1918), "The True Story of Ah Q" (1921–22), and "The New Year's Sacrifice" (1924). The state-of-the-art museum, which stands next to Lu Xun's former Beijing residence, displays manuscripts, letters, and pages from his personal diary. Some 13,000 books from his library are also on display, as well as items of clothing and other memorabilia. This is one of the best designed museums in China. Unfortunately, there are few signs in English. Just beside the museum is Lu Xun's courtyard home, where he lived from 1924 to 1926.
🅰 97 B2 ✉ 19 Gongmenkou Ertiao, Fuchengmennei Dajie, beside Baita Si
☎ 010/6616 4169 or 010/6616 4080
🕐 Closed Mon. 💲 $ 🚇 Metro: Fuchengmen

TEMPLE OF ANCIENT MONARCHS

The little-known Temple of Ancient Monarchs (Lidai Diwang Miao) is a hidden gem. It was

A stone sculpture of a piece of writing paper is on exhibit at the Lu Xun Museum.

built some 470 years ago by Ming-dynasty emperors to worship their ancestors, but the ceremonies came to an end with the fall of the Qing dynasty. Since then it has had various incarnations as schools before it opened to the public in 2004 after undergoing a 36-million-dollar restoration. Ask at the ticket window for the six-page computer-printed introduction to the temple that will guide you through each of its courtyards and halls.

🅰 97 B2 ✉ 131 Fuchengmennei Dajie
☎ 010/6612 0186 🆂 $ 🚌 Bus: 101, 103, 109, 812, 814, 846 to Baita Si

TEMPLE OF MOON

Built to the west of the imperial city in 1530, the Temple of Moon (Yuetan Gongyuan or Yuetan Park) was the site of imperial sacrifices to the moon. Unfortunately, a huge 590-foot-tall (180 m) TV broadcasting tower was erected in the middle of the altar in 1969. The park is divided into the altar area and a nicely landscaped park. The older section is actually quite small. When you enter the **north gate,** you'll see a **bell tower** on your right. The tower was built in 1530, and its original bell is now on exhibit in the Big Bell Temple (Dazhong Si; see p. 180). Just past the tower is a section of the old **Ming-dynasty wall,** now enclosed in protective glass. There are also several old gates in the wall around the altar, but they have been cemented shut. Head east and you'll come to the newly renovated **Jufu Dian,** where the emperor changed his clothing when he came here to make a sacrifice to the moon. Heading south you'll see the **East Holy Gate** on your left. Turn right to reach the east gate of the altar, a prominent three-tiered gate with cloud designs. Walk south and turn right at the corner and you'll come to the **Sacrificial Slaying Pavilion** and the **Sacred Kitchen** and **Sacred Warehouse.** Keep heading south and you'll soon be in the newer section of the park, which is also worth exploring.

🅰 97 A2 ✉ 6 Yuetan Beije ☎ 010/6802 0940 🆂 $ 🚇 Metro: Nan Lishi Lu

WHITE DAGOBA TEMPLE

The 150-foot-high (48 m) Yuan-dynasty Temple of the White Dagoba (Baita Si) stands out in Beijing's northwestern skyline. When construction was completed in 1279, the temple was considered one of the highlights of the Mongols' new capital. A monastery was set up here by Kublai Khan, which was later destroyed and then rebuilt and renamed Miaoying Temple during the Ming dynasty. The temple was seriously damaged during the Cultural Revolution and in the 1976 earthquake, but it has now been renovated. The four remaining halls date back to the Qing dynasty and contain Yuan- and Ming-dynasty Buddhist statues and Tibetan tankas.

🅰 97 B2 ✉ 171 Fuchengmennei Dajie ☎ 010/6616 6099 🆂 $ 🚇 Metro: Fuchengmen

TOMB OF MATTEO RICCI

The Tomb of Matteo Ricci, a Jesuit priest who came to China in the late Ming dynasty, is oddly located in the former Beijing Communist Party School. Ricci is admired for having mastered China's language and, along with his fellow Jesuits, for introducing modern mathematics, geography, and other breakthroughs in Western science to China. According to the rules of the Ming dynasty, foreigners who died in China had to be buried in Macao. The Jesuits asked that an exception be made for Ricci in view of his contributions to China. Emperor Wanli of the Ming dynasty gave his permission and in October 1610, the Italian priest's remains were buried here. The tomb, along with those of other foreign Jesuit missionaries who died in China, has been restored after being damaged twice. Constructed of square bricks and surrounded by a brick wall, it is entered through an iron latticework gate. A pair of carved Ming-dynasty stone vases stands before the tomb, and a stone tiger from the same period stands outside the gate. The gate to the burial place is locked and entrance gained only by prior arrangement. However, it's possible to view the other Jesuit tombs through the gate.

🅰 97 A3 ✉ 6 Chegongzhuang Dajie (inside Beijing Communist Party School) ☎ 010/6800 7279 (Foreign Affairs Office of the Beijing Communist Party School) 🕐 By appt. 🆂 $ 🚇 Metro: Chegongzhuang ■

Once one of Beijing's most colorful areas, Chongwen District (Chongwen Qu) is fading rapidly. However, a slice of the past still exists in its narrow lanes, where some old theaters, acrobatic halls, and traditional shops and restaurants continue to flourish after more than a century.

Chongwen District

Colorful painted umbrellas for sale at a Beijing stall

A Beijing opera performance at the Lao She Teahouse

Chongwen District

ONE OF THE FOUR DISTRICTS THAT ORIGINALLY COMPOSED THE OLD CITY, Chongwen District has a completely different feel from other parts of Beijing, which traditionally have been more residential or historically significant. Still rich in local color and bursting with commercial energy, it also contains some intriguing sights—most notably, the breathtaking Temple of Heaven.

Qianmen Dajie, the street running directly south of Tiananmen Square and the former imperial route to the Temple of Heaven, is located just outside Qianmen, or the Front Gate, which once divided the imperial city from the Chinese ghetto to the south. It has been a bustling commercial area for 500 years. Before the communists took control of the city and curtailed capitalist practices in 1949, the area was packed with street peddlers, small stores, and some of the city's most famous *laozihao,* or old brand-name shops, some dating back more than a hundred years. According to various legends, some emperors would sneak out of the Forbidden City disguised as simple merchants in order to enjoy a normal meal or a night in one of the

"song houses" that used to dot this small, colorful neighborhood.

The area was once busy with magicians and other street performers and its halls crowded with people enjoying an acrobatic show, Peking opera, or comic cross talk, a comedic performance somewhat akin to an Abbott and Costello routine. Spectators enjoyed the shows while slurping hot tea and loudly cracking melon seeds then spitting them on the floor. But the performers never seemed to mind.

Today, the warren of narrow streets around Qianmen that compose Chongwen District is packed with tourists and locals, cars and bicycles, rickshaws and carts, all fighting for every inch of free space. The area is overloaded with peddlers hawking their goods and restaurants spilling out onto the sidewalk. Enter any *hutong* and you'll find yourself immediately rubbing elbows—and a bit more—with everyone else.

In this nearly forgotten little district you'll discover one of the city's most splendid structures, the fabled Temple of Heaven, once the holiest shrine in China. Here, too, awaits the enigmatic Qianmen Underground City, where you can delve beneath the surface of Sino-Soviet relations during the Cold War. The Ming Dynasty City Wall Ruins Park holds a reconstructed section of the city's original inner wall, dating from 1419; now landscaped, it's a popular refuge for city dwellers. Here, too, is the Legation Quarter, the 19th-century foreign enclave where remnants of European-style architecture still survive.

In 2006, Qianmen Dajie and its adjacent alleyways underwent a large-scale renovation that saw many old buildings—even entire streets—disappear. No one knows if the plan to rejuvenate Qianmen Dajie will successfully capture the authentic feel of the old street. The short of it: Go now, before it's too late. ∎

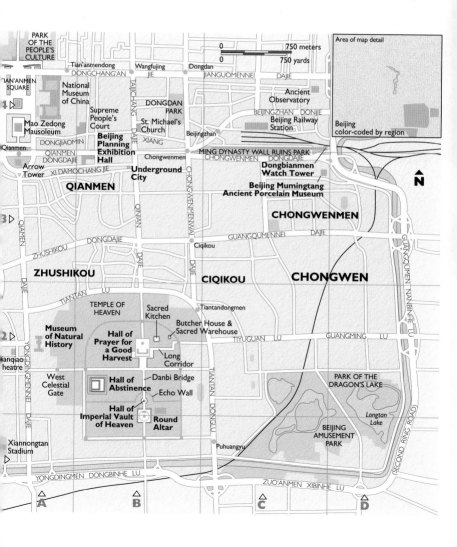

A worker sweeps the ground at the Temple of Heaven.

Temple of Heaven

Temple of Heaven

🗺 115 B1–B2

✉ Yongdingmen Dongjie (south gate)

☎ 010/6702 8866

💲 $ (extra fee for Yuanqiu & Qinian Dian)

🚌 Bus: 2 or 35 to Tiantan Ximen; 36, 53, 120, or 122 to Tiantan Nanmen

THE TEMPLE OF HEAVEN (TIAN TAN) IS ONE OF CHINA'S best examples of religious architecture. Construction began in 1406 during the reign of Yongle and took 14 years to complete. Emperor Qianlong later carried out an extensive renovation of the complex, which has three main buildings, where ritual ceremonies took place, and a host of other Taoist structures associated with sacred rites.

HISTORY

Each year during the winter solstice, Ming- and Qing-dynasty emperors visited the Temple of Heaven in their capacity as the Son of Heaven in order to offer their prayers, make sacrifices for a good harvest, and present the annual ceremonial report to heaven of the events in the past year.

For three days before the rituals began, the emperor would not drink wine, or eat meat or pungent vegetables, such as garlic and scallions. Instead, he ate simple vegetable dishes. He also abstained from sex.

The day before the ceremony, the emperor—carried in a yellow palanquin (litter) that was borne by 16 men—departed the Forbidden City via the Wu Men. He was accompanied by ceremonial elephants, his master of ceremonies, a cavalry escort packing bows and arrows, dancers, musicians, and eunuchs on horseback decked out in gorgeous robes and carrying paraphernalia for the various rites. Following all these were the imperial standard-bearers—in all, more than 200 people composed the procession.

The emperor passed through the neighborhood of Qianmen, its streets cleaned of peddlers and beggars. In fact, all the city's residents were required to remain indoors, keep silent, and, of course, avert their eyes as the imperial procession passed by. A message was also sent to the Legation Quarter (see pp. 122–123), ordering foreigners not to approach or even attempt to look at the imperial procession. The emperor's journey was made even smoother since the deep grooves in the street made by wooden cart wheels had been filled. During the late Qing dynasty, even railway traffic was temporarily halted so that the train's whistle would not destroy the solemnity of the procession.

The procession, which stretched for several miles, continued south all the way to the west gate of the temple complex, where the emperor made his grand entrance. After he arrived, he would take a ritual bath then spend the night before the ceremony fasting in the Hall of Abstinence.

Annual sacrifices to the earth were also performed here on the summer solstice until the reign of Yongle, whose advisers suggested he build a new place for these sacrifices—the Altar of the Earth.

The ceremony of the winter solstice was last held by a Manchu in 1910, during the regency of Puyi (see p. 72), the Last Emperor, who was just 4 years old at the time. Would-be emperor Yuan Shikai, president of the new republic, was the last person to use the hall. He threw on imperial robes during the winter solstice of 1914 to perform the sacrifice for the last time. In 1918 the public was admitted.

VISITING THE TEMPLE

The temple complex lies in the midst of a great park that's popular with Beijing residents. In the morning, the grounds are full of people out for their daily exercise and recreation. You'll see them singing, practicing *tai ji quan,* dancing, playing badminton, and much more.

The temple's design emphasizes the basic tenets of imperial religious belief, with repeating symbols of heaven and earth: circles and squares, for example, and colors such as blue and yellow. Even the shape of the park follows this principle: the northern end is semicircular, for heaven, and the southern end is square, for earth.

As you approach the park you choose to enter through any of several gates (which are set at each point of the compass); if you enter through the south gate and proceed north to the triple pai-lou (or gate), you'll be in front of the Round Altar. From here you can proceed to the Hall of the Imperial Vault of Heaven, Hall of Abstinence, Divine Music Bureau, Hall of Prayer for a Good Harvest (the most famous building here), and the Long Corridor.

ROUND ALTAR

The Round Altar (Yuanqiu Tan or Yuanqiu), also known as the Circular Mound, was added to the temple complex in 1530. It's an open altar erected on three round marble terraces, surrounded by two sets of walls. The outer square wall represents earth, while the inner circular wall represents heaven.

It was at this altar that, on the solstice, the emperor would present his annual ceremonial report to heaven on the events of the past year. In addition to this report, he would offer animal sacrifices to implore of heaven a good harvest in the upcoming year. The most important sacrifice was an unblemished ox, which was ritually burned in the small oven decorated with green tiles that's located in front of the altar; it would then be "delivered" to heaven via smoke. Other sacrifices included a variety of meats, grains, fruits, vegetables, wine, incense, jade, and silk.

HALL OF THE IMPERIAL VAULT OF HEAVEN

Just to the north of the Round Altar is the Hall of the Imperial Vault of Heaven (Huangqiong Yu), which is encircled by the traditional symbol of heaven: a round wall. The structure, which sits on a marble platform, is capped with blue tiles and was once home to the spirit tablets of Shangdi, which were used in the ritual ceremony associated with the Round Altar. In the hall, the emperor would burn incense in front of the tablets and make three genuflections and nine kowtows.

The circular brick wall surrounding the imperial vault is known as the **Echo Wall** (Huiyin Bi) or the Whispering Wall, since its design allows two people standing at opposite points on the wall to hear each other speaking softly. A second phenomenon is the **"echo stones,"** the first three rectangular stones at the foot of the staircase leading up to the imperial vault. If you stand on the first stone at the foot of the incline and clap your hands once, you'll hear one echo. Clap once on the second stone, and you'll hear two echoes. A single clap from the third stone will be answered with three echoes.

Exit the Hall of the Imperial Vault of Heaven at the south gate where you entered. Turn right and look for the path heading east. You'll soon come to a triple gate. Turn right here and walk to the Hall of Abstinence.

The blue, yellow, and green tiles of the Hall of Prayer for a Good Harvest

HALL OF ABSTINENCE

The Hall of Abstinence (Zhai Gong) was where the emperor met his ministers and fasted for three days before the sacred rites were held. It is surrounded by a moat that was once guarded by eunuchs. The main hall is also known as the Beamless Hall because no beams support the roof.

The sleeping quarters behind the main hall contain **two imperial bedrooms.** The emperor slept in the southern chamber during the summer and in the northern one on the night before the winter solstice rituals. The northern room had a *kang,* a brick bed that was heated by wood burning underneath. The kang may have contributed to the fire that destroyed the building in 1807. The hall was immediately rebuilt.

Exit the Hall of Abstinence, and turn back south to the main path. Turn right and walk to the Divine Music Bureau.

DIVINE MUSIC BUREAU

The Divine Music Bureau (Shenyue Shu), which has been rebuilt, was the site of a Taoist temple during the Ming dynasty. When the Temple of Heaven was first built, it included a hall dedicated to Guan Di, the patron saint of Manchu emperors. The structure was enlarged and later turned into a music hall, where musicians and dancers were trained before they took part in the imperial rituals that took place at several altars in Beijing. The complex now houses exhibits on ancient Chinese ritual music, dance, and instruments.

Return to the outside path and turn left. Walk north until you reach the **West Celestial Gate** (Xi Tianmen). Turn right at the gate and proceed down a path, shaded by scholar trees, to the **Danbi Bridge**

(Danbi Qiao), a raised causeway. Turn left after the bridge and proceed to the most impressive structure in the Temple of Heaven complex—the Hall of Prayer for a Good Harvest.

HALL OF PRAYER FOR A GOOD HARVEST

Perhaps the most celebrated building in Beijing, the hall was first built in 1420 during the reign of Yongle. The emperor's

HALL OF PRAYER FOR A GOOD HARVEST

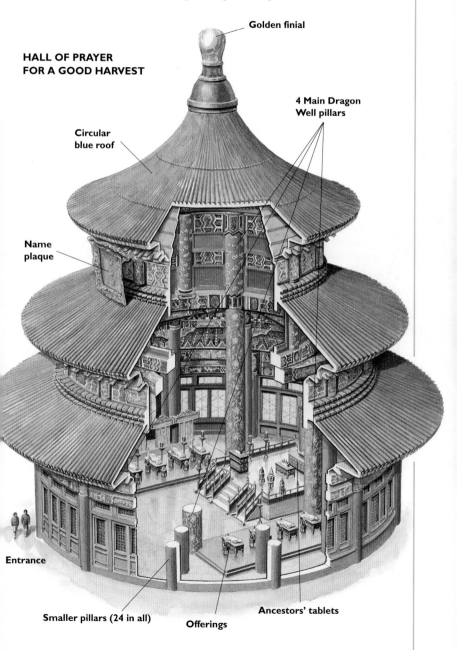

Golden finial

4 Main Dragon Well pillars

Circular blue roof

Name plaque

Entrance

Smaller pillars (24 in all)

Offerings

Ancestors' tablets

geomancers determined this as the exact point where heaven and earth met. The hall was the focus of prayers for fruitful spring harvests. Copies of the spirit tablets in front of which the emperor would offer his prayers stand in the hall.

It was rebuilt in 1545 into a triple-eaved structure that glistened with blue, yellow, and green glazed tiles. This chromatic scheme symbolized, in turn, heaven, earth, and the mortal world. Qing Emperor Qianlong replaced the tiles

Exit through the hall's east gate and walk to the Long Corridor.

LONG CORRIDOR

The Long Corridor (Chang Lang) is a covered walkway that takes you past the **Sacred Kitchen, Butcher House** (Zaisheng Ting), and **Sacred Warehouse** (Shenku), where the products for sacrifice were kept and prepared before the rituals. According to ancient practice, sacrificial animals had to be slaughtered at least

Chinese doing their morning exercises on the grounds of the Temple of Heaven

with the present azure roofing, to symbolize sky. During the reign of Guangxu (*R.*1875–1908), lightning damaged the hall.

The beautiful conical roof symbolizes the extent of heaven. The 120-foot-high (36.5 m) vault was skillfully slotted together without nails. The four inner pillars represent the seasons, and two sets of 12 columns denote the months and the division of the 24-hour day into two-hour units. Be sure to note the phoenix and dragon in the ceiling.

200 steps away from the altar. The 72 bays of the Long Corridor, which linked these buildings, were built to keep the weather from damaging the offerings (note that, in another show of symbolism, the number 72 represented the Earthly Fiends). At midnight on the day of the sacrifice, they were carried from the Long Corridor to the altar.

You can exit the park at the east gate, which is just past the Long Corridor, or return to the south gate where you started. ∎

Underground City

THE MYSTERIOUS UNDERGROUND BOMB SHELTER COMPLEX known as the Underground City (Dixia Cheng) officially opened to tourists in 2000. This labyrinth of tunnels and vaults, said to stretch from the center of Beijing to outlying parts of the city, was built in the late 1960s at the instruction of Mao Zedong, when there were fears that the Soviet Union would attack China.

About 40,000 workers (some sources say 70,000) spent ten years digging the tunnels; the work teams were frequently changed to prevent anyone from having a complete understanding of the project. The tunnels lie about 33 to 39 feet (10–12 m) below street level, and the passageways are wide enough to accommodate large military vehicles. The shelter was built to hold about 40 percent of the city's population (the rest would have been moved to the neighboring hills). Hospitals, shops, restaurants, schools, even movie theaters and a roller-skating rink were built in preparation of a nuclear attack that never came.

When you walk through the limited area open to visitors, you'll see portraits of communist leaders, revolutionary posters, and political slogans from the heady 1960s decorating the walls. Doors along the way are said to be emergency exits leading from courtyard houses above. Signs point in the direction of well-known Beijing streets above. It's said that the government used the tunnels to move the army into place beneath the Forbidden City in 1989, enabling the troops to avoid human roadblocks organized by citizens sympathetic to the student demonstrators.

While most of the tunnels' businesses are now covered in dust, it does house one Suzhou silk shop, where you can observe workers making quilts using cocoon silk.

Few Chinese seem to know about the Underground City, which can be difficult to find. If you take the D exit at the Chongwenmen subway station, find the New World Hotel and walk west down the street on the north side of the hotel, Xi Damachang Jie, until you come to the entrance with a sign that proclaims "Underground City" in English and Chinese. Or you can go to the intersection of Zhengyi Lu and Xi Damachang Jie and turn left, walking in that direction for a few blocks. There are also a bevy of rickshaw drivers in the city who will take you to the Underground City. ■

Underground City

- 🅰 115 B3
- ✉ 62 Xi Damachang Jie
- ☎ 010/6702 2657
- 💲 $
- 🚇 Metro: Chongwenmen

Legation Quarter

Bordering Dongjiaomin Xiang, east of Tiananmen Square, Beijing's Legation Quarter is where a number of foreign powers set up consulates and businesses in the late 19th century. They built lavish, Western-style churches, banks, embassies, and a post office that, alas, suffered severe devastation during the Boxer Rebellion of 1900. Nevertheless, a visit evokes a sense of bygone times.

ORIGINS

Dongjiaomin Xiang, literally Eastern Alley where the People Mingle, has long been a foreign ghetto. The street is thus named because it was here that Manchus hosted envoys from states such as Mongolia, Korea, Vietnam, Burma, and Tibet, who came here to pay their obeisance to China's emperors. During the Yuan dynasty, the street was known as Dongjiangmi Xiang, or Eastern Alley of Glutinous Rice, because boats sailing north on the Grand Canal, carrying rice and other goods, supplied a neighborhood market here. When the Grand Canal fell into disuse, the street's name was changed to its present one.

The Russians—who were among the early traders with China—were the first to open an embassy here, in 1727, although some sources say the Russian presence goes back over a century earlier. It was more than a hundred years later before England and France gained a foothold on the street, only after their soldiers trashed the Old Summer Palace during the Opium War (1856–1860). The right of other countries to establish a mission here was one of the terms of the infamous 1858 Treaty of Tianjin. The court had apparently tried to dupe the foreigners into moving out by the Old Summer Palace, a ruse to keep them outside the city. They refused. Over the years, a number of foreign banks and other businesses set up in the foreign enclave. Each of the architects who built here tried to re-create a piece of his own country, which may explain the clashing architectural styles.

During the Boxer Rebellion of 1900 (see pp. 36–37), the Legation Quarter was under attack by the Boxers (the Group of Righteous Harmony) for nearly two months until the Eight Nation Alliance lifted the siege.

The end came less than two months later when an 18,000-man joint military force, made up of American, British, French, German, Italian, Japanese, and Russian troops, fought its way to Beijing. The resulting 1901 Peace Protocol paved the way for more foreign governments to open consulates and businesses here.

The Legation Quarter continued to serve as an embassy area after liberation and through the 1950s, when many foreign companies withdrew to Taiwan on the heels of the defeated Nationalist government. Some of the embassies that stayed behind—mainly from Eastern bloc countries—moved northeast of here in the late 1950s.

WHAT TO SEE

Among the structures that survived are the twin-spired St. Michael's Church at the corner of Taijichang Dajie and Dongjiaomin Xiang; the buildings of the Belgian Embassy across from the church; and a former French Post Office at 19 Dongjiaomin Xiang. You can also see the arched gate of the entrance to the former Japanese Legation on Zhengyi Lu near the British Legation, which is now part of State Security buildings. The Huafeng Hotel, south on Zhengyi Lu, occupies the former site of the Grand Hotel des Wagons-Lits, dating from 1905. The walk described on pages 124–125 provides an intimate tour of the old quarter. ■

The site of the former Yokohama Species Bank in the old Legation Quarter

LEGATION QUARTER WALKING TOUR

The old French Post Office, now a Sichuan restaurant, on Dongjiaomin Xiang

Legation Quarter walking tour

The Legation Quarter on Dongjiaomin Xiang is today a pale shadow of its former self. This street features a surprising amount of historic European architecture, but it is going fast and in many instances you have to peek over walls or through cracks to see what has survived. Most interesting are the old French Catholic church, St. Michael's, the Yokohama Species Bank, and the former National City Bank of New York.

Begin your walk on Dongjiaomin Xiang. The street can be reached most easily by entering the lobby of the Novotel Xinqiao Hotel and exiting through the back door.

At the intersection of Dongjiaomin Xiang and Taijichang Dajie, formerly known as Rue Marco Polo, you'll come to one of the more prominent landmarks in the neighborhood, **St. Michael's Catholic Church** ❶. Built by French Vincentian priests in 1902, the Gothic church, with nice stained-glass windows and beautiful ceilings, is packed on Sundays—the only time the gate is unlocked for visitors. There are several Masses in Chinese, English, and Korean.

The red building opposite the church is the former **Belgian Embassy** ❷. After liberation in 1949, it became the Burmese Embassy; today it is part of the Ruijin Hotel.

On the north side of the street is No. 15, the location of the former **French Legation** ❸, which was destroyed during the Boxer

Rebellion. This was once the property of a Manchu prince who had fallen on hard times. Former Cambodian leader Prince Sihanouk stayed here during his many visits to China. The old **French Post Office** is now a Sichuan restaurant.

Located at No. 28, **Hongdu Tailors** ❹ is a Beijing laozihao that also served top Communist Party officials. Nearby once stood Keirulf's, the first shop serving foreigners in Beijing. The Chinese were adamantly opposed to the shop opening here as foreign trade was strictly forbidden in the city. But foreign ministers argued that they needed the biscuits, condensed milk, cotton, and horse saddles that the shop offered. Ironically, it was the Chinese who became its most loyal customers.

At the northeast corner of Zhengyi Lu, once known as Rue Meiji, is a grand looking building that was formerly the **Yokohama Species Bank.** It's now a Chinese bank, so feel free to have a look inside.

There's a pleasant patch of greenery running down the center of Zhengyi Lu, which was built in 1925 when the old rice-bearing canal was filled in. Walk down to Qianmen Dong Dajie and cross the street. Here you can plunge through the alleyways to **Li Qun Roast Duck Restaurant,** which is located in an old courtyard house. Stacks of fruitwood piled outside are ready for roasting. A small number of rickshaws will take you to the restaurant or the Underground City (see p. 121) nearby.

Return to Dongjiaomin Xiang and continue walking west. In the middle of the next block on your right is the gleaming new headquarters of China's **High Court** ⑤, the former site of the Russian legation. One original gate remains here.

On the opposite side is the old **Banque de l'Indochine** ⑥, which was first occupied by Americans. A bit farther down the street is a building with thick Roman columns that was first the Russia Asiatic Bank and later the National City Bank of New York, marked by the fading letters "NCB" at the top of the building. Today it has been converted into the **Beijing Police Museum** (*36 Dongjiaomin Xiang, tel 010/8522 5018, $*), which tells the history of police work in the city.

Still farther down the street is the old **French Hospital** ⑦ and opposite is the former **American legation and barracks.**

There are big plans for this corner. Chinese-American property developer Handel Lee is planning to turn the century-old former American complex into an upscale entertainment and shopping venue. The complex, which is expected to open in late 2008, will include a branch of Enoteca Pinchiorri, a Daniel Boulud restaurant, and two restaurants from Hong Kong's Aqua Restaurant Group. The complex will also house a repertory theater, art gallery, café, and outdoor concert space.

From here you can walk down the short flight of steps that leads to **Tiananmen Square** (see pp. 76–78) and visit the old **Arrow Tower** (Jian Lou) and the **Zhengyang Gate** (see p. 78).

Or take a left at the bottom of the steps and start the walking tour along Dashilan Street in the Xuanwu District (see pp. 132–134). ∎

🅜 See area map p. 115
▶ Novotel Xinqiao Hotel
🔁 1.5 miles
🕘 90 minutes
▶ Tiananmen Square

NOT TO BE MISSED
- St. Michael's Catholic Church
- Yokohama Species Bank
- Beijing Police Museum

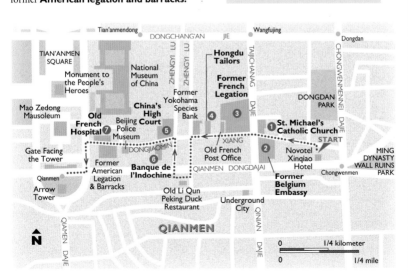

More places to visit in Chongwen District

The Urban Planning museum offers a bird's-eye view of Beijing's layout.

BEIJING MUMINGTANG ANCIENT PORCELAIN MUSEUM

If you like pottery, be sure to visit the Beijing Mumingtang Ancient Porcelain Museum (Beijing Mumingtang Guci Biaoben Bowuguan), which boasts a collection of more than 50,000 pieces of porcelain. Spanning the 7th through the 20th century, the museum's exhibits number more than a thousand.
🏯 115 C3 ✉ 1 Huashi Beili Dongqu
☎ 010/6718 7266 🅂 $ 🚌 Bus: 43, 44, or 800 to Dongbianmen; Bus: 12, 610, or 723 to Baiqiao Dajie

DONGBIANMEN WATCHTOWER

The last remaining watchtower in the city, the imposing Dongbianmen Watchtower today hosts the **Red Gate Gallery,** which exhibits the work of contemporary Chinese artists (see p. 59). The second and third floors are devoted to the history of Chongwen District, with some interesting historic photos and artifacts on display.
🏯 115 C4 ✉ 9 Chongwenmen Dongdajie
☎ 010/6527 0574 🅂 $ 🚌 Metro: Jianguomen then walk south; Metro: Chongwenmen then walk east; or Bus 44 to Dongbianmen

MING DYNASTY CITY WALL RUINS PARK

A reconstructed section of Beijing's old inner-city wall, Ming Dynasty City Wall Ruins Park (Ming Chengqiang Yizhi Gongyuan) is a nicely landscaped area with paths full of Chinese enjoying some time outside.
🏯 115 C4 ✉ Chongwenmen Dongdajie

MUSEUM OF NATURAL HISTORY

The Museum of Natural History (Ziran Bowuguan) presents the evolution and development of man over the last 300 million years, with exhibitions on prehistoric life, as well as the origins of man, dinosaurs, human anatomy, and more.
🏯 115 A2 ✉ 126 Tianqiao Nan Dajie
☎ 010/ 6702 4431 🅂 $ 🚌 Bus: 2, 6, 15, 17, 20, 25,35, 36, 45, 53, 110, or 120 to Tianqiao

URBAN PLANNING EXHIBITION HALL

The Urban Planning Exhibition Hall (Beijing Chengshi Guihua Zhanlanguan) examines the history and future of urban planning in Beijing. Of some interest is a scale model of the entire city, its center partially composed of model buildings and partially of photographs arrayed on a glass floor. A balcony provides a bird's-eye view of Beijing equivalent to viewing the city at 20,000 feet. The hall also has a 3-D cinema showing films about urban planning in Beijing.
🏯 115 B3 ✉ 20 Qianmen Dong Dajie
☎ 010/6701 7074 🅂 $ 🚌 Metro: Qianmen ∎

Much of the charm of Beijing's oldest district has been sacrificed to urban reform, but a good deal of Xuanwu's colorful culture remains alive in the many old shops, temples, and churches that still grace its streets.

Xuanwu District

The dragon and the snake are two of the 12 animals in the Chinese zodiac.

At the Source of Law Temple, a golden Buddha stares out from his perch at a passing monk.

Xuanwu District

THE XUANWU DISTRICT (XUANWU QU) IS CONSIDERED THE BIRTHPLACE OF Beijing. For some 3,000 years Chinese from around the country have come here to make their fortunes. In turn they have helped the city prosper and created history.

During the Qing dynasty, the government decreed that Han Chinese and Manchus must live in separate districts within the city. As Xuanwu was located just outside the imperial inner city, it was the home of the common classes, aristocrats, merchants, and scholars. Provincial guildhalls set up around the district catered to wealthy merchants visiting from all over China and to visiting scholars who came to take part in the imperial civil service exam. The would-be officials whiled away the hours perusing the art shops and bookstores of Liulichang, sometimes selling antiques when they were short of money. Those who passed the exam would spend huge amounts of money on expensive garments, hats, and all the other accessories that go with being an official.

The various people living here all contributed to commerce in the district, and prosperity led to the establishment of more and more shops, many of which continue to do business today. The Dashilan area, which has a history that goes back 570 years, is home to many *laozihao,* or old brand-name shops. The street names that remain today in Xuanwu District are a testimony to the area's once bustling commercialism: Caishi-kou, or vegetable market; Meishijie, or coal market; Guozixiang, or fruit market; and Zhubaoshi, or jewelry market.

Once known as Xuannan, Xuanwu District is also famous as the birthplace of Peking opera. The four Anhui opera troupes came to Beijing to perform during the Qing dynasty.

Adopted from several older traditions, such as the 500-year-old Kunqu opera, Peking opera later evolved into the Anhui opera. Xuanwu District also provided stages for hundreds of opera stars—including the legendary Tan Xinpei, Yang Xiaolou, Mei Lanfang, and Ma Lianliang—who lived in the area's narrow lanes. As a result, out of the city's alleyways grew an entire industry of producing costumes, musical instruments, and props used in opera productions across the city.

In recent years, the district has had an extensive face-lift in preparation for the 2008 Olympics, which unfortunately has erased many old buildings and streets. The area still has much to offer, however. The busy Dashilan area, for example, has its laozihao and old theaters. Liulichang, long the gathering place of the literati, still sells the "Four Treasures of the Studio" (ink, brushes, paper, and inkstones). The bustling Ox Street Mosque is crowded with Beijing's Muslim faithful, while Dashilan is also peppered with colorful ancient Buddhist and Taoist temples—such as the White Cloud Temple—thick with the smell of incense, and Ming-dynasty Catholic churches that are once again crowded on Sunday mornings. ∎

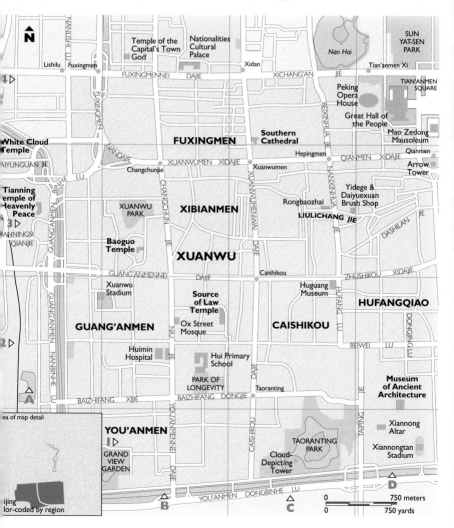

A man examines a calligraphy brush along Liulichang.

Liulichang

LIULICHANG, BEIJING'S OLD ART STREET, IS WHERE THE literati, painters, and calligraphers of the Ming and Qing dynasties gathered to shop for rice paper, calligraphy brushes, inkstones, art, antiques, and other items. It is possible that they even met to compose a few lines of poetry over a pot of tea.

Liulichang

🅰 129 C3

✉ Liulichang Xijie & Liulichang Dongjie

🚇 Metro: Hepingmen then Bus: 7, 14, or 15 to Liulichang

HISTORY

The name Liulichang translates as "glazed tile factory." This lively and beautiful old street was originally famous for its kilns, in which Chinese craftsmen began making glazed tiles in the 13th century during the Yuan dynasty. About a hundred years later, when the emperors of the Ming dynasty

began to build their imperial palaces in Beijing, the tile factory in Liulichang was expanded and became one of five factories under the direction of the Board of Works. Most of the glazed pieces that were used in the Ming-dynasty halls and palaces that were built on the order of Emperor Yongle were made here. Clay and other raw

VISITING LIULICHANG

Once home to the antiquarians, the goods sold on any street were known by the street's name, such as Jade Street, Embroidery Street, Silver Street, and Lantern Street. It was the practice for merchants and artisans who were members of the same guild to live in the same area.

Today this area continues to sell many of the items it was famous for a century ago, and it remains a fun place to explore, despite having been turned into what looks like a touristy and unrealistic set for an old Chinese movie. **Cuiwenge** *(58–60 Liulichang Dongjie)* carves traditional Chinese seals, or chops. At **Yidege** *(67 Liulichang Dongjie)* you can buy old-fashioned India ink sticks, which the company has been making for calligraphers and painters since 1865. Yidege ink is made of high-pigment carbon black using traditional methods. The sticks are rubbed in water on an inkstone until the required consistency is reached.

Selling inkstones and thick calligraphy brushes for close to a century, the **Daiyuexuan Brush Shop** *(73 Liulichang Dongjie)* produces several types of writing brushes, including yang hao (goat hair), lang hao (wolf hair), and zi hao (a mixture of wolf and goat hair). **Xinghai Yuehaixuan Musical Instruments** *(97 Liulichang Dongjie)* is the place to buy traditional musical instruments.

Cross Xinhua to West Liulichang Xijie and stop by **Rongbaozhai** *(19 Liulichang Xijie)* —doing business for more than 200 years—which continues to sell the "Four Treasures of the Studio": ink, brushes, paper, and inkstones. The shop also sells scrolls and woodblock prints. It is said that master painter Qi Baishi could not distinguish a Rongbaozhai wood block from his original. ■

materials needed by the tile factory were brought to the area via the canals nearby.

During the Qing dynasty, Liulichang became a residential neighborhood for Chinese officials who worked for the Manchus. Provincial and prefectural guesthouses were set up to provide lodging for visiting business people and for candidates taking the imperial exams, who would frequently spend hours wandering the shops and selling the tools of the intellectual trade. It is said that, by the late 17th and early 18th centuries, Liulichang had become a bustling cultural center and that the "homes and buildings lined up like fish scales."

Money Street–Dashilan

The Dashilan area of Xuanwu was the home of many Qing-era laozihao, or brand-name shops. An old saying about three of these shops highlights the popularity of brand-name products: "Majuyuan (hats) on your head, Ruifuxiang (cloth) on your body, and Neiliansheng (shoes) on your feet." But it is Volume 7 of *The Collected Works of Mao Zedong* that contains the ultimate testament: "Ruifuxiang and Tongrentang should be preserved for ten thousand years." This walk will take you past—and into—many of these time-honored shops, through some traditional *hutongs*, and up to Liulichang, which is famous for its traditional art supplies and bookshops.

The Zhang Yiyuan Tea Store offers more than a hundred varieties of tea.

The walk begins on the frenetic **Zhubaoshi Jie,** a narrow market street spilling over with small shops selling a myriad of goods. Head down the street until you arrive at a very narrow alleyway on your right—**Qianshi Hutong ❶,** or Money Alley. This is said to be the narrowest hutong in the city, 2.3 feet (0.7 m) at its widest point and just 1.3 feet (40 cm) at its narrowest, where pedestrians must squeeze past one another. During the Qing dynasty and early years of the Republic, this was the official financial market and mint for Beijing, as well as the place where private banks determined the exchange rate between silver and copper cash. The exchange rate was posted on a big board by the banks, and small banks around the city would dispatch staff to consult the board every morning. It's said that the alleyway was deliberately narrow—and a dead-end—to prevent bandits from easily entering and exiting. Nevertheless, soldiers and bandits forced their way in and robbed the place during an uprising in 1912.

At **No. 10** Qianshi Hutong you'll see an interesting old door carved with Chinese characters, while the last building here **(No. 7)** houses the vault. The building, which has very thick beams, is now occupied by a number of families who have slapped up walls to create some private space.

Retrace your steps to Zhubaoshi Jie and continue past the Republican-era buildings on your right just before the stone archway. When you reach **Dashilan Dajie,** turn right and head west along the street.

The first old shop you will run across is **Ruifuxiang Silk Store ❷** *(No. 5),* which began selling bolts of cloth to the royal nobility, high-ranking officials, actors, and women from wealthy families in 1893. The building was burned down by the Eight Allied Armies when they entered Beijing in 1900 to lift the siege on the Legation Quarter, and the present building was built on the same spot one year later. The first national flag unfurled by Mao Zedong at the founding of the People's

Republic of China in 1949 was made from silk that came from this shop. The tailors in this western baroque building can turn out suits for men and *qipaos* for women. On the first floor you'll find bolts of cloth of every imaginable fabric and color. The black-and-white photographs on the walls near the stairs are of old Beijing. There are also posters with English descriptions that tell the history of this famous shop, which got its start in the late 1800s when the Meng family from Shandong first began selling cloth on a nearby street.

The **Zhang Yiyuan Tea Store** at No. 22 was established in 1908 by a merchant from Anhui, who originally sold teas from his own plantation in Fujian Province. Today this shop sells hundreds of different types of tea.

China's most famous traditional Chinese medicine company is **Tongrentang** ❸ *(No. 24)*. The large and colorful building, guarded by two grand *qilins*, is easy to pick out especially because of the thick herbal smell emanating from the front door. Enter the shop and you'll see deer antlers, shark fins, royal jelly (fengwang jiang), dried lizards, sea horses, and

black ants. Bird's nest sells for a whopping $3,300, but that's not the most expensive thing here. *Lingzhi*, a type of grass soaked in wine or cooked in soup with red dates, wolfberry, and pork, will supposedly cure a variety of ailments—diabetes, high blood pressure, cancer, allergies, and more. Such cures don't come cheap, however; a good-size piece of lingzhi will cost you $24,800.

The next shop is **Neiliansheng** ❹ *(No. 34),* the shoemaker to the tsars. Founded

---

△ See area map p. 129
▶ Zhubaoshi Jie
↔ 1.5 miles
⏱ 90 minutes
▶ Liulichang

NOT TO BE MISSED
- Money Alley
- Ruifuxiang Silk Store
- Tongrentang
- Neiliansheng

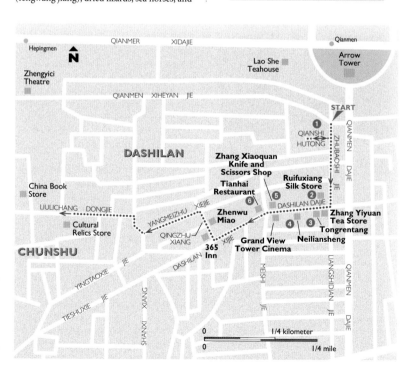

during the Qing dynasty by Zhao Ting, this shop has been making shoes since 1853. When translated into English, the shop's auspicious name means "unstopped promotions in official ranks," and indeed the company earned a good reputation making court boots for top officials. Popular for their bright black satin and the 32 layers of cloth used to make their soles, the court shoes of Neiliansheng soon became a fashion statement in Beijing and a mark of high status.

Neiliansheng sells all sorts of handmade cloth shoes, and just inside the entrance on the

Displayed for customers, a variety of Chinese teas sits in porcelain bowls.

right side are photos of the 20th-century leaders who had their shoes made here: Mao Zedong, Zhou Enlai, and Liu Shaoqi. Copies of the shoes that Mao wore are on display in a glass case. In a room to the left of the entrance you can watch a pair of shoes being made. But don't come here if you need your new shoes in a hurry—it takes three months to have a pair of shoes custom made.

Your next stop on your left, No. 36, the **Grand View Tower Cinema** (Danguanlou Yingyuan), first began showing films in 1905 and it now shows modern movies. A brass

plaque on the left side of the theater entrance explains the history of the building. The lobby has an old projector on display as well as a series of black-and-white photos, some of old movie stars and others showing highlights from the history of Chinese cinema. The café in the rear serves coffee and tea.

The **Zhang Xiaoquan Knife and Scissors Shop** ❺ *(No. 37),* which stands opposite, stocks cutting utensils in all shapes and sizes, many of which you've probably never seen before. The record-setting King Scissors model is 3.8 feet (115 cm) long and weighs 125 pounds (57 kg), while the smallest pair of scissors is only 1.2 inches(3 cm) long. Special scissors can be bought for cracking pine nuts, sunflower seeds, and melon seeds. The shop also carries very long knives for slicing watermelons, the official fruit of Beijing, as well as the latest in ceramic knives. Although relatively new to the Beijing market, Zhang Xiaoquan has been turning out blades in Hangzhou for more than 335 years.

Cross Meishi Jie and proceed down Guanyin Si Jie, which is also known as Dashilan Xijie. On the corner stands the **Tianhai Restaurant** ❻ *(No. 37),* which sells the traditional snacks of old Beijing. In front of the shop is a huge steaming cauldron filled with intestines, a popular food in the city. Farther down this street you'll come to a Republican-era building on your right with bird cages and arches on the upper floor. Next door is a restaurant selling dog meat, another Beijing favorite, especially during the winter.

At No. 55 is **365 Inn** (Anyi Zhijia), which is popular with backpackers. This is a good place to stop for refreshments and tourist information. The small hutong that runs along its east side is called Qingzhu Xiang, or Green Bamboo Lane. **Zhenwu Miao** *(No. 4),* a former Taoist temple along this lane, has been turned into a house. At the end of the street, turn left on Yangmeizhu Xiejie, a traditional hutong with typical old courtyard houses. The famous writer Shen Congwen once lived at **No. 61.** Go straight until you come to **Liulichang** (see pp. 130–131), a good place to browse for books, paper, and artwork. ∎

Source of Law Temple

BUILT BY EMPEROR TAIZONG IN 645, THE SOURCE OF LAW Temple (Fayuan Si) was originally dedicated to soldiers killed in battle. It was transformed into a Buddhist temple during the Qing dynasty. While many temples in Beijing are more akin to museums, this is a functioning place of worship; it is crowded with people burning incense, praying, and meditating. It's also the site of the Chinese Buddhist Academy.

In the first courtyard you'll see the typical drum and bell towers. The first hall is the **Hall of Heavenly Kings** (Tianwang Dian) with a statue of Milefo, or the Laughing Buddha, inside. Walk to the rear and you'll see an interesting statue of Wei Tuo, the protector of Buddhism, squatting slightly as if ready for battle.

Six large steles, their tops hugged by dragons, stand in the second courtyard. The main hall here is the **Daxiong Baodian,** which has a statue of Sakyamuni.

The third courtyard has a large incense burner sitting on an elaborately carved stone base that depicts the mythological beast known as a *qilin*. The **Minzhong Ge** has a gold statue of Sakyamuni holding a lotus cup in his hand.

Located in the sixth and final courtyard, the **Fa Tang** has a magnificent sleeping Buddha made of sandalwood and covered in a golden robe. Small Buddha statues have been placed in notches in the wall by patrons of the temple.

The temple has a wonderful collection of stone and wood sculptures dating from the Liao and Tang dynasties. There's one particularly interesting statue of Guanyin, also known as the goddess of mercy, holding a small child in her hand. Women anxious to get pregnant come to the temple to pray to Guanyin. (At the time of writing, the temple was under construction and the statues were scattered in different halls, so keep an eye out for them as you wander through the courtyards.) ■

Source of Law Temple

- 🗺 129 B2
- ✉ 7 Fayuan Si Qianjie
- ☎ 010/6353 3966
- 💲 $
- 🚇 Metro: Xuanwumen then Bus 54 to Nanhengjie

Ox Street Mosque & Muslim Quarter

Ox Street Mosque

🅰 129 B2

✉ 18 Niujie

☎ 010/6353 2564

💲 $

🚇 Metro: Changchun Jie, then Bus 61 to Libai Si

IN THE LATE SEVENTH CENTURY, CAMEL AND HORSE caravans traveling across the Central Asia steppe brought Muslim merchants and soldiers from the west. Today there is little left of Beijing's once exotic Muslim Quarter, home to the city's Islamic community for more than a thousand years. Few Muslim shops still line the streets, and they are now dwarfed by tall apartment complexes. The streets, however, are packed with bearded men in white skull caps and women in head scarves, and the ancient Ox Street Mosque is crowded with the faithful at prayer time.

OX STREET MOSQUE

The largest of Beijing's mosques, the Ox Street Mosque (Niujie Qingzhen Si or Libai Si) is a living reminder of this neighborhood's once exotic atmosphere. It was built in the Chinese style in 996 by a man named Nasruddin, the son of an Arab cleric. Its present layout dates from the Qing dynasty, when it was enlarged and restored. Today the mosque's front gate is locked, and it is only opened during Ramadan and the lively annual Corban festival, so visitors must enter through the side gate. A traditional Chinese protective gate stands opposite the main entrance.

Just inside the mosque complex is the **Tower for Observing the Moon** (Wangyue Lou). This hexagonal observation tower was once used to make astronomical calculations and to observe the movements of the moon. Behind the tower is the **prayer hall,** which faces west toward Mecca and can accommodate up to a thousand worshippers. Only Muslim men are allowed to enter the hall, but a new

Devout Chinese Muslims kneel in prayer at the Ox Street Mosque, Beijing's oldest.

hall nearby provides a separate place for women to worship.

Facing the prayer hall is the **minaret,** from which the call to prayer summons the faithful each day. It is flanked by two small towers with steles inside said to commemorate the founding of the mosque and its restoration on two occasions, once in 1442 and again in 1692 under Emperor Kangxi. The writing on the stone steles is indistinguishable today.

According to one old story, when Kangxi's spies reported to him that the Muslim community

A Beijing woman wearing a Muslim hat at the Ox Street Mosque

was planning a rebellion, he visited the mosque himself. Upon discovering that the rumor was not true, he issued an imperial order:

Tell the provinces of the country that the governor will have anyone who spreads false tales about the Muslims executed, and then bring a report to me. All the Hui shall follow Islam and may not disobey my commands.

The order is engraved on a plaque stored in the nonpublic part of the mosque, which also holds an 18th-century copy of the Koran that is entirely handwritten.

Nasruddin, the mosque's founder, is buried in a side courtyard along with two imams from Central Asia who came to China via the Silk Road about a thousand years ago to teach the Chinese about Islam. Their fading tombstones are protected in a glass case behind their tombs.

The mosque is crowded at 1 p.m. on Fridays, when hundreds of faithful come here to pray.

A small shop in the complex sells Muslim souvenirs: vases with Arabic writing, bracelets, tea sets, wall hangings, and more. Visitors must dress modestly. The ticket office will provide baggy clothes for those whose outfits are deemed unacceptable to enter the mosque.

MUSLIM QUARTER

The mosque is located in Beijing's Muslim Quarter, which is currently home to about 200,000 Chinese Muslims known as the Hui. Hui men are recognizable for the white caps they wear.

This historic quarter is small, spreading about 1 square mile (2.6 km) around the mosque, but it features the Hui Primary School for Muslim children and the Huimin Hospital. Few tourists visit the area, so enjoy a walk through its streets. Be sure to try one of the authentic Muslim restaurants. Afterward it's just a 15-minute walk to the **Source of Law Temple** (see p. 135). ∎

Muslim food

The Hui, or Chinese Muslims, have made a significant contribution to Chinese cuisine with a wide variety of foods, from sour bean juice and boiled tripe to sticky rice cakes. A number of foods introduced to China from Central Asia, including many of the most popular fruits, spices, and condiments, predate, or were contemporary with, the introduction of Islam to China. These foods and spices gradually formed a new Chinese halal cuisine. (Halal refers to meat slaughtered in accordance with Islamic law.)

By the beginning of the Qing dynasty, in 1644, Ox Street (Niujie) was already an important market for the sale of halal beef and mutton. In fact, the street is so named because of the importance of beef and lamb (but not pork) in the Muslim diet. Many Hui dishes made with lamb—braised lamb, boiled lamb's head, flash-boiled tripe—have become an integral part of Beijing cuisine. Today, halal restaurants in Beijing serve dishes such as lamb coated with sesame, a long-standing favorite, and *shuan yangrou,* rinsed mutton cooked in a brass hot pot heated with charcoal. Warm and hearty, shuan yangrou is especially popular during cold Beijing winters.

The Hui also excel in making many types of tasty *bing,* (baked bread) as well as snack foods, such as deep-fried dough glazed with honey, wife's cake filled with red bean paste, glutinous rice covered with coconut, and "donkey rolling on the ground," a cake made of red bean paste rolled in glutinous rice then covered with ground soy beans.

Visitors can easily identify Hui eating establishments by the green-and-white signs hung on their shop fronts. The signs are adorned with flowing Arabic script and the Chinese characters *qingzhen,* or halal. ∎

A man cooks buns stuffed with halal meat.

Gods & goddesses

China has two main religions, Buddhism and Taoism, each with a host of deities ruling over the sacred domain.

BUDDHIST GODS & GODDESSES

Historical Buddha (Sakyamuni) The founder of Buddhism, the Present Buddha was born Siddhartha Gautama, Prince of Sakyans. At age 35 he attained supreme enlightenment and became the Buddha. For the rest of his life, he was known as Sakyamuni, which means "capability and kindness."

The main hall of every Buddhist temple holds a trinity of golden Buddhas. The Historical Buddha sits in the middle flanked by the Past Buddha on his left and the Future Buddha on his right. The Historical Buddha is often shown reclining.

Past Buddha (Randengfo) The Past Buddha is the one who gave Siddhartha the name Sakyamuni, saying, "In the future, you will become a Buddha named Sakyamuni." He is also typically represented reclining.

Future Buddha (Milefo or Maitreya) The Future Buddha is a bodhisattva (see below) who will eventually manifest himself on earth. Sometimes portrayed with a small group of children, this jovial, golden fellow (also known as Laughing Buddha) will greet you at the entrance to any Buddhist temple. Apparently his chubby incarnation in China is based upon the appearance of a real monk called Chang Dingzi.

Bodhisattva The term refers to the Historical Buddha and to those who are capable of becoming Buddhas; in other words, they have attained a pre-Buddha stage of enlightenment. The most prominent bodhisattvas in China are the goddess Guanyin and the Future Buddha, both of whom typify the essentially compassionate mission of the bodhisattva.

Guanyin (Goddess of mercy) Guanyin, whose name literally means "hearing the sounds of the world," is one of the most popular bodhisattvas in China. Of the Four Great Bodhisattvas, she is the most com-passionate and merciful and always heeds cries for help. Buddhists believe that she can alleviate suffering, so many petition her for money, good luck, and children. In temples, her statue is often located at the rear of the main temple, facing north.

Wenshu (Manjusri) Wenshu is the chief of the Four Great Bodhisattvas. He is also the one with the greatest wisdom. Considered the ninth ancestor of the Historical Buddha, he is especially venerated by pilgrims visiting the Wu Tai Shan in Shansi Province. He is usually depicted riding on a lion.

Puxian (Visvabhadra) Puxian is guardian of the *dhyana,* the fundamental law of all practicing Buddhists. He is always depicted riding on a white elephant. Often he appears to the right of the Historical Buddha, with Wenshu to the left.

Dizangwang (Ksitigarbha) Dizangwang, or Earth Womb, is more popular in the Far East than he ever was in India, where he originated. He is usually depicted standing up, holding a pilgrim's staff in his right hand and a pearl in his left.

Luohan (arhats) The Luohan are perfect humans who have been freed from the cycle of rebirth but who remain on earth in order to preach Buddhist doctrines. There are usually 18 of them, and they are often depicted worshipping Guanyin or ranked in two lines of nine alongside temple walls. Occasionally they appear as a gilded group of 500, as in the Temple of the Azure Clouds (Biyun Si; see pp. 176–177). They remain in this world until the coming of the next Buddha.

Weituo The defender of the Buddhist faith can be found standing with a staff behind the Future Buddha at the entrance to a temple.

Four Heavenly Kings Large and ferocious, the Four Heavenly Kings are dressed in armor and carry musical instruments. They are usually represented in pairs on either side of the Future Buddha and Weituo.

Weituo, the guardian of Buddhism, covers the back of the Laughing Buddha.

TAOIST GODS

Laozi Born in the seventh century B.C., Laozi was the founder of philosophical Taoism. He is always shown in Taoist temples, and he is often depicted riding an ox and holding his classic book, the *Daodejing (Classic of the Way of Power)*.

Jade Emperor (Yu Huang Dadi) Frequently represented with a black beard and seated on a dragon throne, the Jade Emperor is the supreme god of Taoism. Together with Laozi and the Yellow Emperor, he is part of the San Qing, or Three Pure Ones.

God of War (Guandi) This god, typically red-faced, adorned with a black beard, and clad in armor, is also the god of literature and represents both civil and military aspects.

Taoist door gods Taoist temples have similar defenses against evil spirits as those found in Buddhist temples. The Green Dragon and the White Tiger are Taoist door gods. ■

White Cloud Temple

CONSIDERED THE CENTER OF TAOISM WHEN IT WAS FIRST built in 739, this sacred complex, with its myriad small and large halls dedicated to various Taoist gods, is one of Beijing's most colorful temples. When you arrive, you will probably be pursued by people selling incense sticks and other Taoist items. You might even be approached by a Taoist master or two offering to tell your fortune. The Chinese Taoist College and the Chinese Taoist Association are also found here.

A woman carries a burning incense stick in the White Cloud Temple.

Inside the temple complex, you will find Taoist faithful decked out in traditional costumes with their hair tied up and small wispy beards drooping down from their chins.

The complex is laid out on three parallel axes, with the main structures located on the central axis. Brief English descriptions in front of each structure provide basic information.

In order to enter the temple, you must pass under a three-tiered gate guarded by lions. In the first courtyard there are two *huabiao*. These marble ornamental pillars with slithering dragons and stylized clouds running down the sides are normally placed in front of imperial buildings.

After you pass through an inner gate with three rounded doors—the stone frame covered with carvings of cranes—you'll come to the small **Wofeng Bridge.** Under the bridge hang two large coins, each with two small bells in their holes. On the coins is written, "When the bell rings it is the omen of happiness." It has become a custom during the spring festival season to try and make the bells ring by throwing coins through the holes.

The main hall is the **Shrine Hall for the Tutelary God** (Lingguan Dian), which is fronted by a large incense burner flanked by four impressive steles sitting on the backs of tortoises. The hall, which was erected in 1443 and rebuilt in 1662, is where sacrifices are made to Wang Guangling, the god of protecting Taoism. This god has a heavy responsibility: to maintain kindness and eliminate evil on earth and in heaven. The wooden statue has three eyes, and like other gods here, he has a horsehair beard.

There are drum and bell towers in the third courtyard, the site of the **Jade Emperor Hall** (Yuhuang Dian). The building was erected in 1438 and rebuilt in 1662 and again in 1778, and it features a statue of the Jade Emperor sitting on his throne, hands clasped, shoulders draped in a gold cloth. The hall on the left is the **God of Wealth Hall** (Caishen Dian). Inside are three gold statues, all with horsehair beards growing from their wooden chins. On the right side is the **Temple of Three Emperors** (Sanguan Dian), which is dedicated to the god of heaven (who brings good luck and reduces suffering), the god of earth (who pardons blame and releases grievances), and the god of water (who eliminates all diseases, bad luck, and disasters).

One of the oldest halls is the **Lao Lu Temple,** which is located in the fourth courtyard. Built in 1456, this hall holds seven statues representing the seven disciples of Wang Chongyang. The hall on the left is the **God of Medicine Temple** (Yaowang Dian), dedicated to Sun Simiao who is said to

have been able to cure diseases and to raise the dead. On the right is the **Temple of the God of Releasing Sufferers** (Jiuku Dian).

In the fifth courtyard, the **Temple of Founder Qiu** (Qiu Zu Dian) dates back to 1228. The hall is dedicated to Qiu Chuji or Qiu Changchun, a Yuan-dynasty monk who is said to be buried beneath the hall. The interior walls

The bearded Taoist god of medicine sits in the White Cloud Temple.

are filled with elaborate scenes from the *Book of Qiu.*

The sixth and final courtyard along the main axis is the **Temple of Four Emperors** (Siyu Dian), where the clay statues date back to the Qing dynasty.

If you have the time and willingness, visit the smaller halls to the left of the fifth courtyard. Especially noteworthy is the **Temple of the God of Thunder,** with bronze statues of the Four Heavenly Kings, including the god of thunder.

Walk north to the garden, cut across to the west side of the temple, and walk back down south on the opposite side looking at the various temples. In one yard you'll see representations of China's 12 figures of the zodiac, as well as famous Chinese folktales. ∎

White Cloud Temple

🗺 129 A3

✉ Baiyunguan Jie, Binhe Lu

☎ 010/6346 3531

💲 $

🚇 Metro: Nanlishi Lu, plus 15-min. walk or taxi; or Metro: Changchunjie, then Bus 9 to Baiyun Qiaoxi

More places to visit in Xuanwu District

Posters and artwork for sale at the bustling Baoguo Temple Saturday market

BAOGUO TEMPLE

This 1466 Buddhist Baoguo Temple (Baoguo Si) was converted into a smelting factory after liberation in 1949. Today it is a busy flea market (see p. 261), where hawkers lay out goods on the ground, on bicycle carts, and in small make-shift rooms. Items include Cultural Revolution kitsch, old coins and stamps, jade, and books. Government offices occupy some of the other halls.

🅰 129 B3 ✉ 1 Baoguo Si, Guang'anmennei Dajie ☎ 010/6317 3169 🚇 Metro: Xuanwumen, then Bus 109 to Guang'anmen

MUSEUM OF ANCIENT ARCHITECTURE

This is the site of the Xiannong Tan, or Altar of Agriculture, where Qing-dynasty emperors held lunar equinox ceremonies. The halls are as im-pressive as the famous architecture that runs along the old capital's north–south axis. The Museum of Ancient Architecture (Gudai Jianzhu Bowuguan) displays architectural models of all eras, from ancient thatched huts to the magnificent structures of the Qing dynasty. The displays feature English captions. This is a great place to visit before heading out to see Beijing's architectural wonders.

🅰 129 D2 ✉ 21 Dongjing Lu ☎ 010/6317 2150 or 010/6301 7620 💲 $ 🚌 Bus: 803 to Nanwei Lu, near north gate of Xiannong Tan

SOUTHERN CATHEDRAL

Known as the Xuanwumen Catholic Church, the Southern Cathedral (Nantang) was built during the Ming dynasty, making it Beijing's oldest Catholic church. First con-structed by Italian Jesuit Matteo Ricci in 1605, it was large enough to accommodate only a hundred or so Chinese converts. It was rebuilt by the German Jesuit Adam von Bell in the 17th century. The present structure was rebuilt in 1904 after the Boxer Rebellion.

🅰 129 C4 ✉ 141 Qianmen Xi Dajie ☎ 010/6603 7139 🚇 Metro: Xuanwumen

TIANNING TEMPLE OF HEAVENLY PEACE

The first Tianning Temple of Heavenly Peace (Tianning Si) was originally built during the Northern Wei dynasty (386–543), while the pagoda was added a millennium later. The pagoda is the oldest structure in Beijing. Three layers of carved lotus petals support its first story. Above are 13 levels of eaves.

🅰 129 A3 ✉ 3A Tianningsi Qianjie, Guang'anmenwai Dajie ☎ 010/6343 2507 🚇 Metro: Nanlishi Lu, then Bus 42–46 ■

Chaoyang District (Chaoyang Qu) is Beijing's biggest and busiest district, but few traces of the imperial city's colorful past remain. Nevertheless, this is the face of New China and the place where you'll find lots to do, from quiet walks in tree-shaded parks, to shopping and dancing.

Chaoyang District

**A lotus in Beijing's ancient
Ritan Park**

The Green Tea House is a stylish restaurant serving nouveau Chinese cuisine.

Chaoyang District

OCCUPYING THE AREAS NORTH, EAST, AND SOUTH OF THE EASTERN SECOND Ring Road, sprawling Chaoyang District has traditionally been home to the working-class residents of government housing compounds. These days their number is dwindling, however, as the homes are bulldozed to make way for sleek new high-rise apartment buildings intended for Beijing's growing middle class. Fast becoming a hub of international business, the area is in the midst of a construction renaissance, as glass towers, high-class international hotels, new malls, and commercial complexes are going up seemingly overnight—most notably in the Central Business District (CBD). Here, too, is the Olympic Park built for the 2008 Summer Olympics.

In the district's eastern urban section, between the Third and Fourth Ring Roads, the Beijing CBD area is soaring to new heights—literally. Among the skyscrapers going up in this developing show of business might is Rem Koolhaas's ambitious plan for the CCTV headquarters. It will not be a traditional tower but a continous square-shaped loop rising 755 feet (234 m). Here, too, is the 41-floor Beijing TV Center and the 74-floor China World Trade Center Tower 3, among many other futuristic high-rises.

China's past and present meet in the large parks of Chaoyang District. In the morning, gaggles of people enjoy both the traditional and the new pastimes of China, moving gracefully with ancient Chinese architecture serving as a backdrop. Among the favorites is Ritan Park, dating from 1530 and once part of a network of imperial altars used to worship the natural world. Here the emperor made sacrificial offerings to the sun god. All traces of the altar are gone, but the park remains a tranquil spot for a pleasant stroll.

Continuing on the theme of old and new, Dongyue Temple, founded in 1319, is a popular Taoist temple just north of the park,

while, in a completely different world, sea critters roam the underwater realm of the nearby Blue Zoo aquarium. Farther afield, Dashanzi Art District houses a thriving artist community located within 50-year-old factory buildings; it's often compared to New York's SoHo or Greenwich Village.

Amid all the bustle, high-end bars and clubs draw China's beautiful people for a sophisticated evening out. ∎

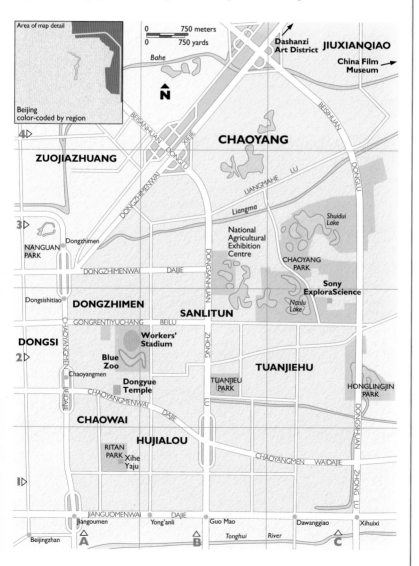

Ritan Park

Ritan Park

⬛ 147 A1
✉ 6 Ritan Bei Lu
☎ 010/8561 6301
🚇 Metro: Jianguo-
menwai; Bus: Ritan Lu

RITAN PARK (RITAN GONGYUAN), ALSO KNOWN AS SUN Altar Park, was built in 1530, making it one of the city's oldest recreational areas. Today this former sacred site is the central location for the meeting between old and new China.

Father and son peer into a lotus pond in Ritan Park.

Enter the park through its **north gate** and pass under a looming *pai-lou*, or archway. The emperor entered from the west, beneath a triple archway, his procession moving toward the center of the park, where there is a red circular wall topped with green tiles. Inside, the square, white marble **altar** was once used for imperial sacrifices to the sun.

This once hallowed site has since been taken over by young couples playing badminton and elderly kite hobbyists holding long reels of string, squinting against the sun to see their "swallows" rise and fall in the distance.

Sprinkled throughout the park are little stone monuments and historical sites, such as the place where the emperor would change

**Young women
practice the
ribbon dance.**

his robes and the hall where
musical instruments and sacrificial
objects were stored. Pockets of

green solitude are ideal for a picnic
or for quiet contemplation on one
of the benches.

Among the park's many restaurants is **Xihe Yaju,** in the northeast
corner, which serves Cantonese
and Sichuanese fare in an outdoor
setting. **Xiao Wangfu's** dishes
out home-style cooking near the
north gate, with a nice rooftop
dining area.

Ancient
tai ji quan

Health and serenity are the
aims of *tai ji quan,* the slow
motion routine that scores of
people practice in Ritan Park,
indeed, in parks around the
world. Sometimes called a moving meditation, it's a traditional
form of martial arts in which
more than one hundred possible movements and positions
are performed in a slow, graceful manner. You can stick to a
few, or do the whole range. ■

Kids love the small playground,
two rock-climbing walls (one easy,
the other a bit more daring), minigolf course, bumper cars, and, of
course, the chance to fish for
chubby goldfish. ■

Dongyue Temple

Dongyue Temple

 147 A2

✉ 141 Chaoyang-
menwai Dajie

☎ 010/6551 0151

💲 $

🚇 Metro: Chaoyangmen;
Bus: 101, 109, 112,
750, 846, 858, or
855 to Shenlu Jie

DONGYUE TEMPLE (DONGYUE MIAO), ONE OF BEIJING'S
most colorful Taoist temples, is dedicated to the Supreme Celestial
Emperor of Taishan Mountain—the Eastern Peak Equal to Heaven—
the guardian of the offices of hell who oversees the good and evil that
people do.

Built between 1314 and 1320,
Dongyue Temple—which is still an
active place of worship—was once
one of the largest Taoist temples in
the city. Destroyed by fire, it was
rebuilt during the Ming dynasty.
Although the current complex
dates from the Qing dynasty, it still
retains its earlier style.

Like many Chinese temples, its

showcasing statues of the Supreme Celestial Emperor of Taishan and his senior attendants. A corner of this hall is occupied by the God of Writing, to whom all those keen to excel in literature bring offerings of brushes and ink slabs.

The complex also has hundreds of frightening **life-size sculptures** of those who suffer in the 18 Layers of Hell—the frightening King of Hell holds the register of Life and Death, and presides over the tortures of the damned—or serve in the 72 departments. "When you go in the Dongyue Miao," warns one ancient inscription, "you encounter the gates of the seventy-two offices and are immediately fearful." Each of the vestibules display different officials—many of them extremely grotesque —handing out punishments to miscreants, a kind of Dante's *Inferno* with fascinating, if morbid, Chinese elements.

The minor shrines here are filled with deities that control diseases, because as author Juliet Bredon pointed out in the early 1900s, gods exist governing "every part of the body from the hair to the toe nails."

Don't miss the **Museum of Beijing Folk Custom,** located in the back of the temple complex. The captions for the exhibits are all in Chinese, but you won't miss them: The interesting items on display speak for themselves.

Despite its darker aspects, Dongyue Temple is a wonderful place to visit during festival season, especially Chinese New Year, when you can sample one of Beijing's traditional temple fairs. At that time, the old complex pulses with stilt walkers—heavily made-up young children walking on long stilts—and a number of people selling old folk crafts and traditional Beijing snacks. ∎

Large fairs are held at temples throughout Beijing to celebrate the Chinese New Year.

gateway is guarded by two sacred custodians, General Heng and General Ha, two deities wearing fierce facial expressions.

On the left (west) side is a large **abacus,** a reminder that everyone's good and bad behavior will be calculated some day. Running along the sides of the first courtyard are small cubicles that house the Taoist deities that hand out penalties.

In the main courtyard stands the **Hall of Taishan** (one of China's five sacred mountains),

2008 Olympics

The 2008 Olympics have become a source of immense pride for China's 1.3 billion people, a coming-out party for the world's newest economic powerhouse and a metaphor for its rapid rise. It's no wonder that the government has pulled out all the stops to make this the "best games ever."

In the summer of 2008, Beijing will be thrown into the spotlight for two exciting weeks, when an estimated two million visitors descend on the city. Anxious to make a good impression on the world, the government has carried out what may be the most ambitious urban makeover seen in modern times. The face of Beijing seems to change daily, with new roads, swirling flyovers, modern malls, and sleek high-rises appearing throughout the city, and with a greatly expanded transport system ready to serve the Olympic crowds.

China has invested some 40 billion dollars in 14 new venues and another dozen or so upgrades—more than double the 16 billion dollars Greece spent to prepare Athens for the 2004 Summer Games. And the total investment could climb as high as 67 billion dollars after all the projects are completed.

Several of the Olympic projects have been designed by top-notch international architects, and they have already begun attracting tourists more than a year before the games officially open.

The jewel in the crown is the 386-million-dollar **National Stadium.** This space-age-looking stadium, made of bands of gray steel intertwined like twigs, has been dubbed the "bird's nest" for obvious reasons. The stadium was designed by the Swiss firm Herzog & de Meuron Architekten with input from Chinese artist Ai Weiwei.

Beijing's eye-catching National Stadium, a venue capable of seating 90,000

Equally impressive is the stunning **National Aquatics Center.** Wrapped in a skin like bubble wrap, the building is popularly known as the "water cube." The 125-million-dollar design utilizes the newest plastic material for an eye-catching visual and sensory effect. The facility, which seats 11,000 spectators, was designed by PTW Architects of Australia.

The state-of-the-art **Olympic Water Park** is the third largest arena for gold-vying athletes in the world. As many as 32 gold medals will be contested here, including canoeing and kayaking. It is also the first venue to have a flat-water area and a slalom course, and the builders claim it is the most advanced in the world for rowing.

The government has mandated that the major Olympic venues have a life after the Olympics. The Olympic Water Park, which will become the largest resort in northeastern Beijing, will be used for competitions, recreation, and fitness. The National Olympic Center and the National Aquatics Center will likewise be turned over to public use.

The Olympic Games, however, are not all concrete, iron, steel, and glass. Dubbed the Five Friendlies, the Olympic mascots embody the natural characteristics of four of China's most popular animals—the fish, the panda, the Tibetan antelope, and the swallow—and the Olympic flame.

The government is also planning to deal with something that everyone talks about—the weather. Officials are hard at work on a project that they say could delay or push away disruptive rain clouds during the games. According to the local media, an array of chemical-infused rockets, cannon, and planes will zap dangerous clouds out of the sky.

An even bigger challenge will be changing human nature. Worried about its image, Beijing has launched a public relations campaign to put an end to bad habits like spitting, smoking, and littering. And it has designated the 11th of each month as "queuing day," a reminder to the city's often impatient populace that it needs to stay in line.

Just about everything has been done to ensure a successful Olympics, including the selection of an auspicious time and date for the opening ceremony, August 8, 2008, at 8:08 p.m. The number 8 is a lucky in Chinese because it sounds similar to the word for wealth or prosperity.

For up-to-date information, visit the official website at http://en.beijing2008.cn/.

Traditional Chinese knotting with an Olympics theme

ACCOMODATIONS

If you manage to get tickets for your favorite event, finding a room may pose a larger problem. Many of the top hotels are reserving rooms for important guests and all will be significantly raising their room rates during the two weeks. Some of the city's low-end hotels have increased their rates ten times, while the five-star hotels will probably triple their rates to at least $800 per night. ∎

Opening ceremony: August 8, 2008
Closing ceremony: August 24, 2008
Number of sports: 28
Events: 302
Athletes: 10,500
Visitors: 2,000,000
Accredited media: 21,600
Volunteers needed: 70,000
Average Beijing temperature
   in August: 77°F (25°C)

Blue Zoo

SOME 5,000 OCEAN CREATURES—FROM DANGEROUS SHARKS and piranhas to marvelous rays—swim just beneath the surface of a dried-up, man-made lake in the Workers' Stadium. Called the Blue Zoo (Fuguo Haidi Shijie), this magnificent underworld sea is a 23.5-million-dollar facility stocked with exotic sea creatures.

Blue Zoo

- 147 A2
- 141 Gongti Nanlu (S entrance of Workers' stadium)
- 010/6591 3397
- $$$
- Bus: 101, 109, 112, 750, 846, 848, or 855 to Shenlu Jie; Bus: 43, 110, 118, 120, 403, or 813 to Chaoyang Yiyuan

The huge main tank at the Blue Zoo is home to sand tigers, soldier-fish, barramundi cod, and coral trout, as well as endangered sucker fish and sturgeon—many of them collected by Chinese fishermen. Two open exhibition tanks hold sharks and rays, which swim just inches from your reach. There are also rock pools featuring animals found in China's coastal areas.

The aquarium has a 360-foot (110 m) movable walkway that allows visitors to take a ten-minute trip through an underwater tunnel, giving them a spectacular fish-eye view of this exotic world. Watch as a large mother shark swims just above the glass, several babies swimming under her belly. A school of fish swims past in the opposite direction, followed by a huge flat fish, his wide body brushing the roof of the tunnel as visitors crane their necks for a look.

You should schedule your visit around the two daily feeding times—10 a.m. and 2:30 p.m.—when brightly dressed divers jump into the tank to feed the sea creatures by hand. Feeding the sharks requires more care. A diver holds a long spear with a small fish on its end to feed these predatory animals. Feeding time also provides an opportunity for the divers to check the health of the fish.

A complete ecosystem has been established to make sure that the fish live in an environment that is as natural as possible, and a full-time curator is on hand to balance the fish communities and manage their marine environments. The salt water is artificial, and is made of water from Beijing mixed with salt imported from Israel's Red Sea.

PADI scuba lessons are given here in the early morning hours (*SinoScuba, tel 86/1369 3028 913*). ∎

Dashanzi Art District

MORE POPULARLY KNOWN AS THE 798 FACTORY, THE Dashanzi Art District (Dashanzi Yishu Qu) is located in an old factory complex now converted into galleries, restaurants, and nightlife spots. Whether or not you love art, this is a great place to see some of the cooler aspects of Chinese culture. New contemporary art exhibitions are held regularly—from oil paintings and installation art to ceramics and sculpture. It's best to go to Dashanzi late on a weekend afternoon, when you can browse the galleries until it gets dark, and then have dinner at one of the hip restaurants or coffee shops.

Dashanzi Art District
www.798space.com
🗺 147 C4
✉ 4 Jiuxianqiao Lu
☎ 010/6438 4862
🕐 Closed Mon.
🚍 Best reached by taxi; Bus: Dashanzi Lukou Nan

This complex of Bauhaus-style factories was built in 1953 under the auspices of the East Germans, and on some of the walls it's still possible to see fading political slogans from the Cultural Revolution. When business declined in the 1980s, the factories began pulling out, and by the late 1990s, many of the buildings were vacant. It was perfect timing. Around the same time, a group of daring independent artists, who had ruffled the feathers of the cultural czars, were kicked out of their commune at the Old Summer Palace, where they had been based for some ten years. Around 2000, a number of Beijing's best artists flocked to Dashanzi, attracted by the large spaces, cheap rents, and ample natural light pouring through the huge ceiling windows. The artists were soon followed by hip coffee shops and Western and Chinese restaurants. The Dashanzi Art District also has the best English-language art bookstore in Beijing: **Timezone 8** (24-AZ Meishuguan Dongjie, tel 010/ 6400 4427).

Taxis are not usually allowed inside, so you'll have to get out at the main gate. Start from the end of the main road. All **galleries** welcome visitors, and some may have maps available. The best galleries to explore are: Beijing Commune, Marella Gallery, 798

Photo Gallery, Beijing Tokyo Art Projects, Chinese Art Seasons, Chinese Contemporary, Contrasts Gallery, Galleria Continua, New Long March Space, Star Gallery, and White Space.

The annual **Dashanzi International Art Festival** is held here every May. ∎

A socialist-themed sculpture stands in the Dashanzi Art District.

More places to visit in Chaoyang District

The skyline of the Central Business District rises beyond Chaoyang Park.

CHAOYANG PARK

This huge and pleasant park—Chaoyang Gongyuan—does not have the imperial history of the city's other parks, but it has plenty to offer in terms of recreation. About one-fourth of the park is water, so there are opportunities for boating (primarily paddleboats). There's also a nice swimming pool, as well as beach volleyball grounds, tennis courts, a gymnasium, and a small amusement park. You can rent a slow-going electromobile (*$ for 30 min.*) to get around this sprawling park. Numerous stands serve food, or walk around to the west gate, where you'll find a street with popular Western and Chinese eateries.
147 C2 ✉ 1 Chaoyang Gongyuan Nanlu ☎ 010/6506 5409 $ Bus: 117, 302, 406, 419, 608, 703, 705, or 710 to Chaoyang Gongyuan Qiaoxi

CHINA FILM MUSEUM

The China Film Museum (Zhongguo Dianying Bowuguan) is located in a hip, ultra-modern building in the far outskirts of northeastern Chaoyang District near Beijing's railway testing yard. The building, shaped like a black box, has screening rooms, a four-story circular walkway, and Beijing's first IMAX. The development of the Chinese film industry exhibition is good but does not mention several of the international blockbusters that

government censors did not approve for showing at home. The presentation is top-notch, with good Chinese explanations and brief English translations for each section.
147 C4 ✉ 9 Nanying Lu ☎ 010/6438 1229 Closed Mon. $ Best reached by taxi; Bus: 402, 418, 909, or 973 to Nangao

SONY EXPLORASCIENCE

Inquisitive children and adults will enjoy a visit to Sony ExploraScience (Sony Tanmeng), an interactive science and technology museum —with a focus on Sony's latest digital technologies. The museum, located in Chaoyang Park, is divided into four sections: **Illusion,** where visitors can experience the unique nature of optical illusions; **Refraction/Reflection,** where they can see how light travels through space to deliver information; **Light/Colors,** which uses spectroscopes and computer processing to demonstrate how the light is made up of various wavelengths; and **Sounds.** Special exhibits change every two months. Interactive, bilingual screens around the museum turn the trip into a fun learning experience.
147 C2 ✉ 1 Chaoyang Gongyuan Nanlu ☎ 010/6501 8800 Closed 2–3 days each month, call before going Bus: 117, 302, 406, 419, 608, 703, 705, or 710 to Chaoyang Gongyuan Qiaoxi ∎

Home to intellectuals, important temples, palaces, and gardens, Haidian District is located in the northwest corner of the city. It is almost an hour from the city center, and some choose to visit Haidian by boat.

Haidian District

A painting from the Long Corridor at the Summer Palace

The Bridge of Pastoral Poems at the Summer Palace

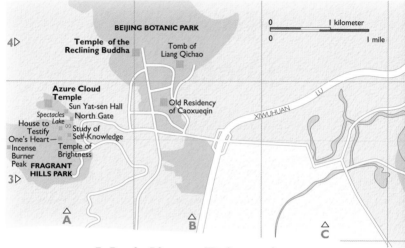

BEIJING BOTANIC PARK

Temple of the
Reclining Buddha

Tomb of
Liang Qichao

0   I kilometer

0   I mile

Azure Cloud
Temple

Sun Yat-sen Hall

Old Residency
of Caoxueqin

Spectacles Lake   North Gate

House to
Testify   Study of
One's Heart—   Self-Knowledge

Incense   Temple of
Burner   Brightness

Peak   **FRAGRANT**
HILLS PARK

XIMUHUAN

LU

△
A

△
B

△
C

Haidian District

HAIDIAN DISTRICT (HAIDIAN QU) IS HOME TO SOME OF CHINA'S BEST
universities, including Peking University and Tsinghua University. Both universities date
back more than a century and count the country's most prominent figures among their
graduates. This busy area is also home to China's version of Silicon Valley, and many high-
tech multinational corporations—such as Microsoft, Lenovo, Siemens, Huawei, NEC, and
Sun Microsystems—have offices here.

Over the past 20 years, China has seen an
explosion in the number of high-tech
companies. Eager to take advantage of the
synergy between technology and local
universities, many have established themselves in Haidian, giving this once sleepy
area a whole new look.

    Name-brand electronics can be signif-
icantly more expensive in China, but if you're

looking for high-tech gadgets, then Zhongguancun is the perfect place. Known as the
Silicon Valley of China, this area has row after
row of electronics shops. The huge five-story
Hailong Electronic City is the place to go for
no-frills computers, MP3 players, wireless
cards, and many other components. But buyer
beware—the quality is often uneven.

    Haidian District is not all work and no

play, however. Just like any university area, the district is packed with student bars, cafés, and restaurants. Wudaokou has a bustling night scene reminiscent of college towns all over the world. You can stop for dinner at one of the many international restaurants—Korean, Mexican, Japanese, Italian, American—and then go out for a night on the town.

A good deal of old Beijing is also still alive here in Haidian, including the Summer Palace —the emperor's hot weather retreat. Other historic sites in this area provide some surprises as well

as a number of Beijing's oldest temples and parks: the rustic Dajue Temple, dating from the Liao dynasty, the Biyun Temple—built during the Yuan dynasty, the Jietai Ordination Temple, and the Big Bell Temple.

Haidian also has dozens of gardens designed by Ming- and Qing-dynasty emperors, including the Summer Palace, the popular Old Summer Palace (Yuanmingyuan), and the Fragrant Hills. ■

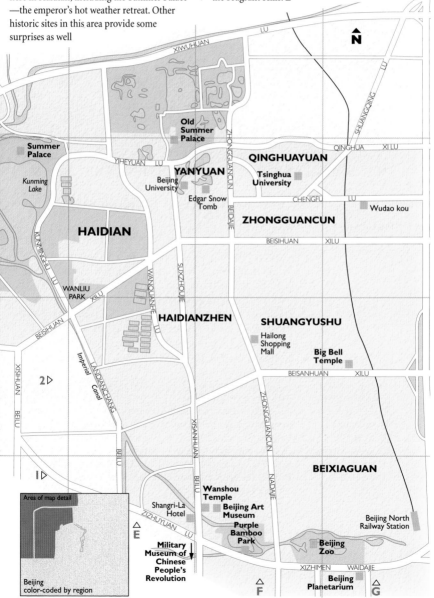

Students crowd a study hall at the prestigious Tsinghua University.

Tsinghua University

TSINGHUA UNIVERSITY (TSINGHUA XUETANG) IS OFTEN called the MIT of China. Founded in 1911 as a preparatory school, it became a university in 1925. During the Japanese occupation of Beijing, the university's students retreated to Kunming in southern China until after Japan's surrender. After the founding of the People's Republic of China in 1949, the country's hard-nosed communist leaders changed the university's focus to engineering and science. Eager to become more comprehensive, the university began adding humanities courses in the late 1970s.

Tsinghua University
www.tsinghua.edu.cn/eng/
🗺 159 F3
✉ Qinghua Yuan
☎ 010/6278 9437
🚈 Light Rail: 13 (East Gate) to Wudaokou

The university campus is located in an idyllic area near the Summer Palace and the Old Summer Palace. It was a private garden during the Ming dynasty, and during the reigns of Kangxi and Qianlong it was part of the Old Summer Palace (see p. 171). The campus today is a mixture of traditional and modern architecture, rolling hills, shady trees, lakes, and streams, and has many sites worth visiting.

The **West Gate,** which is guarded by two stone lions, was built in 1933. During the December 9th Anti-Japanese Student Movement in 1935, school authorities used this white stone gate to block nationalist police from entering the campus.

The **Jinchun Garden** was reduced to a deserted island in 1860 following the invasion of the Anglo-French Army. But by 1927, Zhu Ziqing (a university professor and one of China's most talented writers) was inspired to pen his moving essay, "The Moonlit Lotus

Pond," after walking past this blissful garden one evening.

Completed in 1909, the elaborate **Memorial Gate** is the oldest gate on campus. The structure was destroyed at the start of the Cultural Revolution, but it was restored in 1991.

The redbrick **Auditorium,** a mixture of Greek and Roman architecture, is one of the most eye-catching Western-style structures on campus. The stately building—with its domed roof, bronze gate, and four large marble columns—was completed in 1920.

Located to the southeast of the green area near the Auditorium, the **Tsinghua Xuetang,** or Original Classroom, was completed shortly after the university was founded. The two-story structure, built in the German classical style, first served as classrooms then as an administrative building. Later it was the site of the Institute of Chinese Classics, where leading scholars lectured in the 1920s.

The **Gongzi Courtyard,** an H-shaped hall, was originally the home of the Emperor Xianfeng. Today it serves as the university's main administrative office.

Other modern buildings on the campus include the new **Library wing** and the impressive glass **Natatorium.** Construction on the Stalinist-looking **Main Academic Building,** which was modeled on the main building of Moscow University, began in 1960, before relations between the two communist giants turned sour.

The area around the university has a lively café and bar scene. One of the most popular student hangouts is **Sculpting in Time** (Diaoke Shiguang, *7 Weigongcan Xi Kou),* outside the South Gate just across the street from the Wudaokou Light Rail Station. This large coffee shop—its tables and sofas usually packed with foreign and international students—serves typical Western dishes and desserts and offers free Wi-fi. ∎

An officer adjusts a student's hat during annual military training for university students.

Campus life

Today's Chinese students are similar in many ways to their counterparts in the West. The streets around Peking University are lined with bookstores, coffee shops, bars, and small eateries. Students sneak a kiss outdoors and lie on the grass, reading textbooks or chatting. But similarities to the West stop there. Chinese students must contend with regulations and restrictions that Western students would find suffocating.

Today's generation of Chinese college students is the first to enjoy previously unknown freedoms, but the pressures that accompany these freedoms can be overwhelming. Products of China's one-child policy, they are often pampered and protected at home only to face tough living conditions—crowded dormitories, poor food, and inadequate washing facilities—on campus.

Fang Xin, a Peking University psychologist who has been working with college students for 12 years, says that students today are "victims of a changing society," in which parents put extraordinary pressure on their only child to succeed.

"Parents tell their children if they work hard they'll get into a better university, and if they graduate from a better university, they'll get a better job, and if they get a better job, they'll earn more money," she says.

But some observers worry that China's pampered "little emperors" are ill prepared for the real world. Most new students have never been away from home, and many have not had a romantic relationship. There are also media reports of parents moving to Beijing with their college child in order to take care of him; some families go so far as to hire "nannies" to care for their university-age sons and daughters.

Fang blames protective parents for spoiling their children. "They're 18 years old, but their psychological age is just 8 or 9," she says of students today. "This is because Mom is always telling them, 'You needn't do anything. I'll wash your clothes, I'll cook for you.'" Yet as they struggle to gain independence against the conflicting stresses imposed by family and society, today's university students find their intellectual and physical freedoms curtailed.

Most university campuses in China are walled and gated. Students are normally required to live in dormitories, whose doors are locked each evening. As many as six students may be crowded into one small room, with toilet facilities down the hall. Hot water is turned off at 11 p.m. Lights also may be shut off at 11 p.m., so students have to move into the hallway for late night studying. There they sit on stacks of books and use chairs as makeshift desks.

Chinese universities also have strict rules regarding relations between male and female students. Some institutions forbid men from entering women's dormitories and vice versa. "The guard at our building has such a keen eye that even a male fly would not be able to sneak in," jokes one female student.

Students take the restrictions seriously, and for good reason. Some have been kicked out of colleges just because they were caught kissing.

Chinese students also face a good deal of political indoctrination as part of their education. The summer before their freshman year, all students take part in obligatory military training. Standing in the sun for hours may not be pleasant, but by the end of the training, they have usually bonded with their instructors. Some are even said to have tears in their eyes when they leave.

Students must also take courses in basic communist philosophy, including Marxism, Maoism, and the theories of Deng Xiaoping. Few students—or professors for that matter—appear to take these courses seriously.

In recent years, the Ministry of Education has begun to relax its grip on university life. For example, it appears to have softened the requirement that all students live on campus; the current regulation is vague and implies that students might be allowed to choose where they want to live. The ministry also lifted the decades-old ban on student marriage, a move welcomed by a *China Daily* commentator. "It is as if an old lady is reluctantly loosening her grip on her naughty grown-up children," the commentator writes, adding that the move was "a trend that should be encouraged." The author went on that excessive supervision by schools and parents limits the opportunity to learn from one's mistakes.

Meanwhile, however, the Communist Party of China has responded to changes on the nation's campuses with a characteristic call for a heavier hand in dealing with university students. The government has shut down popular Internet bulletin boards, and at some universities, Internet usage has been restricted to people who are physically on campus. Students have also been told that they must register with their real names in order to use the Internet, a move that no doubt has had an intimidating effect on cyber rebels.

But in the real world, students continue to skirt campus rules intended to keep them on a tight leash. "There's no way to force a 20-year-old," says one university student. "If you want to go out every night, no one can watch you all the time. And I don't think it's necessary. We're mature enough to make our own decisions and we know what we want." ∎

Students have been participating in campus life at Peking University since 1898.

On the way to classes on the campus of Peking University

A walk around Peking University

The first national comprehensive university in China, Peking University (PKU) was founded in 1898 in Shatan, not far from the Forbidden City. It moved to Yan Yuan (or the Garden of Yan), adjacent to the Summer Palace, in 1952. The campus has a large green area, many trees, winding paths, traditional architecture, and beautiful places like Weiming Lake and Boya Tower. This walk will take you on a tour of the old part of the campus. When you've finished, take a stroll to the other parts of the university.

Enter the university via the bright red **West Gate ❶**, a traditional Chinese gate guarded by two lions. The gate was first built in 1926; it was repaired in 1998 to celebrate the hundredth anniversary of the university. The characters on the gate proclaiming "Beijing Daxue," or Beijing University (the school continues to use the old spelling for its official English name), were written by Chairman Mao.

Just inside the gate you'll come to a stone bridge that crosses a pond. Walk straight ahead on the main path, which is flanked by two *huabiao* ❷, or decorative pillars. Believed to have been made in 1742, they once stood in the Summer Palace.

Straight ahead is the **Administration Building ❸**, which was built in 1926 and is guarded by two qilin, which came from the Old Summer Palace. The Chinese unicorn and vermilion steps in front of the building are also relics from the destruction of the Old Summer Palace.

Turn left and walk straight ahead. Turn left at the first corner to visit the **Arthur Sackler Museum of Art and Archaeology ❹** (*tel

010/6275 1667, $). Its worthwhile collection of artifacts from all over China covers 280,000 years: from the Paleolithic era to the Qing dynasty in the 20th century.

Retrace your steps and take the path to the left just before the Administration Building. On your right you'll see **Weiming Lake ❺**, where hawkers sell a variety of PKU souvenirs, from pens and notebooks to T-shirts, all emblazoned with the university logo.

Walk along the south side of the lake, where, in the lake, you'll see the **Stone Fish with Curled Tail ❻** (Fan Wei Shi Yu). A relic from Changchun Garden in the Summer Palace, the stone fish was sold to Zaitao, younger brother of Emperor Guangxu. In 1930, students of Yanjing University, the former name of PKU, bought the fish and donated it to the school—it's remained in the lake ever since.

Continue straight along the south path that cuts away from the lake until you reach the **Bronze Statue of Cai Yuanpei ❼**, the president of PKU from 1916 to 1927. On the left is **Qianlong's Poem Tablet ❽**, on which is carved a poem describing a happy day of archery at the Changchun Garden in the Summer Palace.

Head up the small hill, then descend back to the lakeside and continue walking north. Facing the lake stands **Ciji Si** 9, or Flower God Temple. The nicely carved decorations above the door are worth a look.

Edgar Snow's Tomb 10 stands on the opposite side of the path. An American journalist, Snow (1905–1972) lived in China during the 1920s and 1930s and taught journalism at the university.

In 1934, Snow made the treacherous journey—through nationalist lines—to Yan'an, the communist revolutionary base in the northwest, to interview Chairman Mao, as recounted in his 1937 book, *Red Star over China*. Snow was the first Westerner to tell Mao's story, and the interview propelled Mao onto the international scene.

In front of you is **Boya Tower** 11. Made of brick, the tower was built over a well dug on the north side of the lake in 1924. Its crystal clear water once shot some 10 feet (3 m) out of the ground.

Turn left and continue around the eastern end of the lake then move west, walking past the willow trees that hang over the lake. Cross the small bridge on your left, then bear left until you reach what looks like the base of a **stone boat.** This is a perfect place to stop and enjoy the wonderful view of the pagoda reflected in the water. Ahead on the right, just past a stone arched bridge, you'll see **four stone screens** 12, each with poetic descriptions of scenic spots in the Old Summer Palace, their original home.

Continue around to the other side of the island and return to the main path. ∎

> 🗺 See area map pp. 158–159
> ▶ West Gate of Peking University
> ↔ 1 mile
> 🕐 45 minutes
> ▶ Stone screens

NOT TO BE MISSED
- Arthur Sackler Museum of Art and Archaeology
- Edgar Snow's Tomb

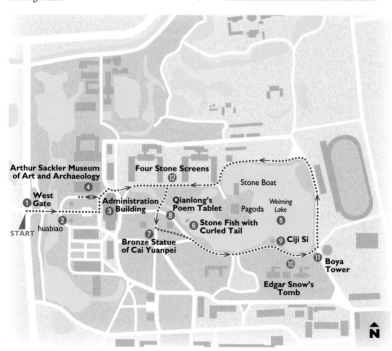

Summer Palace

Summer Palace

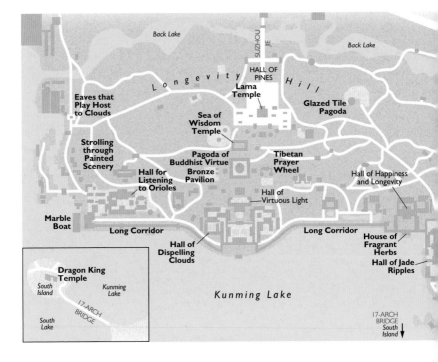

159 D3

Xinjian Gongmen Lu

010/6288 1610

$ (extra fees for sites inside park)

Bus: 332, 333, 346, 362, 374, or 375

BUILT AS A RETREAT FROM BEIJING'S INTENSE SUMMER heat, the Summer Palace (Yihe Yuan) is a sprawling imperial complex set in a large park around the vast Kunming Lake. Its temples, halls, and pavilions date back 800 years. The first emperor of the Jin dynasty (1115–1234) built the Gold Mountain Palace on Longevity Hill; succeeding dynasties added new structures and landscaping.

MAIN PALACE COMPLEX

The imperial family used to arrive at the Summer Palace via a boat that left from the northwest part of the city wall, stopping to rest at Wanshou Temple (see pp. 178–179) along the way.

Today, anyone can enter the park at the **East Palace Gate.** Inside the grounds, directly opposite the gate, stands the **Hall of Benevolence and Longevity** (Renshou Dian), which was burned by British and French soldiers who swarmed through the Summer Palace in 1860 during the Second

Opium War; it was rebuilt 18 years later. This is where Emperor Guangxu and the Empress Dowager Cixi administered state affairs, and where Cixi hatched her intrigues. It is also where emperors of the late Qing dynasty received ambassadors from other countries.

Cixi's throne still sits inside the hall, but the hall's interior is fenced off and inaccessible to visitors. The fascinating bronze statues in front of the hall include a qilin, a mythical creature that is part dragon, part lion, and part deer, among other creatures. The qilin

was often used as decoration in Confucian and imperial buildings. To the left of the hall stand statues

of a dragon (meant to represent the emperor) and a phoenix (symbolic of the empress).

On your right, to the north of the hall, is the **Garden of Harmonious Virtue** (Dehe Yuan), which has what was reputed to be one of the best Peking opera halls in the country. Cixi was a huge opera fan and watched many performances by the palace troupe here on her private stage. When you reach the small well, turn right and follow the path until you reach the **Violet Vapors from the East** (Ziqi Donglai Chengguan), a martial-like tower that was once guarded by eunuchs. Pass through the opening, and continue walking until you reach the peaceful **Garden of Harmonious Interests** (Xiequ Yuan), an imitation of a garden in Wuxi, in Jiangsu Province, that was loved by Emperor Yongzheng. His son Qianlong built the garden here for his father in 1754. Take a walk around the small lake before returning to the main path, which

The arched Mirror Bridge at the Summer Palace

Map labels:
0 150 meters
0 150 yards
YIHEYUAN LU
ongevity Hall
Garden of Harmonious Interests
KUNMINGHU LU
ion of Great piness
Violet Vapors
Garden of Harmonious Virtue
East Palace Gate
of Benevolence Longevity
N

River rides

Travel to the Summer Palace the way the emperor did—via the Changhe Canal. The rides begin at the Beijing Zoo (see p. 182), passing by the Five Pagoda Temple, the Wanshou Temple, and Purple Bamboo Park, a shallow area where you must transfer to a smaller boat. As you float along, you'll pass beneath willow trees and many moon-shaped bridges. Enjoy also the many historic sights that overlook the river. The ticket for the ride includes entrance to the Beijing Zoo. The dock is located at the north end of the zoo, behind the Elephant Hall. The ride takes one hour, punctuated the entire way by a Chinese-speaking tour guide. You can buy a ticket for the Summer Palace on the boat, which will take you in through the south gate. The company, Yunhe Travel Agency *(behind Beijing Zoo, 137 Xizhimenwai Dajie, tel 010/8836 3576, closed Nov.–March, $$, Bus: 7, 15, 19, 27, 45, 102, 103, 105, 111, 332, 334, 347, 380, 812, 808, or T4 to Dongwu Yuan)*, offers two other water tours to the Summer Palace. ∎

leads across a very short bridge over the water.

LONGEVITY HILL

The most important sites in the Summer Palace are on Longevity Hill, which is bounded by **Back Lake** (Houhu) to the north. Walk along the narrow path with the lake on your left until you reach a bridge, then cross the water onto Longevity Hill. When you reach a T-intersection, turn left and walk for just a few minutes until you come to a path on your right that

will lead you to the **Glazed Tile Pagoda** (Duobao Ta), which, like many things here, dates back to the reign of Qianlong. The pagoda is inlaid with glazed bricks of blue, green, and yellow.

From the pagoda, turn left and head west on the main path along the shore to the **Hall of Pines** (Song Tang), a large square at the bottom of a flight of stairs, where you'll find Chinese dancing, flying kites, and playing other games. Just to the north is **Suzhou Street** (Suzhou Jie). Connecting the Hall of Pines with the opposite shore, the street was built by Qianlong so that the members of his court could pretend they were in the canal town of Suzhou. The shops here were even filled with products from Suzhou. *(An extra ticket is required to enter this area.)*

Cross back over the lake and proceed south through the open square. Hike the steps up to the **Lama Temple** (Sida Buzhou or Xiangyan Zongyin Zhige). Once at the top, take the path to the **Sea of Wisdom Temple** (Zhihui Hai). This temple is covered with small glazed-tile Buddhas, many of which (especially on the lower tiers) had their heads smashed by French and British troops in 1860. The foreign troops returned and caused more damage after the Boxer Rebellion in 1900. Wander around the temple grounds for wonderful views of **Kunming Lake,** which lies on the south side of Longevity Hill.

From the temple move west along the path until you reach a pavilion called **Strolling through Painted Scenery** (Huazhong You), then head northwest to the next intersection. Turn left and proceed to the bottom of the hill, passing through a fort-like gate known as **Eaves that Play Host to Clouds** (Suyun Yan). Turn left and head south. On your right, you'll see a bridge that crosses over a small inlet. The bridge is a good vantage point for viewing the infamous **Marble Boat** (Qingyan Fang or Shi Fang), of which only the hull is marble. Cixi was long alleged to have built the "boat," thus squandering the funds that were meant to establish a real navy. But it was actually Qianlong who built it as a warning to his children. "Water can carry a boat," he said, "and it can also capsize a boat." Cixi renovated the "boat" in 1893, adding paddle wheels and a Western-like cabin.

LONG CORRIDOR

Continue south along the path toward Kunming Lake until you reach the far western edge of the Long Corridor (Chang Lang), which was built by Qianlong in order to protect his mother from the elements while she strolled along the lake. The beams of the corridor—which is 2,388 feet (728 m) long—have been painted in bright colors and depict scenes from Chinese myth, literature, drama, and history.

Follow the corridor east, and you'll pass a number of traditional structures, including the **Hall for Listening to Orioles** (Tingli Guan), which is now a restaurant, and the **Hall of Dispelling Clouds** (Paiyun Dian). The imposing **Pagoda of Buddhist Virtue** (Foxiang Ge), where Qianlong erected a temple as a gift to his mother on her 60th birthday, is set back on the hill. You can walk up a path to visit the pagoda, which is flanked by the **Bronze Pavilion** (Baoyun Ge or Tongting) and the **Tibetan Prayer Wheel** (Zhuanlun Zang).

Walk to the end of the Long Corridor and then follow the path past the **House of Fragrant**

A young boy enjoys a run along the Long Corridor at the Summer Palace.

Herbs (Yiyun Guan), where Emperor Guangxu's wife resided. Turn south to visit the **Hall of Jade Ripples** (Yulan Tang), where the Empress Dowager held her nephew Guangxu under house arrest following his involvement in the 100 Days Reform Movement. He remained here until he died in 1908, one day before his aunt, amid rumors that she had him poisoned.

SOUTH ISLAND

Follow the contour of Kunming Lake to the graceful 492-foot-long

(150 m) **17-arch Bridge** (Shiqi Kong Qiao). Cross the bridge to **South Island** (Nanhu Dao).

Here you'll find the **Dragon King Temple** (Longwang Miao), where the Empress Dowager would come to pray for rain. Alongside the temple is the pier where she would alight from her boat. Inside you can catch a glimpse of the Dragon King. From here, walk back to the East Palace Gate.

Expect to spend at least half the day exploring the palace, and be sure to wear comfortable walking shoes. ∎

Where do ducks come from?

Peking duck dates from the Yuan dynasty (1206–1368), when it was first listed among the imperial dishes in *Complete Recipes for Dishes and Beverages*, a collection created in 1330 by Hu Sihui, an inspector of the imperial kitchen.

A chef deftly slices roast duck at the Dadong Restaurant in Nanxincang.

It is rumored that the best ducks come from farms located in the suburbs near the Summer Palace, an area that locals say is blessed with rich earth and excellent water. The Qinglongqiao Duck Farm has been raising ducks here along the Jingmi Irrigation Canal for more than 40 years.

"They say the water is quite good here," reports one manager, adding that it comes from Jade Spring Mountain (Yuquan Shan), which she points to in the distance. "And it's the water the emperors drank, so it's also good for ducks."

This is no exaggeration. For hundreds of years, the water from the springs on Jade Spring Mountain was delivered every day to the emperors in the Forbidden City, who even took jars of it on their sojourns around the country.

As she talks about the farm, Ms. Jian jots down phone orders on a blackboard, including one for a hundred ducks to be delivered the next day to a roast duck restaurant in Haidian District. "The white ducks are more tender. They're fat, but not greasy," she explains.

Out in the yard, the ducks are divided by age. Farmers holding long staffs and making trilling noises gently coax the ducks, who move in the right direction, more or less obediently, quacking all the while. It takes 38 to 40 days to raise a duck for market. During the last few weeks, the ducks are fed a special diet of millet, mung beans, sorghum, and wheat chaff. A duck is ready for market when it reaches a weight of about 4.5 pounds (2 kg).

Despite its popularity, there are some Beijingers who can actually resist the appeal of a molasses-coated roast duck. "When you raise ducks day after day for 20 years, you don't feel like eating them when you get home," confesses Section Chief Lu, who has worked at the duck farm since she was 20 years old. "I almost never eat roast duck." ∎

Old Summer Palace

A visitor stands atop one of the stone ruins at the **Old Summer Palace.**

A WALK AROUND THE ENCHANTING OLD SUMMER PALACE is the perfect antidote to the mayhem of the metropolis. Move away from the grinding snarl of Beijing's traffic by walking leisurely along the palace's shaded paths, meandering past ponds thick with lilies.

The Old Summer Palace is a lovely complex of three gardens that was constructed during the reigns of Emperors Kangxi, Yongzheng, and Qianlong—who were father, son, and grandson. The original palace, designed by Jesuit priests serving the imperial court, was a large estate, with more than 200 buildings and a circumference of 4.5 miles (7 km).

The park was destroyed in 1860 by Anglo-French troops and again in 1900 by Western soldiers, who filled their knapsacks with treasures that still pass through auction houses and private collections in Europe and the United States.

When several animal heads were auctioned off by Sotheby's in Hong Kong in 2000, it caused a national outrage in China. However, the Poly Group bought them and put them on display at Beijing's new Poly Art Museum (see p. 94).

Today the Old Summer Palace is a collection of fallen stone columns, marble pillars, and plinths that are scattered in the **Eternal Spring Garden.** While some have argued that the park should be rebuilt, the nationalist minded among the Chinese prefer that it remain in ruins, a bitter historical reminder of the evils of foreign imperialism. ∎

Old Summer Palace
- 🅰 159 E3–E4
- ✉ 28 Qinghua Xilu
- ☎ 010/6262 8501
- 💲 $
- 🚌 Bus: 331, 365, 375, 717, 801, 810, or 973 to Yuanmingyuan Nanmen

Dancing in the streets

Cruise just about any area of Beijing in the evening, and you are likely to find yourself within earshot of the cacophonous clash of drums and gongs punctuating the early evening darkness. If you follow the beat of the music—a rhythm so pervasive it occasionally crosses across different neighborhoods—you will soon come upon a circle of dancers, accompanied by musicians, parading along a wide expanse of pavement, in a park, or possibly under a bridge. You have stumbled upon Beijing's most popular fad—the revival of the popular *yangge* folk dance.

Yangge is a typical Han folk dance and very popular in China's northern area, having originated among peasants in rural areas. Translated, the term means "the song sung while transplanting rice." The People's Liberation Army, which learned it from peasants in the 1940s, brought the traditional dance to Beijing in 1949.

The dancers, mostly retired women (and some men) in their 50s and 60s, appear to have discovered the fountain of youth. Boldly made-up and dressed in brightly colored traditional costumes, these smiling senior citizens look more like high-school girls than grannies as they sway their hips and wave ornate fans and handkerchiefs.

To the uninitiated observer, yangge looks a bit monotonous. Dancers make circle after circle, seemingly performing the same steps over and over again. Not so, says Granny Pang, the leader of the Shougang Yangge Troupe, one of Beijing's most active. The 60-year-old Pang says the steps change at the start of each new circle and that more than 30 different routines can be performed.

Practitioners say yangge is not just a popular folk art form but, equally important, a form of exercise and a chance to socialize with neighbors. And neither the bitterest winter night nor the hottest summer evenings appear to be much of a deterrent.

After spending the day in their apartments, cooking and looking after their grandchildren, many of Beijing's senior citizens take pleasure in getting out of their apartments for some exercise and a chance to mingle with their neighbors as soon as the evening meal is over.

"I watch my grandson all day long, do the shopping for groceries, and then cook dinner," says Granny Pang, whose family encourages her to take part in the dancing. "After dinner, my husband shoos me out of the house, and I head for the park to dance with my friends."

Song Mei-ying, Pang's number two in the Shougang Yangge Troupe, chips in. "We worked hard for so many years and now we are retired with little to do," she says. "Yangge dancing gives us a chance to get together with friends. It's a good form of exercise for old people, and it's fun."

Yangge advocates point out that participation is inexpensive and the style very easy to learn, encumbered by none of the complicated steps found in ballroom dancing, which is also popular in parks each morning all over the country. The yangge craze is also boosted by growing feelings of nostalgia in the capital city. As China continues down the road toward reform, say academics, it is natural that some people take solace in the more familiar, traditional customs of the past, when life moved at a slower pace.

While, in the past, ceremonies marking the opening of new business ventures would not have been complete without a performance by the local high-school band or lion dance team, more and more companies—including foreign ones—are inviting yangge groups to perform at their openings.

City officials, concerned that the revelry of older residents may keep the younger ones awake nights, are trying to work out a compromise to accommodate this popular form of recreation for senior citizens. Under consideration is the suggestion that tape players be used, with the volume turned a few decibels lower than the original instruments—a suggestion that so far has not been met with much enthusiasm.

Regardless of where the music comes from, the yangge renaissance is putting a spring back into the step of Beijing's old folks and delighting spectators of all ages. ∎

Elderly women practice in the cold for Beijing's New Year's celebration.

A young girl blows bubbles at the Beijing Botanical Garden.

Beijing Botanical Garden

Beijing Botanical Garden

🅰 158 A4–B4

✉ Wofosi Lu, Xiangshan

☎ 010/6259 1283

💲 $ (plus $ for Temple of the Reclining Buddha)

🚌 Bus: 318, 331, or 360 to Zhiwuyuan/ Wofo Si

PERCHED AT THE FOOT OF THE WESTERN HILLS IN Beijing's northwestern suburbs, the Beijing Botanical Garden (Beijing Zhiwuyuan), established in 1955, houses China's largest plant collection: 6,000 different plant species from all over northern China, including 2,000 types of trees and bushes, more than 1,600 species of tropical and subtropical plants, 1,900 kinds of fruit trees, and 500 flower species. Along with a state-of-the-art greenhouse and a variety of different gardens, this is a pleasant place to stroll, especially in spring, when the peach and pear trees burst with pretty blooms. An added feature is the striking Temple of the Reclining Buddha, boasting an enormous statue that, it's said, took 7,000 slaves to build.

Road signs at every corner indicate what's where, so just wander around the park and go wherever your interest takes you. Of interest: a number of exhibition districts and halls including the tree garden, a perennial bulb garden, a wild fruit resources district, a rose garden, a traditional Chinese medical herb garden, a water and vine plant district, an endangered plant district, and a peony garden.

Also of note is the huge glass **Tropical Conservatory,** which has a dozen rooms filled with a variety of plant species, from palms to tropical aquatic plants. A number of tea gardens offer a pleasant place to take a break.

Also here, on the garden's eastern side, is a **memorial to Cao Xueqin** (1715–1763), author of *The Dream of the Red Chamber*, China's most popular novel. Cao wrote his book in a house at the foot of the Fragrant Hills that has since been torn down.

TEMPLE OF THE RECLINING BUDDHA

The Temple of the Reclining Buddha (Wofo Si) is located within the garden grounds, a 15-minute walk from the front gate. Originally built during the Tang dynasty, it was rebuilt and renamed several times during the Yuan, Ming, and Qing dynasties. The name comes from the huge bronze statue of a Sleeping Buddha at the back of the complex.

The temple entrance is a pleasant stone incline, framed by cypress trees, that leads to a triple-arched red gate with yellow and green tiles.

Drum and bell towers flank the first courtyard, where you'll see two steles. In the **first hall** stand statues of General Ha and General Heng, one of whom emits white clouds from his nostrils and the other yellow smoke from his mouth, in order to subdue their enemies—look at their faces and see if you can tell which one wields which power. In the **second hall** a statue of a red-caped Maitreya, the Future Buddha, stands among the Four Heavenly Kings, each holding his distinctive weapon: thunder, wind, rain, and harmony. Behind the Future Buddha is a statue of Weituo, the guardian of Buddhism. The **third hall** is devoted to Sakyamuni, who sits here with his hands in his lap as if in meditation.

The **Hall of the Sleeping Buddha** is the temple's main attraction. Inside, a 14th-century bronze statue of a reclining Sakyamuni Buddha is surrounded by 12 of his disciples. A long red robe covers the statue, which stretches more than 17 feet (5 m) in length.

An interesting exhibition just behind the hall features photos of Sleeping Buddhas from all over China, as well as a model showing how this statue was cast. ∎

Workers restore the windows of the Temple of the Reclining Buddha.

Fragrant Hills Park

Fragrant Hills Park

🏛 158 A3

✉ 40 Maimai Jie, Xiangshan

☎ 010/6259 1155

💲 $

🚌 Bus: 90, 318, 360, 714, 733, 737, or 833

LESS THAN AN HOUR'S DRIVE FROM THE CENTER OF THE city, Fragrant Hills Park (Xiangshan Gongyuan) was built in 1168 during the Jin dynasty and served as an imperial retreat for hundreds of years. Like the Summer Palace (see pp. 166–170) and the Old Summer Palace (see p. 171), it was destroyed by foreign forces in 1860 and then again in 1900. Today it is a pleasantly laid-out park with numerous pools, pavilions, and temples, as well as row upon row of apricot, pear, and peach trees. The best time to visit is in late autumn, when the leaves of the smoke tree turn a fiery red.

Sakyamuni, the Historical Buddha, is surrounded by his attendants at the Temple of the Azure Clouds.

Many of the park's highlights are located at its northern end, which can be reached more easily via the north gate, near the Temple of the Azure Clouds.

TEMPLE OF THE AZURE CLOUDS

The Temple of the Azure Clouds (Biyun Si) is just to the right after you enter Fragrant Hills Park.

Originally built by two Ming-dynasty eunuchs, who hoped to make it their burial grounds, it was converted into a Buddhist temple in 1366. The complex was expanded twice during the Ming dynasty and once more during the Qing dynasty. One of the most interesting temples in Beijing, it features a number of wonderful halls, as well as six courtyards rising in succession up the mountain slope.

As in many other temples, you'll be welcomed into the temple at the **Gate Hall** by General Ha and General Heng. The next hall is the **Hall of Milefo** (Milefo Dian or Tianwang Dian), featuring a statue of the Laughing Buddha.

Cross a small stone bridge to the **Hall of Lokapalas** (Daxiong Baodian). Inside is a statue of Sakyamuni sitting in a lotus blossom, flanked by 18 *luohan*, or arhats, nine on each side. At the back of the temple is a statue of Guanyin holding a vase.

Next is the **Hall of Bodhi-sattvas**. Built during the Ming dynasty, it houses statues of five bodhisattvas with five different beasts, including a blue lion, a unicorn, a white elephant, and one simply called "freak."

Behind here is **Sun Yat-sen Hall,** where the former leader's body was placed in 1925 before being taken to his final resting place in Nanjing, four years later when his grand mausoleum in the former nationalist capital was completed. The hall displays some of his personal effects.

Turn left to reach the **Hall of Arhats** (Luohan Tang). Built in 1748, the hall holds 508 unique, life-size statues of luohan, each with a completely different facial expression and physical pose.

Behind the hall a flight of stairs leads up to a large triple archway. The three panels have been carved with white dragons, while stone lions and carvings of musicians decorate the wall. The steles bear inscriptions in Manchu, Chinese, Mongolian, and Tibetan marking the 1748 construction of the **Vajrasma Pagoda,** which is located on the next level.

The pagoda is decorated with Buddhist images and reliefs of dragons, phoenixes, clouds, lions, and elephants. There are nice panoramic views from the top, where you'll also find four flask-shaped stupas decorated with small Tibetan images.

Work your way back down the slope to the entrance, taking time to examine the side halls.

MORE SIGHTS

From the park entrance, you can also visit **Spectacles Lake** or Eyeglasses Lake (Yanjing Hu), built in 1745. The name derives from its shape—a bridge that divides the lake in two gives it the look of a pair of eyeglasses.

To the west of the lake awaits **House to Testify One's Heart** (Jianxin Zhai). Built during the Jiajing period of the Ming dynasty, the house features a semicircular pond and a pavilion. A rounded wall and promenade surround the entire complex.

Built in 1780 during the reign of Qianlong, the **Temple of Brightness** (Zhao Miao) was a Tibetan-style lamasery that is purported to have been a residence for the sixth Panchen Lama during his visits to the emperor. On the temple's east side stands a white marble triple memorial archway with green tiles; a pagoda with yellow and green glazed tiles stands beside it. Bells hanging from the eaves of the pagoda frequently chime.

With an elevation of 1,827 feet (557 m), **Incense Burner Peak** (Xianglu Peak) is the highest peak in Fragrant Hills Park and offers great vistas of the surrounding area, including the Summer Palace.

Weekends at the peak are crowded with visitors, however, so it's best to visit during the week or as early as possible on weekends. If you're not up to the climb, you can take the chairlift to the top from the North Gate. ■

Prayers written on red cloth cover a fence in the Wanshou Temple.

Wanshou Temple & Beijing Art Museum

Wanshou Temple & Beijing Art Museum

🚇 159 Fl

✉ Xi Sanhuan Beilu (S of China Grand Theater, No. 16)

☎ 010/6842 3380 or 010/6842 3565

💲 $

🚌 Bus: 300, 323, 374, or 830 to Wanshou Si

WANSHOU TEMPLE (WANSHOU SI), SOMETIMES THOUGHT OF as a miniature Forbidden City, dates back to 1577, when it was built by a wealthy eunuch, who later fell from power as a result of the court intrigues that plagued the end of the Ming dynasty. Originally, the temple was divided into three sections: the middle was devoted to Buddhist activities, the west wing was a temporary dwelling for emperors, and monks occupied the east part. The north end was an orchard, where the monks worked the land. One of many structures restored by Emperor Qianlong, the temple overlooks Changhe Canal.

During the Ming and Qing dynasties, the emperor and his entourage would board the imperial barge at Gaoliang Bridge, which was just outside Xizhimen Gate to journey to the Summer Palace.

Vermiliion robed monks kneel before the temple gates....

The **drum tower** inside the main gate contains an exhibit with photographs of Empress Dowager Cixi and the temple's original plan. There is also a **bell tower** nearby.

The first hall is the **Hall of Deva Kings** (Tianwang Dian). Maps of the Changhe Canal are on exhibit here, but unfortunately there are no statues of the gods of the four directions.

The **Sakyamuni Shrine** (Daxiong Baodian) is dedicated to Buddhas of the Past, Historic, and Future, and has 18 luohans standing on the side. Just behind the three Buddhas is a statue of Guanyin, the goddess of mercy.

Behind this hall is the three-story **Hall of Ten Thousand Ages** (Wanshou Ge), which is now filled with porcelain objects. A tea shop may soon open here.

The hall to the left exhibits Ming- and Qing-dynasty porcelain bowls, vases, and plates, with different glazes—blue-and-white, blue, yellow, celadon. The hall on the right has statues of the bodhisattva cast in bronze. The head of Vajradhara Buddha, or Jingang Pusa in Chinese, is colored blue.

The **Beijing Art Museum,** which was established on the grounds of the temple in 1985, has a permanent collection of ancient calligraphy, imperial weavings, bronzes, jade, pottery, porcelain, furniture, coins, paintings, ceramics, lacquerware, ivory, and embroidery. The museum also has more than 50,000 Neolithic artifacts. ■

Midway between the gate and the Summer Palace stood the willow-draped Wanshou Temple, which became a resting place for members of the imperial family when they were making the trip. It was also a place where the imperial family celebrated birthdays, most notable was the huge party that Qianlong threw for his mother's 70th birthday, in which some one thousand monks participated. The emperor refers to the temple in one poem:

Wanshou Temple is barely two li distant
High over its walls embroidered banners flutter.

Blue and white porcelain vase from the collection in the Hall of Ten Thousand Ages

A diversity of bell sizes are found in the 700-bell collection, from as tall as a two-story house to the size of a small cup.

Big Bell Temple

Big Bell Temple
- 159 G2
- 31 Beisanhuan Xilu
- 010/6255 0843
- $
- Light Rail: Dazhong Si; Bus: 361, 367, 718, 727, or 730 to Dazhong Si

BUILT IN 1733, BIG BELL TEMPLE (DAZHONG SI) WAS ORI-ginally called Juesheng Temple, or the Temple of Awakening to a Sense of a Former Existence. One year later, however, a huge bell was installed, and the name of this small, charming temple was changed. Since then, the temple has amassed 700 bells, some of them dating back to ancient times.

During the Qing dynasty, a ceremony was held in the temple every year to pray for rain. Several emperors came to the temple during the ceremony in order to pray. Farmers also usually participated, and each year large numbers of them, donning willow wreaths (since the willow is associated with water), visited the temple. There they prayed to the Dragon King, who controls rain. According to one Manchu observer, for ten days each year men and women flocked here "in groups like clouds" to see the ceremony.

Like most temples, the Big Bell Temple, which is also known as the Great Bell Temple, is set on a north–south axis. The **first hall** introduces visitors to the history of the temple. A stele here bears an edict written by Yongzheng, who ordered the temple built. More exhibitions of Chinese bells are on display through the other halls.

The **second hall** has a collection of bells from the Warring States period, while Buddhist and Taoist bells are featured in the **third hall.** The **fourth hall** has Ming- and Qing-dynasty bells on display, each of them a good example of the large and elaborate bells that graced Buddhist and Taoist temples. Many of them are decorated with traditional Chinese motifs, such as dragons and clouds.

The giant **Yongle Bell** is located in the last hall. It's believed to have been cast in the Ming dynasty, during the reign of Yongle, which would make it more than 550 years old. More than 23 feet (7 m) tall, the bell has been inscribed with an entire sacred verse.

The temple features an exhibit on the casting of bells, including the production of molds and the melting of bronze, as well as exhibits of bells from other countries around the world. ■

Military Museum of Chinese People's Revolution

PRESENTING 5,000 YEARS OF CHINESE MILITARY HISTORY, the collection housed at the Military Museum of Chinese People's Revolution (Zhongguo Renmin Geming Junshi Bowuguan) includes everything from ancient weaponry to the tools of modern warfare. It also boasts a bit of nostalgia: Zhou Enlai's airplane, Mao's limo (a gift from Stalin), and U.S. tanks captured during the Korean War.

Military Museum of Chinese People's Revolution

🅰 159 E1
✉ 9 Fuxing Lu
☎ 010/6686 6244
💲 $
🚇 Metro: Junshi Bowuguan; Bus: 1, 4, 21, or 337 to Junshi Bowuguan

Visitors are welcomed into the museum by a pair of imposing revolutionary sculptures located in the large square in front of the museum. The building itself is vintage Soviet-era architecture, its center adorned with a large red star and the Chinese characters *ba yi*, which refer to August 1, the founding date of the People's Liberation Army. A huge red star decorates the museum's interior ceiling dome.

Step inside the main hall, where a larger-than-life-size **statue of Mao** greets you inside the cavernous hall with huge marble columns. The **first floor** of the museum displays military uniforms and weapons used in the 1927 Autumn Harvest Uprising. The **second floor** focuses on the War of Resistance against Japan and the "war for liberation," while the **third floor** explores modern warfare as well as the Opium Wars of the mid-1800s.

The topic of ancient warfare dominates the **fourth floor.** The objects on display include a model of a war chariot, Ming-dynasty weapons, and lacquer shields from the Warring States period.

Other interesting items in the museum's collection include a variety of American, Japanese, and Soviet tanks, several fighter planes, and Chinese missiles. ■

MiG jet fighters and tanks face off at Beijing's Military Museum.

More places to visit in Haidian District

BEIJING PLANETARIUM

Built in 2004 beside the original building, the new Beijing Planetarium (Beijing Tianwen Guan) utilizes the latest in high-tech equipment. The large complex has three theaters, two observatories, and a solar exhibition hall. Take a 45-minute journey through the stars via the Planetarium's SGI Digital Universe Theatre and view more than 30,000 galaxies, constellations, nebulae, planets, and spacecraft. Or enjoy the three-dimensional space-shuttle simulator.
159 G1 ✉ 138 Xizhimenwai Dajie ☎ 010/6835 2453 or 010/6831 2517 Closed Mon. & Tues. $ $ (extra fee for shows & special exhibits) Bus: 7, 15, 65, 102, 103, 107, 111, or 334 to Dongwuyuan

have looked run-down in the past, recent improvements have made it an enjoyable place for animal lovers of all ages.
159 F1 ✉ 137 Xizhimenwai Dajie ☎ 010/6831 4411 $ $ (extra fee to visit Giant Panda House) Bus: 7, 15, 19, 27, 45, 102, 103, 105, 111, 332, 334, 808, 812, or T4 to Dongwuyuan

PURPLE BAMBOO PARK

Purple Bamboo Park (Zizhuyuan Gongyuan) comprises three lakes built during the Yuan dynasty to control the flow of water pouring into Beijing's moats. This is one of the places where you can book a boat ride to the Summer Palace (see pp. 166–170). Or hire a small boat and sail around the park's vast

A panda carefully negotiates his way down a log at the Beijing Zoo.

BEIJING ZOO

In 1906, the imperial court opened an experimental farm and zoo called the Garden of Ten Thousand Animals, and two years later it opened to the public. Today the Beijing Zoo (Beijing Dongwu Yuan) has thousands of animals and a number of special halls, including the **Giant Panda House, Bird Garden,** and **Aquarium.** While the zoo may

canals. The family-friendly park also has a playground and offers a painting and pottery workshop for children. Enter from the south gate and exit at the north gate to go to **Wan-shou Temple** (see pp. 178–179), about a 20-minute walk away.
159 F1 ✉ 35 Zhongguancun Nan Dajie ☎ 010/6842 5851 Metro: Baishi Qiao (east gate); Metro: Zizhu Qiao (west gate) ■

The ultimate engineering feat, the Great Wall of China is on everyone's must-see list. But that's not all that awaits north of Beijing: Temples, tombs, museums, and beach resorts are worthy destinations as well.

Excursions north to the Great Wall

Guarding the Spirit Way

Excursions north to the Great Wall

THE NORTHERN AREAS OF GREATER BEIJING OFFER A WIDE VARIETY OF opportunities to climb the Great Wall, from the renovated—and crowded—sections, such as Badaling and Mutianyu, to isolated areas, where you can walk, and sometimes claw and crawl, your way over the crumbling structure. Or stand on a military fortification in Shanhaiguan and watch the rising sun throw its first rays on the starting point of the Great Wall.

While the Great Wall is the most significant attraction for most tourists traveling north of Beijing, there are several other places near the wall worth a visit. Many visitors to the Great Wall at Badaling—northwest of Beijing—combine their excursion with a stop at the Ming-dynasty imperial tomb complex, Shisanling, in Changping District. The principles of feng shui guided the design of the entire complex, from site selection to landscaping to tomb architecture. Three of the 13 tombs—Changling, Dingling, and Zhaoling—are open to the public. The site was designated a World Heritage site in 2003.

Like today's tourists, China's emperors frequently ventured north of Beijing and stopped at the temples nestled in the hills of this rural and sparsely populated area. Qing

The Great Wall in Simatai stands in relative seclusion.

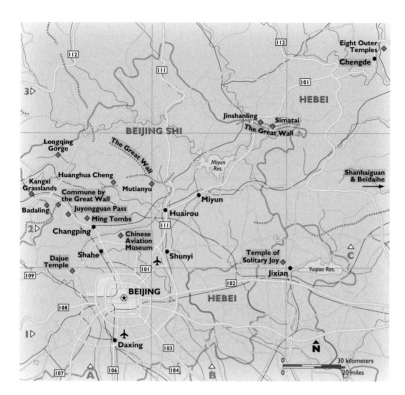

emperors especially favored the Tang-dynasty Temple of Solitary Joy. Made entirely of wood, the temple stuns modern visitors with beautiful painted murals and a wooden statue of Guanyin, said to be one of the largest in the world. The natural beauty of the grounds at Dajue Temple echoes its quiet solemnity. Here visitors can burn a stick of incense to the Future Buddha then enjoy a taste of some local food. From the 18th century, many emperors escaped the summer heat at the Chengde Imperial Mountain Resort, a complex of pavilions and temples set on a sheltered river plain ringed by mountains.

In the past, countless threats laid in the mountainous region north of Beijing, making defensive fortifications like the Great Wall essential. Located just south of Badaling, Juyongguan Pass—a strategically important gateway to China's northern border during the Yuan and Ming dynasties—overlooks some magnificent scenery. Located where the Great Wall meets the sea, the former garrison town of Shanhaiguan is a short train or bus trip east

from Beijing. The museum in this pleasant town is dedicated to the history of the wall. Nearby the popular beach resort of Beidaihe on the Hebei Coast offers a retreat from the dry and dusty Beijing summer.

Lovers of military history, as well as aviation buffs, will enjoy a visit to the impressive collection of historic aircraft housed at the China Aviation Museum.

But a visit to the Great Wall region does not have to be entirely about the past. Architecture enthusiasts will not want to miss the Commune by the Great Wall, a luxury hotel near Badaling, where 12 of Asia's best young architects designed villas showcasing new trends and twists on old styles.

The scenic beauty of Longqing Gorge makes for a top destination but its wealth of outdoor activities is just as alluring. There you can hike, kayak, boat, ice-skate, horseback ride, and even bungee jump. The Kangxi Grasslands, located less than two hours northwest of Beijing, is the place to go if you crave a taste of nomadic life. ■

The Great Wall

COLOSSAL ENDEAVOR, BRAVE FOLLY, FUTILE CONTRIVANCE, or splendid achievement, the Great Wall (Changcheng) inspires awe no matter how you look at it. Straddling northern China from the Yellow Sea in the east to its crumbling finale beyond Jiayuguan in the Gobi desert of Gansu, its entirety measures nearly 4,000 miles (6,430 km) long. Several sections have been restored outside Beijing, the most popular being Badaling and Mutianyu. For those with a little more time, the wilder parts, particularly Jinshanling, Simatai, and Huanghua Cheng, are worth the jaunt.

HISTORY

The Great Wall was built to prevent hostile nomadic groups from the north—like the Huns, Khitans, Jurchens, Mongols, and Manchus, all of whom threatened China at one time or another—from riding their horses south to invade and plunder. Not so much one wall as an articulation of ramparts, most of the Great Wall's sections were built independently of the others during different dynasties. The earliest parts date back to the seventh century B.C., when many ducal states began buildings walls along their boundaries.

The wall did not take on its gargantuan character until the third century B.C., when China became a united nation. Emperor Qin Shihuang (R.221–210 B.C.), of terra-cotta warrior fame, ordered Gen. Meng Tian to incorporate existing walls into his own defense network, threading together the ramparts, erecting watchtowers, and constructing beacons to alert the capital (near present-day Xi'an) of attack. His creation became the first Ten Thousand Li Great Wall.

The wall advanced during the Han dynasty, whose emperors extended Qin Shihuang's efforts into the Gobi desert. Little was done to lengthen the wall during the flourishing Tang and Song dynasties, but the Jin and Ming dynasties heralded a spate of enthusiastic construction—most of the wall we see today dates from the Ming dynasty. In some areas, two walls built in two different dynasties can

Blowing smoke

Towers built along the wall were used as signal towers to report enemy sightings and attacks. Drums were the main form of communication in the Warring States period (475–221 B.C.), but during the Han dynasty (206 B.C.–A.D. 220) the Chinese began to develop and use basic smoke signals, sent during the daylight hours. Every tower along the wall had a ready supply of materials that could be burned to create the signals. At night, lanterns and fires were used. The Tang dynasty (618–970) adopted a more advanced method of smoke signaling involving wolf dung, which gave off a black smoke that stayed in the air longer and was clear from long distances. With the heralding of the Ming dynasty (1368–1643) and the invention of gunpowder, the signaling system was greatly enhanced because the sound of firing cannon could carry over a long distance. ■

**Opposite:
Student musicians
perform on the
Great Wall.**

be seen running side by side over the hills and mountains.

Based on the different technologies available to different dynasties, construction methods varied through the centuries. In general, the wall's foundation consisted of layer upon layer of tamped earth, sometimes mixed with sticks, pebbles, or reeds. The Ming encased exterior sections of the wall in brick that had been fired in local kilns. Many of the kilns can still be found in the valleys around the outskirts of Beijing.

The Great Wall's average height is 32 feet (10 m), with an average width of 16 feet (5 m)—wide enough for ten soldiers or five horses to stand abreast. Natural features such as mountain ridges, river gorges, and narrow passes were incorporated into the design. Watchtowers, signal towers, and moats are regularly spaced. Three overlapping layers protected extremely strategic areas.

SECURITY BREACH

Despite the care taken by the Chinese to erect an impenetrable

A lone walker
explores an
unrestored
section of the
Great Wall
at Jinshanling.

structure, the wall failed spectacularly, most notably with the incursions of nomadic groups from the north that established the dynasties of the Jin (Jurchen) in the 12th century, the Yuan (Mongol) in the 13th century, and the Qing (Manchu) in the 17th century.

The Ming dynasty fell to a peasant rebellion in 1644, but the new regime was short-lived. Gen. Wu Sangui, who commanded the forces guarding the Great Wall in Shanhaiguan, decided to throw his lot in with the nomadic Manchus from the north and opened the gates. Manchu forces poured into China. The early Manchu rulers debated the need for such border defenses and apparently decided not to put any more effort or money into them. Eventually they were too occupied with the onslaught of Western forces and European Catholic missionaries that was coming from the coast to spend time maintaining the wall. Ultimately, the wall was superseded by technology and circumvented by (continued on p. 192)

The disappearing wall

According to a survey conducted in 2006 by the Great Wall Society of China, only 20 percent of the Great Wall is in "reasonable" condition, and another 30 percent lies in ruins. The rest has already disappeared.

In Gansu Province, a portion of the wall was rented to farmers, who "restored" it by sealing the section with cement and installing a gate so they could charge admission. A short distance away, tourists have pulled grass from

Workers repair a broken section of the Great Wall at Jinshanling.

These numbers are not surprising when you consider that in the 20th century alone the wall has suffered from decades of government neglect and intentional destruction.

During the 1950s, for example, Mao Zedong exhorted the Chinese people to "allow the past to serve the present" (known in Chinese as *"Gu wei zhong yong"*). He had farmers demolish parts of the wall and use the bricks for building houses and pigpens.

When capitalism began making an inroad during the 1980s, many officials believed that the tourist industry would save the wall. But today tourism may be its biggest threat.

Poorly executed restoration efforts have left some sections near Beijing looking like a Hollywood set. Entrepreneurs have set up cable cars, souvenir stalls, fast-food restaurants, amusement facilities, villas, and crowded parking lots—all within a stone's throw of the wall.

rammed-earth walls—among the wall's oldest and most endangered segments. And Christmas lights have been nailed to the 14th-century towers guarding the gate at Jiayuguan.

For his 2007 book, *The Great Wall Revisited,* expert William Lindesay gathered hundreds of photos of the wall taken at the turn of the 20th century. He then set out to rephotograph 150 of the locations, some of which he found had already disappeared. The result was a sobering reminder of how much the wall suffered in just a single century.

In 2002, when the New York–based World Monuments Fund put the Great Wall on its list of the World's 100 Most Endangered Sites, Chinese government officials finally sat up and took notice of their national treasure.

In 2003 Beijing announced its first regulations to protect the wall near the capital. Then in December 2006, the central government announced a new national law. It is

A hiker picks her way across a broken section of the disappearing wall.

now illegal to remove bricks or stones, carve into the wall, or build a house against it. The law also states that "all citizens, legal entities, and organizations" have the responsibility to protect the wall and report illegal activity to government agencies. On December 3, 2006, a construction company—which had taken apart large pieces of the wall in order to make way for an illegal highway—was the first fined under the new law.

Still the wall's biggest problem today may be the lack of understanding among some Chinese, especially in poor areas outside Beijing. Parts of the wall have been covered in Chinese graffiti, and farmers continue to cart bricks away as they've done for decades.

According to Dong Yaohui, of the Great Wall Society of China, "Trying to get the significance of the wall across to a people worried about their survival is not easy." ∎

A guard tower overlooks the mountain ridges in Jinshanling.

Badaling

- 185 A2
- 010/6912 1737
- $$
- Bus: 919 from Deshengmen; or Tour Bus 1 from Qianmen (Beijing Sightseeing Bus Center, west of Tiananmen Square, 6:30 a.m.–10 a.m.; tel 010/8353 1111)

Mutianyu

- 185 A2
- Mutianyu Town
- 010/6162 6505
- $$
- Taxi is the best. Bus: 916 or 936 from Dongzhimen Station to Huairou International Conference Center, then minibus; or Tour Bus 6 from Xuanwumen on weekends & national holidays.

(continued from p. 189)

forces that moved into China from other directions, such as the Japanese and the Western powers that mustered along the coastline. Though much preservation work needs to be done, the Great Wall became a UNESCO World Heritage site in 1987. The sections you can realistically visit have been rebuilt and cosmetically touched up for the benefit of visitors; this gives a false impression of the condition of the wall (in large measure derelict). The fortresslike segments viewable around Beijing quickly peter out. But that doesn't make a visit here any less impressive.

BADALING

Most day-trippers from Beijing visit the Great Wall at Badaling, 43 miles (70 km) northwest of the capital city. A hallmark of Ming-dynasty construction, the wall here undulates dramatically peak to peak, punctuated occasionally by watchtowers and gates. Some parts of the wall here can be extremely steep, so wear good shoes. To the west, this stretch eventually dissolves into ruins.

Most times of the year, Badaling is besieged by tourists and commercialization, so don't expect a romantic sojourn with just you and

the wall. If you visit in midwinter, however, you will be rewarded with relative peace and quiet and a wonderfully frosted landscape. In addition, you won't be surrounded by a crowd of T-shirt sellers. Just be sure to wrap up—the wind howls here, and it's bitter cold.

Entrance to the **Great Wall Museum,** which covers the wall's long history, is included in the ticket for the wall. Also be sure to check out the **International Friendship Forest.** This landscaped path is not well known or marked, so it's usually empty. At the top of the small hill leading from the parking lot toward the steps to the wall, look for the opening to the walkway on the left, just where the souvenir stands begin. Follow the path to a deserted guard tower and nice views of the wall from below.

Nearby **Juyongguan Pass** (see p. 195) is a popular addition to a Badaling visit.

MUTIANYU

Originally built in the sixth century, Mutianyu is one of the most popular sites for today's tourists. It is also one of the closest, located about 56 miles (90 km) from downtown Beijing. As a result, Mutianyu is one of the wall's most overdeveloped and crowded sections. Nevertheless, once you climb the wall and move away from the crowds, it offers picture-postcard views of the Great Wall and the surrounding countryside.

The portion of the wall located at Mutianyu was given renewed attention after the fall of the Yuan dynasty in 1368, when the new Ming government focused its attention on security along the northern border. This section, which is just a mile long (1.6 km), was repaired and expanded twice during this period, first in the 14th century and then again in 1570, when the structure grew to the size you see today. You can take a cable car to the top of the wall, then slide back down again on a small toboggan track.

JINSHANLING & SIMATAI

Located about 60 miles (100 km) from Beijing, Jinshanling dates back to the sixth century; the portion of wall that stands here is a product of Ming-dynasty engineers. This is one of the few sections of the wall that allow visitors to spend the night. You can sleep in a tent or under the stars in the warmer months, but beware: Mice rule this part of the Great Wall after dark.

One of the most secluded and historically authentic parts of the Great Wall can be found at Simatai, which has been only partially restored. Dotted with no fewer than 15 watchtowers, this section was once a Ming-dynasty fortress of the same name. The powerful landscape makes for a marvelous backdrop while hiking along the crumbling remains. Be careful, however: The wall can be dangerously steep in parts and occasionally comes to an abrupt halt over a dangerous drop.

Trekking

Jinshanling and Simatai are much farther away from Beijing than

Jinshanling & Simatai

🅰 185 B3

✉ Miyun District

☎ 010/8402 4628 & 010/6903 5025

$ $$

🚌 Jinshanling
Bus: From Dongzhimen bus station to Chengde then taxi Simatai
Bus: 980 from Dongzhimen to Miyun, then bus to Simatai.

Camping out on the Great Wall

Cable cars whisk visitors to the top of the wall at Simatai.

Huanghua Cheng

🅰 185 A2

✉ NW of Huangrou District

💲 No gate, but local farmers will sometimes try to charge visitors who wish to climb on the wall

🚌 Bus: 916 from Dongzhimen to Huairou, then switch to the minibus, or hire a taxi.

either Badaling or Mutianyu, and the distance has protected both places from overexposure to tour groups and restoration projects. The four-hour walk between the two sites is highly popular. As you leave one site and head for the other—you can go in either direction—the physical condition of the wall grows gradually worse, and the vendors fall by the wayside. This is not an easy walk, and in some spots you'll have to cross narrow remnants of the wall or climb around areas that have been heavily damaged. Don't attempt

Debunking the space myth

Despite common belief, astronauts cannot see the wall from space. Astronaut William Pogue, who reported that he had seen it from Skylab, discovered he was actually looking at the Grand Canal near Beijing. ■

the walk unless you're in relatively good physical shape and wearing proper hiking shoes.

Jinshanling and Simatai are best reached by taxi. If you plan to walk between the two sites, have the driver wait for you at your destination. Or organize your visit through the Peking Downtown Backpackers Hostel (Dongtang Kezhang, *85 Nanluogu Xiang, tel 010/8400 2429, $$$$$*). Trips leave every other day at 7 a.m.

HUANGHUA CHENG

Located about 40 miles (65 km) north of downtown Beijing, Huanghua Cheng is less developed than other sections of the wall, and in some places it is heavily damaged. The entire segment, which is nearly 7 miles long (11 km), joins with Mutianyu Great Wall in the east and Juyongguan Pass and Badaling in the west. Despite the challenge it gives hikers—it has no stone steps or single pathway—this section is becoming increasingly popular. ■

Juyongguan Pass

ONE OF TWO IMPORTANT MOUNTAIN PASSES INTO BEIJING
and the interior of China, Juyongguan Pass became a vital possession for Beijing. While fortifications may have existed here as early as
the sixth century (before Beijing even existed), it was during the Ming
dynasty that an impenetrable fortified gate system was constructed
here as part of the Great Wall.

Juyongguan Pass
- 185 A2
- Nankou Town, Changping District
- 010/6977 1665
- $$
- Bus: 919 from Deshengmen

Not that it kept invaders out. It
was at this pass that Li Zicheng led
his peasant army into Beijing in
1644 to overthrow the last Ming-
dynasty emperor.

Having undergone a massive
renovation between 1993 and 1997,
the strategic fortress gate, with walls
and towers protecting the sur-
rounding mountains, is a popular
destination, especially given its
proximity to Beijing—just 37 miles
(60 km) northwest of Beijing.

Be sure to stop at the **Cloud
Platform,** also known as Crossing
Street Tower, in the middle of the
pass. Erected during the Yuan
dynasty to protect the road leading
north to Mongol territories, the
Cloud Platform is made of white
marble and features numerous
Yuan-style architectural details
around the top. Men, horses, and
carriages could pass through the
hexagonal arched gateway in the
middle of the platform base. ■

**International
cyclists race
along Juyongguan
Pass near the
Great Wall.**

Tourists enjoy a boat ride through the striking Longqing Gorge.

Kangxi Grasslands
- ▲ 185 A2
- ✉ W of Badaling Great Wall, Yanqing County
- ☎ 010/6353 2564
- 💲 $
- 🚌 Bus: 919 from Deshengmen

Longqing Gorge
- ▲ 185 A2
- ✉ Longqing Xia, Yanqing County
- ☎ 010/6353 2564
- 🕐 Closed Nov.—Dec.
- 💲 $$
- 🚌 Bus: 919 from Deshengmen to Yanqing Station, then bus 920 or take taxi

Kangxi Grasslands & Longqing Gorge

BEYOND THE GREAT WALL AT BADALING AWAITS A COUPLE of lesser known areas that combine stunning landscapes with the promise of adventure.

KANGXI GRASSLANDS
Experience a bit of Mongolia on the Kangxi Grasslands, the largest grassland in the Beijing area. Located just west of the Great Wall at Badaling, this extensive plain peppered with yurt villages was once a favorite hunting spot of Qing-dynasty emperors. Take a ride on one of the Yili horses from Xinjiang, or even a camel. You can also spend a few nights in a yurt hotel. Wildlife on the plain is most striking May through September.

LONGQING GORGE
Offering a great afternoon respite from a morning spent at Badaling,

Longqing Gorge (Longqing Xia) is often called the Little Three Gorges. Take the escalator 1,150 feet (350 m) to the reservoir at the top of the biggest dam in northern China, where you can catch a boat for a 30-minute cruise through the gorge. In addition to lovely scenery, the area also offers horseback riding, kayaking, and rock climbing. If you can't make it all the way to Harbin in northern China for the winter Ice Festival, Longqing Gorge, which is just 50 miles (80 km) from Beijing, is an easy substitute. The **Longqing Gorge Ice Sculpture Festival** is held every January and February. ■

Commune by the Great Wall

ONE OF THE MORE INTERESTING ARCHITECTURAL PROjects in the Beijing area is Soho China's Commune by the Great Wall (Changcheng Jiaoxia De Gongshe). The project, which was the brainchild of Zhang Xin and Pan Shiyi, husband and wife property developers, is part commercial enterprise, part artistic endeavor. The hotel won a prize at the 2002 Venice Biennial, when it was unveiled to great international acclaim. Zhang says it was designed in part to fill China's gap in architectural awareness.

Commune by the Great Wall
www.commune.com.cn/en
- 185 A2
- Badaling Highway
- 010/5878 8328
- By appointment
- $$
- Bus: 919 from Deshengmen, then take taxi

Staff at the hotel wear bright red stars on their hats and uniforms, but there's nothing communist about this fashionable enclave, which features 12 luxury villas and more than 45 guest rooms. The structures were designed by Asia's most talented young architects, with two stipulations: The designs had to be as flamboyant as possible, and the architects had to agree to accept a small design fee of $12,000 (88,765RMB).

The most impressive of the villas is the **Bamboo Wall,** designed by Japanese architect Kengo Kuma. The structure's interior and exterior walls, and some floors, are made of bamboo, while the elegant but sparsely decorated rooms create a Japanese aesthetic. One of the most interesting parts of the house is the meditation space. The dining room door opens onto a granite bridge that spans a shallow moat within the house, leading to a bamboo cage comprised of sliding doors. The view of the Great Wall from inside the cage is magnificent.

The **Split House,** designed by mainland architect Yung Ho Chang, is split down the middle to create various angles and spaces. A small stream meanders up to the front door then flows beneath the glass walkway into the vestibule. This wood-framed house was built in the Chinese tradition, and its ecological impact on the countryside is minimal. The earthen walls act as insulation, keeping the house warm in the winter and cool in the summer.

Designed by Hong Kong architect Gary Change, the **Suitcase House** is just as its name suggests. Pneumatic panels on the floor open up to reveal hidden bedrooms as well as a submerged kitchen and bathroom. There are hidden work and storage spaces throughout the house, and even a hidden sauna and shower. Wall panels slide back and forth to provide privacy.

The villas at the Commune by the Great Wall are available as accommodations, but visitors are welcome to admire their exteriors any time and to look inside when the villas are vacant. The somewhat pricey restaurant serves classic Beijing, Sichuan, and Cantonese dishes and offers great views of the surrounding countryside. ∎

The deck of the Cantilever House offers a grand view of the countryside.

Dajue Temple

Dajue Temple

🅰 185 AI

✉ Bei'anhe Nankou
Haidian District

☎ 010/6245 6162 or
010/6245 6163

$ $; English audio $

🚌 Bus: 346 from
Summer Palace to
Bei'anhe Nankou,
then a mile (2 km)
walk to temple

NESTLED AT THE FOOT OF YANGTAI MOUNTAIN, SOME 50 miles (80 km) northwest of Beijing, Dajue Temple (Dajue Si) is a serene and rustic spot that dates back nearly a thousand years. This pleasant temple was built during the Liao dynasty, rebuilt during the Ming dynasty, and renovated several times during the Qing dynasty.

Unlike most Chinese Buddhist temples, which face south, Dajue Temple, or Temple of Great Enlightenment, faces east, a reflection of the Khitan (Liao) custom of "turning to the sun." After entering the temple you'll cross a bridge over a small pond filled with turtles and goldfish. Drum and bell towers stand on either side of the courtyard.

The first building is the **Hall of Deva Kings** (Tianwang Dian), in which Milefo, the Future Buddha (see p. 140), is protected by the Four Heavenly Kings. Weituo stands behind the Future Buddha in his normal fighting pose.

The **Mahavira Hall** (Daxiong Baodian), which dates back to the Ming dynasty, is made of wood. This is a rarity in modern temple architecture, where almost everything is made of cement and bricks. Inside the hall, where the paint is peeling from the walls, there are images of three Buddhas.

The calligraphy of Emperor Qianlong—a frequent visitor during the Qing dynasty—hangs over the entrance to **Amitabha Hall,** proclaiming "Change and Quietude are Balanced." The temple houses images of Amitabha Buddha and Guanyin Bodhisattva, and a wall at the back displays a diorama made of painted mud.

To the right of the last hall is a Liao-dynasty stele that tells the temple's history. The carving is blurred and the stele is broken in several places, but most of the inscription remains clear.

OUTSIDE COURTYARDS

Follow the steps to the right of the stele and walk up to the next level, where you'll find a large white dagoba, with elaborate dragons, clouds, and flowers carved on its base. Walk south and take the steps down, noticing the narrow stone gutter that serves as a channel for the water flowing down to the pond. Just past the elegant **Minghui Teahouse**—which is decorated with traditional furniture—is a pleasant restaurant, which serves Shaoxing cuisine from Zhejiang Province. Turn left and take the steps ahead of you, which will return you to the main courtyard. A simple courtyard-style hotel in this area offers rooms for the night.

Dajue Temple is also known for its natural beauty. A small spring flows gracefully down the hill behind the temple and along the walkways via a small aqueduct, finishing its journey in the **Lotus Pool** just inside the temple entrance. Scattered around the temple grow yulan magnolia and ginkgo trees. One of the yulan magnolias is said to have been planted by a monk around 300 years ago. There's also a ginkgo tree that many believe dates back about a thousand years.

A small market in front of the temple sells fresh local produce and other goods, including pumpkins, peaches, dates, corn, almonds, *luva*, gourds, and pomegranates. You can also buy long incense sticks, some of which are as thick as salami. ∎

Opposite: A hiker strolls past the Dajue Temple.

Ming Tombs

Ming Tombs

⚑ 185 A2

✉ Shisanling Changping County

☎ 010/6076 1423

$ $$, plus $$ to visit Sacred Way & each of the tombs

🚌 Bus: 1–5 (before 9 a.m.) or 345, then transfer to 314

THIRTEEN OF THE SIXTEEN MING-DYNASTY EMPERORS ARE buried in the Ming Tombs (Ming Shisanling), which are located in a valley about 30 miles (48 km) northwest of Beijing. Three tombs in the valley are open to the public: Changling, Dingling, and Zhaoling.

SPIRIT WAY

After an emperor died, his body was placed in a coffin and carried to his tomb along an impressive pathway called the Spirit Way (Shen Dao or Ling Dao). The body was accompanied by 24 carved stone statues: six pairs of animals—lions, *xiechi* (a mythical beast), camels, elephants, unicorns, and horses— and three pairs of humans—scholars, administrators, and soldiers.

In order to reach the tombs, you must also walk along the Spirit Way, which begins beneath a stone portico with five carved archways and continues through the **Great Red Gate** (Da Hongmen Do Gongmen). The gate's central archway was reserved solely for the coffins of deceased emperors. Next is the **Stele Pavilion** (Bei Ting), which holds a large stele eulogizing the Ming-dynasty emperors. The Spirit Way comes to an end at the **Dragon and Phoenix Gate** (Lingxing Men and Longfeng Men), which the dead emperor passed on his way to the tomb.

After crossing the arched bridge, you can visit the tombs, which are scattered around the valley.

THE TOMBS

Changling is the first tomb ahead. Considered the most important in the valley, it is the tomb of Emperor Yongle, who died in 1424. Although the tomb itself has not been excavated, you can visit the imposing Hall of Sacrifice, which is supported by 32 huge pillars, each of which was carved from a single tree and transported from Yunnan Province.

Dingling, the tomb of Emperor Wanli (*R.*1573–1620) and his two concubines, was excavated in 1958. The excavation team found a number of underground vaults and around 300 garments and many pieces of jewelry, curios, and porcelain packed in 26 lacquer chests, all of which are now displayed in two exhibition halls outside.

Zhaoling is the tomb of Ming-dynasty Emperor Longqing (*R.*1567–1572).

The remainder of the tombs are awaiting excavation. ∎

A stone camel guards the Spirit Way leading to the Ming tombs.

China's Y-5 transport aircraft, modeled on a Soviet design

China Aviation Museum

THE CHINA AVIATION MUSEUM (ZHONGGUO HANGKONG Bowuguan), which boasts more than 200 aircraft of a hundred different types, may just be the largest collection of retired military and civilian aircraft on display anywhere in the world. An hour's ride from Beijing, the museum is located on an airbase hidden at the foot of a mountain, Datangshan. While its collection may be a bit dusty, it does offer military and aviation buffs an interesting walk through modern Chinese history.

The museum opened in 1989, on the occasion of the 40th anniversary of the Chinese Air Force. It's divided into two sections.

AIRFIELD

Begin your visit outside, where dozens of MiG fighters, crew transports, and helicopters stand ready on the airfield. Radar, anti-aircraft guns, and a battery of Red Flag No. 3 missiles stare straight up into the sky, as if ready to thwart an imminent attack.

Here also sit the personal aircraft of Chairman Mao Zedong and Premier Zhou Enlai. In 1956, Mao used the looming **Lear 2** to inspect Guangzhou, Changsha,

Wuhan, and other areas, and it was the plane he used ten years later when he flew to Nanjing to make his celebrated swim in the Yangtze River. But it is the **IL-18** that is reported to have been Mao's favorite; he used it 23 times in 1957 and 1958 to conduct inspections around the country. Walk up the steps to the plane and peek through the Plexiglas for a look at how Mao traveled in those days. Some of the Chairman's personal items are displayed in the plane, including his teacup, blankets, and bed.

Also outside are several **B-29** strategic bombers dating back to the 1940s. One of them has been fitted with a large circular radar

China Aviation Museum

🄰 185 A2

✉ Datangshan, Xiaotangshan, Changping District

☎ 010/6178 4882

🅂 $$

🚌 Bus: 912 from Andingmen

device that bears a close resemblance to the AWACS (Airborne Warning and Control System) used by the United States Air Force. Opposite stands one of the Chinese Air Force's most revered aircraft, a **Red Flag F20** fighter—the first to shoot down enemy aircraft during the Korean War. Standing on a concrete slab in a small pond nearby is a smart-looking **Be-6** aircraft. Produced in the former Soviet Union, the water-ready plane joined the Chinese Navy in 1955 and was used for antisubmarine warfare.

MAIN COLLECTION

Made of reinforced concrete and fitted with antiblast doors at both ends, the huge cavelike hangar—with high, rounded ceilings—houses copies of vintage aircraft, as well as restorations, and the mangled remains of planes that either crashed or were not treated well by time. Some of those on display are missing propellers, a wing, or other important parts.

The first thing you will see after entering the hangar is a **statue of China's first female military aviators.** The six women, who are depicted standing shoulder to shoulder, flew in formation over Tiananmen Square during National Day celebrations in 1952.

The indoor collection begins with some rather old aircraft. For example, you will find on display the biplane of Chinese aviation pioneer Feng Ru. A contemporary of the Wright brothers, Feng Ru put his plane together in the United States and flew it for the first time in 1910. According to the museum, the **Feng Ru No. 2** was made of bamboo. Feng died several years after his first flight, when his plane crashed in China.

During the 1920s, Chinese leader Sun Yat-sen presented *The Rosamonde* to his young wife, Madame Song Qing-ling. It is on display in the museum and still bears the blue-and-white nationalist symbol under its double wings. And then there is the first aircraft owned by the People's Liberation Army—the **Lenin Plane**—which was used to drop propaganda leaflets.

Also on display inside the museum are a variety of war planes from Japan and the United States that were either captured or shot down during World War II, the Chinese civil war, the Korean War, or later conflicts. The aircraft on display include a **Tachikawa Ki-36,** used by the Japanese against Chinese guerrilla fighters; a U.S. **Mustang fighter,** circa 1943, which was captured from the nationalists in the summer of 1949; and copies of the **Huey** and **Apache helicopters,** which gained fame in the Vietnam War.

Of interest to history buffs are the **P-40** fighters, made famous by the Flying Tigers, who inflicted severe damage on the Japanese in late 1941 and early 1942. The volunteer American pilots, who flew under the Chinese flag, received $500 for every Japanese plane they shot down.

The museum also has an extensive collection of Soviet-made aircraft, including the **La-11** fighter, **Tu-2** bombers, **IL-10** attack planes, a machine-gun-laden **Mi-4** helicopter (which was designed by the Soviets and first flown in 1952), and **Yak** domestic aircraft. The museum's holdings include an interesting selection of aircraft flown by nationalist pilots, most of whom either defected or were shot down. Also on display are a **de Havilland Beaver** (made of wood), a **Lockheed T-33** jet trainer, a **Corvair 240** transport, and rows of rusting **MiGs.** ∎

Temple of Solitary Joy

A FINE EXAMPLE OF AN ANCIENT CHINESE TEMPLE MADE of wood, the Temple of Solitary Joy (Dule Si)—which is located outside Jixian, a county about three hours north of Tianjin—was built during the Tang dynasty and renovated in 924 during the Liao dynasty. Despite its age, the temple remains in excellent condition.

Temple of Solitary Joy

- 185 B2
- 41 Wuding Jie, Jixian, Tianjin
- 010/2914 2904
- $$
- Bus: Tianjin's northeastern bus station to Jixian County

Enter at the **temple gate,** which is decorated with two mythical beasts on its east and west corners. You will be greeted by two fierce-looking door guards, General Heng and General Ha, both brandishing swords as they defend the goddess of mercy, Guanyin. The Four Heavenly Kings are painted on the wall.

Inside **Guanyin Pavilion** (Guanyin Ge) is a 52-foot-high (16 m) statue of the goddess of mercy, said to be one of the largest existing terra-cotta figures in China. The statue rises from the center of the hall, climbing past the second and third floors until it almost touches the octagonal ceiling. It was carved out of wood and then plastered with clay that was mixed with egg white and glutinous rice. Ten small Guanyin heads were added to the sculpture to portray the 11-headed Guanyin, a savior deity.

The painted mural of the luohan, which was created during the Yuan dynasty, is quite rare and noted for its unique composition, color, and style. Behind the 11-headed Guanyin is a representation of Guanyin crossing the sea.

A smaller pavilion housing a statue of **Weituo,** the guardian of Buddhism, is located nearby, as is the **Baoen Hall** (Baoen Yuan), which contains a statue of the Future Buddha accompanied by the four "mad" Buddhas.

On the east side of the temple is the **Qing Dynasty Villa,** where Qing-dynasty emperors would rest on their way to worship their ancestors in the Eastern Qing Tombs. There are 28 steles here with inscriptions by Emperor Qianlong. To the south of the temple is the **Dule Temple Pagoda** (Dulesi Ta), also known as the Jixian White Pagoda, which dates back more than a thousand years. The pagoda was severely damaged during the 1976 Tangshan earthquake, and during its restoration, workers discovered one tower within another, and more than a hundred ancient artifacts. ■

The statue of the 11-headed bodhisattva Guanyin, Dule Si

Chengde Imperial Mountain Resort

Chengde

 185 C3

LOCATED 159 MILES (225 KM) NORTHEAST OF BEIJING, Chengde Imperial Mountain Resort is a sprawling 18th-century complex of palaces, pavilions, temples, and monasteries (the latter two known together as the Eight Outer Temples). Although a number of the buildings are in ruins, much survives, offering visitors an impressive architectural museum.

Chengde Imperial Mountain Resort is known in Chinese as Bishu Shanzhuang, literally "mountain villa for escaping the heat." Established during the reign of Emperor Kangxi (*R.*1662–1722), the resort was much expanded during the reign of Kangxi's grandson, Qianlong (*R.*1736–1795). Work continued during the reign of Emperor Jiaqing (*R.*1796–1820), but his death from a fire at the resort (ignited by a bolt of lightning, rumors said) tarnished Chengde's reputation, which was ruined after the death of Emperor Xianfeng in 1861 under suspicious circumstances. Even the Last Emperor Puyi refused to visit the resort.

Originally a 6-mile (10 km) wall enclosed the resort, whose chief entrance is called **Lizheng Men;** another entrance—**Dehui Men**—pierces the wall to the east. The **Main Palace** (Zheng Gong), with its nine courtyards (nine being the number of heaven) set amid pines and rocks, houses a museum of imperial memorabilia that includes furniture, costumes, and period weapons.

Leaving the palace by the north gate will bring you to the main park, which is threaded by lakes. From here, you can see the wooded area to the west. The plain that stretches to the north was the site of imperial hunting parties and archery competitions, and the lake to the east (divided into Ideal Lake and Clear Lake) is studded with temples and pavilions. The **Hall of**

Mist and Rain (Yanyu Lou) sits on a small island hill in the north of the lake. The hall was once an imperial study.

On the lake's eastern shore is **Gold Mountain** (Jinshan), a small hill topped by the **Pavilion of God** (Shangdi Ge), an elegant hexagonal pagoda and temple built for Emperor Kangxi in imitation of the Jinshan Temple in Zhenjiang. Also on the lake are the **Water's Heart Pavilions** (Shuixin Xie), which were erected for Qianlong as one of his 36 spots of beauty on the grounds of the resort.

Nearby is the **Temple of Eternal Blessing** (Yongyou Si), and on **Canglang Island** (Canglang Yu) you will find a copy of one of Suzhou's famous gardens.

EIGHT OUTER TEMPLES

From the front of the imperial garden, catch a bus to the Eight Outer Temples (Wai Ba Miao), which lie a couple miles to the north and northeast. Of the original 12 temples, 8 remain today, built mainly between 1750 and 1780 during the reign of Qianlong. Most were designed in non-Han

A man burns an offering at the Putuo Zongcheng Temple in Chengde.

A lotus pond at the Mountain Villa for Escaping the Heat

Temple of Universal Tranquility

✉ Just off Puning Si Lu

☎ 031/4205 8209

💲 $$

🚍 Bus: 6 or 118

Puyou Temple

✉ Beside Puning Si

☎ 031/4216 0935

💲 $

🚍 Bus: 6 or 118

style to impress visiting Tibetan and Mongol envoys.

The temples have suffered the ravages of time. Some were damaged during the Chinese civil war of the 1930s and 1940s, and some were marred by the war with Japan, while others fell victim to the iconoclastic Cultural Revolution. This neglect is being slowly reversed, but you may find that some temples are closed or partially off-limits. Sadly, all have been ransacked of their former treasures.

Tibetan motifs dominate the peaceful **Temple of Universal Tranquility** (Puning Si), which was built in 1755 and styled after a Tibetan monastery. Inside, the magnificent statue of Guanyin, the

goddess of mercy, stands 75 feet (23 m) in height and is said to be the largest statue of the goddess in the world. This temple is also of interest because it's still a working temple with real devotees who come to worship here.

To the east stands the **Puyou Temple** (Puyou Si), which once had a collection of 500 luohan statues, many of which were destroyed during the war with Japan in the 1930s and 1940s.

Located in the hills to the north of the imperial complex, **Putuo Zongcheng Temple** (Putuo Zongcheng Zhi Miao) is the largest of the eight temples. It was built in 1771 by the very religious Emperor Qianlong to mark his 60th birthday

Culture clash

In 1793, Lord Macartney and his embassy from Britain arrived at Chengde for an audience with Emperor Qianlong. Macartney's brief was to make diplomatic overtures to the Chinese and secure trade links with the Middle Kingdom.

The audience went awkwardly. Lord Macartney would only kowtow to the Chinese emperor if the emperor would likewise bow in front of a portrait of the English sovereign. The Chinese emperor refused. Despite the extravagant gifts presented to the emperor, his final message was, "We possess all things. I set no value on objects strange or ingenious, and have no use for your country's manufactures." This marked the beginning of a war of wills that saw Britain try to force trade on China. Ultimately, China would reluctantly buckle and accept things foreign. ∎

Putuo Zongcheng Temple
- ✉ Shizi Gou Lu
- ☎ 031/4216 3072 or 031/4216 5169
- 💲 $$
- 🚌 Bus: 118

Temple of Sumeru Happiness and Longevity
- ✉ Shizi Gou Lu
- ☎ 031/4216 2972
- 💲 $
- 🚌 Bus: 118

Temple of Universal Happiness
- ✉ Just off Hedong Lu
- ☎ 031/4205 7557
- 💲 $
- 🚌 Bus: 10

Temple of Appeasing the Distant
- ✉ To the north of Pule Si
- ☎ 031/4205 7809
- 💲 $
- 🚌 Bus: 10

and with the hope that the Dalai Lama would visit Chengde (he didn't). The dagoba-topped temple—known as the mini-Potala, a reference to Potala Palace in Lhasa—contains 60 halls.

To the east is the **Temple of Sumeru Happiness and Longevity** (Xumi Fushou Zhi Miao), which imitated the monastery of the sixth Panchen Lama in Shigatse. High outer walls with many windows surround the magnificent temple, whose huge roof is covered with dragons.

Just to the south is the **Temple of Universal Happiness** (Pule Si), which resembles Beijing's Hall of Prayer for a Good Harvest at the Temple of Heaven (see pp. 119–120). The temple, which has a circular, two-tiered roof, was built in 1776 to entertain envoys.

Featuring an unusual black-tiled roof, the **Temple of Appeasing the Distant** (Anyuan Miao), to the east of the Wulie River, is a copy of a temple in northwest China. Built to assuage Mongol tribes that had settled in the area, the huge, quadrilateral temple is decorated with decayed Buddhist frescoes.

Other temples in the complex include the Chinese-style **Temple of Extensive Benevolence** (Puren Si), which is said to be the oldest of the temples, and the **Shuxiang Temple** (Shuxiang Si), located northwest of the complex. Neither is open to the public. ∎

Shanhaiguan & Beidaihe

Shanhaiguan
- 185 C2
- Qinhuangdao City, Shanhaiguan District
- 033/5505 1106 or 033/5515 2996
- $$

Beidaihe
- Train: D517 from Beijing; or bus from Shanhaiguan

A THREE-HOUR TRAIN RIDE FROM BEIJING, SHANHAIGUAN offers history and spectacular views of the Great Wall. Combine your visit with a stop at the seaside resort of Beidaihe.

SHANHAIGUAN

Shanhaiguan, which means the "pass between the mountains and the sea," is a fortress town located where the Great Wall dips down from the mountains in the west and plunges east into the sea. Built in 1381 by Ming-dynasty Gen. Xu Da to keep marauders out of the northeast, this square fortress now draws visitors from all over China.

The fortress at Shanhaiguan played a key role in Chinese history,

A family plays in the sand at Beidaihe.

but not exactly what General Xu intended, for at the end of the Ming dynasty, it failed to prevent the Manchus from entering.

The east gate in Shanhaiguan's city wall, called the **First Pass under Heaven** (Tianxia Diyi Guan), also passes through the Great Wall. The adjacent **Great Wall Museum** has exhibits of armor, weapons, and photographs related to the history of the wall and a scale model of the entire area.

A nice place to view the sunrise, **Old Dragon's Head** (Lao Longtou)—the easternmost portion of the wall built during the

Ming dynasty—has been nicely restored. The old **Navy Barracks** along the shore have also been rebuilt. The Qing-dynasty **Temple of the Sea God** (Haishen Miao), on the other side of the beach, is a good place to view the wall.

Jiao Shan is a very steep section of the Great Wall just 2.5 miles (4 km) outside the city. From its apex you'll have wonderful views of the city and Old Dragon's Head plunging into the sea. For those who can't climb, there is a chairlift that makes the ascent.

BEIDAIHE

Foreigners living in the Beijing legations and the Tianjin concession areas established the popular beach resort of Beidaihe during the 19th century as a respite from city life. After the diplomats, businessmen, and missionaries left, the Communist Party stepped in quickly to fill the gap. Chairman Mao, renowned for his love of swimming, came here for a dip in the ocean, and the top party leadership held secretive meetings here each August, until they were canceled in 2003. Many senior officials own beach villas in this small oceanfront town.

Beidaihe, one of few worthwhile beaches along China's coast, sits along the Hebei Coast just an hour away from Shanhaiguan. The sand and water here are not much to talk about, but this resort remains a pleasant and quick getaway from the hustle and bustle of Beijing. Come here to soak up some sun, swim, walk along the beach, and eat plenty of seafood. ■

South and west of Beijing lie temples, museums, ancient architectural sites, and the former foreign concession of Tianjin. Plan a half day—or several days—for exploring.

Excursions south

Burning incense at Tanzhe Temple

Excursions South

IF YOU HAVE A BIT OF EXTRA TIME DURING YOUR VISIT TO BEIJING, YOU CAN significantly deepen your experience in China by taking advantage of any one of the numerous historical and cultural attractions located within one or a few hours' drive of the old imperial capital.

The imperial tombs offer fascinating insight into the lives and loves—and sometimes intrigues—of China's former emperors. Make a trip to see some of the many imperial tombs set in nearby Hebei Province, such as the fine Eastern Qing Tombs, which are located 78 miles (125 km) northeast of Beijing, and the Western Qing Tombs, 68 miles (110 km) southwest of the city. The tombs are home to nine emperors plus their empresses and concubines. Or visit the tomb of a Han-dynasty prince who died almost 2,000 years ago.

To learn about someone even older, visit the caves of Zhoukoudian, the home of Peking Man, who roamed this neighborhood 30 miles (48 km) southwest of Beijing some half a million years ago.

Because Beijing was an ancient center of Buddhism, the mountain areas ringing the city are rich in rustic old temples, many dating back more than 500 years. Completed in the 15th century, Fahai Temple, which lies to the west of the capital, will impress visitors with its gorgeous interior frescoes. The grounds of the sacred complex of Badachu, in the Western Hills, are rich with magnolias, cypresses, pines, ginkgos, and other beautiful trees.

Jump on one of the many trains to the city of Tianjin, just an hour southeast, and explore one of Beijing's urban neighbors. Walk around the old European-controlled parts of the city, peeking into hundred-year-old Catholic churches and a Qing-dynasty mosque.

For a nice escape from the city, explore Cuandixia, a village where farmers still live in century-old courtyard houses.

Opposite: One of the oldest temples in the Western Hills, the Buddhist Tanzhe Temple features a series of arched roofs.

For those who enjoy outdoor life, the scenic area of Shidu, about 31 miles (50 km) south of Beijing, provides many opportunities for hiking, kayaking, boating, ice-skating, horseback riding, and even bungee jumping. ∎

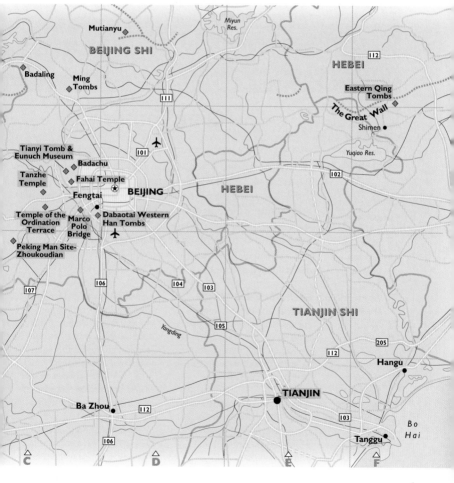

The Tomb of the Empress Dowager Cixi cost 2.27 million tales of silver to build.

Eastern Qing Tombs

⛰ 211 F4

✉ Malan Yu, Zunhua County, Hebei Province

☎ 031/5694 9851 or 031/5694 5471

💲 $$$

🚌 Bus: from Sihui Long Distance Bus Terminal (just S of Sihui Subway Station) toward Zunhua. Get off at Shimen, then taxi

Qing Tombs

UNLIKE MING-DYNASTY EMPERORS, WHO HAD JUST ONE burial place, the rulers of the Qing dynasty had two: the Eastern and Western Qing Tombs. The idea of two burial places probably began with Emperor Yongzheng (R.1723–1735), who some historians now believe usurped the throne from his brother by claiming that he himself was the chosen heir of Emperor Kangxi (R.1662–1722). Wary of being buried alongside those he had betrayed, Yongzheng ordered that a second Qing-dynasty tomb be built. Later, Emperor Qianlong decreed that burials should alternate between the two sites.

EASTERN QING TOMBS

Five Qing-dynasty emperors, 15 empresses, 3 princes, 2 princesses, and 136 concubines are interred at the Eastern Qing Tombs (Qing Dongling), which are located about 78 miles (125 km) east of the old imperial capital. The layout is similar to that of the Ming Tombs (see p. 200), although most of the Qing Tombs have their own personal Spirit Way lined with a series of stone gates.

All of the 15 Eastern Qing Tombs are open to the public.

Emperor Qianlong and Empress Dowager Cixi spent the most money constructing their burial places, so theirs are the best ones to visit. Unfortunately, these two tombs were also looted in 1928. All of their imperial treasures were snapped up, and the Empress Dowager's bones were scattered around the tomb.

Puyi, the last emperor of the Qing dynasty, was cremated after his death in 1967 and buried in a cemetery in western Beijing. In 1995 his ashes were brought to

Xiling for burial in a cemetery not far from his imperial ancestors.

Yuling

Yuling—the underground tomb of Emperor Qianlong—is the finest of the Eastern Qing Tombs. Its interior walls, high arched ceilings, and huge marble doors are decorated with beautiful carved images of the Buddha, the Four Heavenly Kings, and bodhisattvas, as well as passages from Buddhist scriptures in both Sanskrit and Tibetan. The emperor is buried here along with his empresses and consorts.

Ding Dong Ling

The tomb of the Empress Dowager Cixi has many reminders of the Forbidden City. The carved ramp leading to her sacrificial hall depicts the phoenix (representing the empress) above the dragon (the emperor), reflecting her final years in the imperial court when she ruled from behind the proverbial screen. **Longen Hall,** located just before her burial chamber, features elaborate wooden carvings of gold-painted bats and dragons. Cixi's tomb is located next to the tomb of her co-regent Ci'an. Two small museums have been set up in the sacrificial halls of both tombs.

WESTERN QING TOMBS

The Western Qing Tombs (Qing Xiling), located 87 miles west of Beijing, are the final resting place for four emperors—Yongzheng, Jiaqing, Daoguang, and Guangxu—who are buried here with 9 empresses, 76 princes, and 57 imperial concubines.

Tailing

Tailing is the tomb of Emperor Yongzheng and the largest in the complex. It has its own 2-mile-long (3 km) **Spirit Way,** attended by 40 flanking ministers, generals, and animals, all made of stone. The tomb's gateways and buildings were used during the various Buddhist rituals and sacrifices held in memory of the emperor.

Muling

The tomb that Emperor Daoguang (R.1821–1850) built for himself is small and relatively modest compared to Tailing. It also has neither a Spirit Way nor a stele pavilion. Shortly after taking the throne, Daoguang began planning his burial at a site in the Eastern Qing Tombs, according to the alternation plan. One year after it was finished, however, the underground chamber was flooded, and the superstitious Daoguang turned to the Western Qing Tombs to select a new and more auspicious site for himself. Convinced that the flooding was because several dragons had lost their homes, he included many pleasing dragon images in his second tomb. He is buried along with three empresses. Another empress is interred nearby.

Chongling

The tomb of Emperor Guangxu (R.1875–1908) was not yet finished when the Qing dynasty collapsed in 1911, and it would not be complete for another four years. Guangxu was the nephew of Cixi, who held him under house arrest in the Summer Palace during his final years because of the emperor's support for the reform movement. He died mysteriously, and it's widely believed that the Empress Dowager had him poisoned. His tomb has wonderful stone doors carved with bodhisattvas. Keeping him company in an adjoining tomb is Zhenfei, the Pearl Concubine, who is probably best known for allegedly being forced down a well in the Forbidden City after upsetting the Empress Dowager. ■

Western Qing Tombs

🔺 210 B2

✉ Yixian County, Hebei Province

☎ 031/2471 0012

💲 $$$

🚌 Bus: from Lizeqiao Long Distance Bus Terminal to Yixian County then taxi

Manchus

sheltering doorway to watch the procession. The sight of such grandeur was an event in their dull lives, pleasantly frequent and arousing not envy but pride.

Alas, many Manchus, shorn of their fine feathers, are now in actual want. Unable to conceive that their allowances would ever be reduced, they weren't fit to earn a living after they lost military caste privileges in 1911. Too long they had been taught to despise work and neglect scholarship; they had abandoned even their favorite pursuits of arms, archery, and riding, which once made them a vigorous race and for centuries sustained them. As for the higher classes, they made the mistake of forgetting that it was necessary to be men as well as noblemen.

Manchu women, in the days of prosperity, lent a charming note of color and vivacity to the gray old capital. To this day, they have a distinctive costume and coiffure— the long straight gown and waistcoat of bright pink or lavender, the quaint shoes with the heel in the middle of the sole, and the hair done in a high knot or mounted on a satin-covered board that stands up crosswise and ends in prominent wings. Bands of beadwork, handsome pins, and real or artificial flowers—sometimes with fringes of pearls—enhance this odd and, one imagines, uncomfortable arrangement. Its chief charm is the way in which the hair is made to serve as an elaborate frame, well suited to Manchu features and throwing into relief faces heavily powdered and rouged in remembrance of the ethnic origins they claim. Manchu women were constantly seen in public, walking with stately grace accompanied by their servants. They gathered in groups, like birds of bright plumage, to gossip at temple fairs. They paid their visits or went to court in carts or chairs, and a pretty face or a brilliant headdress might frequently be glimpsed through the window of a passing vehicle. ∎

Descendants of the indigenous Jurched tribe of Manchuria, the Manchus conquered China and established the Qing dynasty in 1644, dominating the country with vigor and potency until 1911. The status of the Manchus declined rapidly after the formation of the Republic of China, and today few Manchus—whose traditional customs have all but disappeared—exist in China.

The old-style Manchu cut a striking figure: tall and dignified in his official hat, his long robes of silk or sable, and his richly embroidered undergown. And when he went to or from the palace in his green sedan chair, or in his closed Peking cart surrounded by outriders, no wonder the simple folk looked on him with respectful awe. How the whole patchwork of idlers—the bent old men and the pretty children with gleaming eyes and miniature pigtails—hastily pressed themselves flat against a wall or slipped into a

Manchu women can be recognized by their dress and hairstyles (above). Three Manchu women share an umbrella to avoid the rain in Chengde (right).

Tianjin

Tianjin
- 211 E1
- 022/8837 3183
- Trains from the Beijing Railway Station

Xikai Cathedral
- 9 Xining Dao, Heping Districtt
- 022/2781 1929

Notre Dame Des Victoires Catholic Cathedral
- 292 Shizilin Dajie
- 022/2635 1172
- Inside closed for renovation
- Bus: Shizilinqiao

Ancient Culture Street
- Dongbei Jiao, Nankai District
- 022/2735 8682
- Bus: Dongbeijiao

AT FIRST GLANCE, TIANJIN (TIANJIN SHI) MIGH APPEAR AS an uninviting industrial city. A closer look at the center of town, however, reveals a patchwork of European, Russian, and Japanese architecture in this former foreign concession city.

Tianjin lies just 60 miles (97 km) southeast of Beijing and has a long history as an urban and trading center. Established as a walled garrison in 1404, it became the economic heart of northern China by the early Qing dynasty. The 1858 Treaty of Tianjin—ending the Second Opium War—opened the city to British and French concessions and construction by other Western nations along the Hai River. Foreign troops shelled and occupied the city during the Boxer Rebellion (see pp. 36–37), destroying its old walls. Following that Westerners turned Tianjin into a hub for trade and industry. In the late 1970s, it became one of the first cities opened to foreign investment, and today it is the biggest shipping port in northern China.

Located in the center of the Bohai Bay Rim is the Tianjin Economic-Technological Development Area (TEDA), which is home to more than 3,300 foreign-funded companies, including Motorola, Samsung, and Toyota. Local officials hope that Binhai New District—which includes TEDA, Tianjin Port, and the Tianjin Port Free Trade Zone—will spark the economic growth of the entire Bohai Bay Rim area, a region that covers about 321,000 square miles (516,000 sq km) with a population of 230 million people.

VISITING THE TOWN
Starting on the north side, the **Notre Dame des Victoires**

Catholic Cathedral (Shengmu Desheng Tang or Wanghailou Jiaotang), Tianjin's earliest cathedral, was first built in 1869. It was destroyed during the Boxer Rebellion and again in 1976 by the brutal Tangshan earthquake. The cathedral was rebuilt in 1983.

Head southwest of the church to search for souvenirs and elusive historic relics in the **Ancient Culture Street** (Gu Wenhua Jie). Meant to re-create the structures that once stood on this old

street, the buildings here have carved balconies, red-and-green painted shops, and curling tile roofs. The stalls offer a colorful array of items including documents from the Cultural Revolution, kites, and clay figurines (a local handicraft). The Nirenzhang Clay Figurine Shop and Yang Liuqing New Year Woodblock Prints Shop are worth a visit.

Peeking out through the bric-a-brac for sale on Ancient Culture Street is the wonderful little **Tianhou Temple** (Tianhou Gong). Dedicated to Tianhou, the goddess of the sea, the temple, built in 1326, has undergone numerous renovations. The restored frescoes show scenes from the life of Tainhou (Haishen Niangniang or Mazu).

Also on display are models of Ming- and Qing-dynasty ships from the coastal provinces of Fujian and Zhejiang (where Tianhou is most actively worshipped). The fierce-looking weapons on either side are meant to protect the goddess. In the rear is a small temple dedicated to Guanyin—goddess of mercy.

One block west of Ancient Culture Street stands the **Confucius Temple** (Wen Miao), a rather staid monument to the Great Sage. A statue of Confucius sits on the altar, surrounded by ancient musical instruments. The temple, built in 1436, has been restored many times and reopened most recently in 1993.

EUROPEAN LEGACY

The Romanesque **Xikai Cathedral** (Xikai Jiaotang) was

Confucius Temple

✉ 1 Dongmenli, Nankai District

☎ 022/2727 2812 or 022/2727 2978

🕒 Closed for renovations until mid 2008

Ⓜ Metro: Xibeijiao or Xinanjiao

European-style buildings line the banks of the Hai River.

The beautiful interior of Tianjin's Xikai Catholic Church, built in 1916

Xikai Cathedral

✉ 9 Xining Dao
Heping District
☎ 022/2781 1929

Central Park

✉ Huayuan Lu
Heping District
☎ 022/2712 4668
🚌 Bus: Zhongxin Gongyuan;
Metro: Binjiangdao

Grand Mosque

✉ Qingzhen Xiang Zhenbu Jie
Hongqiao District
☎ 022/2727 1056
🚇 Metro: Xibeijiao

built in 1916 in the shape of a crucifix. Dedicated to St. Vincent de Paul, the cathedral—a copy of Notre Dame de la Garde in Marseille, France—was originally managed by missionary priests.

The area south of the Hai River was home to the former European and Japanese concessions. **Central Park,** on Huayuan Lu, was located in the old French concession (Jiefang Lu), where typical French chateaux line the streets. Some of the city's best examples of European architecture can be found here.

Farther down Huayuan Lu, the British concession reveals grand Edwardian establishments. The **New World Astor Hotel** (Lishunde Dafandian, *33 Taierzhuang Lu, Heping District, tel 022/2331 1688),* sitting on the riverbank, is worth a look. Last Emperor Puyi came here regularly to dance after he was forced out of the Forbidden City in 1924. Although it's seen better days, the hotel has held up better than other

European buildings in the city. Nearby were the offices of great British commercial houses, such as Jardine & Matheson. Across the river lay the Russian concession.

The **Shenyandao Antiques Market** *(Shenyang Dao)* is open every Thursday from 4 a.m. and has a wide variety of real and factory-fresh antiques. As usual, unless you're an expert, steer away from the antiquities.

The **Grand Mosque** (Tianjin Qingzhen Dasi), which adds a bit of exotic variety to Tianjin's cityscape, is believed to have been built in 1644, right at the start of the Qing dynasty. This impressive structure, which has been renovated and expanded over the past several hundred years, is an excellent example of Chinese Muslim architecture, a style that emerged during the Ming dynasty. The mosque is still an active place of worship for the city's Muslims; while guests are allowed to roam the complex, certain halls of worship are off-limits to visitors. ■

Dabaotai Western Han Tombs

THE ARCHAEOLOGISTS WHO EXCAVATED THE DABAOTAI Western Han Tombs (Dabaotai Xihan Mu Bowuguan) were not able to say for sure who is buried here. Since this type of tomb was normally built for Han-dynasty princes and princesses, an educated guess suggests it was a prince of the Liu clan who died sometime around 45 B.C. Located 30 minutes south of Beijing's city center, the site is of great significance for students of ancient Chinese history.

Dabaotai Western Han Tombs

🅰 211 C3

✉ Guogongzhuang, Fengtai District (S of World Park)

☎ 010/8361 3073

🕐 Closed Mon.

🚌 Bus: 692 or 967 to Shijie Gongyuan Nanmen (Dabaotai is about 2.5 miles, 4 km, S of Fengtai Railway Station)

Archaeologists discovered two tombs when they excavated the site in 1975. An underground palace of sorts, **Tomb No. 1** measures 80 feet (24 m) long, 56 feet (18 m) wide, and 14.5 feet (4.5 m) deep. Originally sealed with plaster to keep out moisture—which may explain why it was so well preserved —the tomb includes three inner and outer wooden coffins surrounded by tens of thousands of square beams.

In the tomb, archaeologists discovered more than 400 funeral objects made of pottery, bronze, iron, jade, and bone. The most interesting items are the three lacquered chariots and 11 horses that were buried alive along with them. Large models of the chariots stand on display outside, and the site's small **museum** features several burial objects, including miniature wooden burial figurines, bronze incense burners, and a bronze door decoration which resembles a beast.

Tomb No. 2 contained the remains of the queen consort, but it was plundered and destroyed by fire, leaving little behind for modern archaeologists. ∎

One of three chariots with accompanying horses found in Tomb No. 1.

Marco Polo Bridge

Marco Polo Bridge
- 211 C3
- 77 Wanping Chengnan Jie Lugou Qiao
- 010/8389 4614
- $ ($ extra to visit tower)
- Metro: Qianmen, then Bus: 301 to Kangzhan Diaosu Yuan; or Wukesong, then Bus: 624

Pedestrians have worn smooth the bridge's stones over centuries of use.

THE MARCO POLO BRIDGE (LUGOU QIAO) IS SO NAMED because of its mention in the Italian explorer's famous travelogue. The bridge, wrote Marco Polo, "is a very fine stone bridge, so fine indeed, that it has very few equals in the world." Erected in 1189, the elaborate structure is Beijing's oldest marble bridge.

The Marco Polo Bridge stretches 873 feet (266 m) over what used to be the Yongding River (which is now usually dry). Its original thick stone slabs have survived on the center surface of the bridge. More than 500 carved **stone lions** run across the balustrade; **imperial steles** stand at both ends. The bridge, with its 11 **arches,** can best be seen from the riverside.

The bridge is perhaps most famous as the site of the Marco Polo Bridge Incident of 1937, when Japanese troops in the area exchanged gunfire with Chinese soldiers. The Japanese used this incident as a pretext for Japan's occupation of China.

On one side of the bridge is the **Memorial Hall of the War of Resistance Against Japan** (Zhongguo Renmin Kangri Zhanzheng Jinianguan). The adjacent old walled town of **Wanping** is worth a visit. ∎

Peking Man may
have lived in a
cave like this one
at Zhoukoudian.

Zhoukoudian Peking Man Site & Shidu

THE ZHOUKOUDIAN PEKING MAN SITE (ZHOUKOUDIAN
Yizhi Bowuguan) will fascinate not only archaeologists and anthropologists, but anyone interested in the lives of ancient humans.
Located about 30 miles (48 km) southwest of Beijing, the site was
once home to Peking Man, or Homo erectus pekinensis, who roamed
the area half a million years ago.

In 1929, Chinese archaeologist Pei
Wenzhong discovered a number of
skulls belonging to Peking Man and
his neighbors. These early humans
could stand upright, hunt, make a
fire, and use simple tools made of
chipped stone. Pei's find has been
called one of the most important
paleontological finds of the 20th
century. Unfortunately, the bones
mysteriously disappeared soon after

they were discovered (see p. 222).

The trails at Zhoukoudian
Peking Man Site will lead you
through several areas of excavation and past the caves where this
primitive man lived The small
museum displays artifacts related to the excavations, including
flint tools, bone needles, and animal parts. Although this is a
UNESCO World Heritage site, it

**Zhoukoudian
Peking Man Site**
🔼 211 C2
✉ 1 Zhoukoudian Dajie
☎ 010/6930 1272
💲 $
🚌 Bus: 917 from
Tianqiao Bus Station
to Fangshan, then
taxi

Shidu
🔼 210 B2
✉ Shidu Fangshan
District
☎ 010/6134 9009
💲 $$
🚆 Train: 6095 from
Beijing West Railway
Station to Shidu
Station; or Bus: 917
from Tianqiao

The disappearance of Peking Man & the ongoing search

It has the makings of a great mystery story or, better yet, an Indiana Jones movie. At the height of the war with Japan, archaeologists—worried that Peking Man fossils might fall into Japanese hands—put the 5 skulls, 147 teeth, and a number of other bones into two large wooden boxes and turned them over to the U.S. Marine Corps for safekeeping and eventual transport to the United States.

Although there was some discussion of moving the bones earlier, after the Japanese invasion in 1937, they were apparently assumed to be safe because they were housed in the American-run Peking Union Medical Hospital, which oversaw the Cenozoic Research Lab. Some claim they were later shipped to the offices of the American Legation, but there is no evidence that this claim is true.

The plan to transport the fossils to the United States was interrupted when the Japanese bombed Pearl Harbor on December 7, 1941. Sometime shortly after, the fossils disappeared, never to be seen again.

The fate of Peking Man has been the subject of much speculation. According to one theory, the boxes went to a sea grave when the *Awa Maru* was sunk by the Americans in the Taiwan Strait. An underwater search of the site found nothing. Then, in 1966, a Japanese soldier "admitted" on his deathbed that he buried the bones under a tree in Ritan Park (see pp. 148–149) at the end of the war, but they were not found there either. In 2005 the Chinese government announced a new investigation. It seems that the beguiling mystery of Peking Man continues. ∎

has not been well taken care of and there is little information available in English.

SHIDU

Located about 68 miles (110 km) southwest of Beijing, Shidu sits on the winding Juma River near the Zhoukoudian Peking Man Site. Like the city of Guilin in southwestern China, the location features karst (a kind of limestone) formations and a river. Easy paths in the area wander past the karst formations, or you can tour the place on horseback. You may also find it worthwhile to walk around the small villages and soak up some of the local

This skull is a copy of the one excavated at Zhoukoudian Peking Man Site in 1929.

culture. If you wish, you can rent a room in a private home.

For the adventurous traveler, Shidu is famous for its outdoor activities—especially its bungee-jumping facilities. This is also an excellent place for those interested in rock climbing. ∎

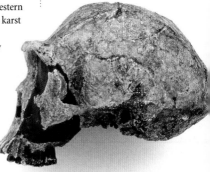

Tomb of Tianyi

DEDICATED TO THE POWERFUL EUNUCH TIANYI (1534–1605), the Tomb of Tianyi (Tianyi Mu) is a tiny, out-of-the-way complex located on the western edge of Beijing. Tianyi was a close confidant and friend of Emperor Wanli (*R.*1573–1620), and when he died, the grief-stricken Wanli canceled all court meetings for three days and had this tomb built in his friend's honor. It is the only eunuch's tomb in China to feature large steles of carved stone.

One of the numerous statues that adorn the tomb area.

Tianyi, who attended three different emperors, was castrated at the age of nine. He served as a eunuch for 63 years, rising through the ranks to become a director of ceremonies, the fourth highest position in the civil service structure at the time.

When you enter the front gate of his tomb complex, you will be greeted by two large **stone statues,** one of a military officer and the other of a civil official, facing each other and guarding the tomb. Beyond them are **three pavilions,** where carved stone steles commemorating the life of Tianyi have been erected.

In addition to Tianyi's tomb, there are four **other tombs** at the site, each dedicated to a eunuch from the Ming dynasty. Their remains were placed in marble tombs on either side of Tianyi. The tombs are wonderfully decorated with carved scenes from old tales, as well as auspicious creatures and plants. Centered between them is the entrance to the underground tomb of Tianyi, which was robbed in the early 20th century. The body disappeared and all that remains are some wooden planks.

The **Eunuch Museum** (Huangguan Bowuguan) features photographs of famous eunuchs from the Qing dynasty, a picture of the knife used for castrations, a gruesome explanation of the castration process, and some photos of Empress Dowager Cixi relaxing at the Summer Palace with

her eunuch attendants. There are also some photos of Sun Yaoting, China's last eunuch, who was castrated at the age of eight, just months before Puyi stepped down, ending Sun's dreams of making it rich in the imperial court as many eunuchs had done before him. He visited the impressive Fahai Temple (see p. 226)—which is only a ten-minute walk from the tomb—just before he died in 1996. ∎

Tomb of Tianyi

⚠ 211 C3

✉ 80 Moshikou Dajie, Shijingshan District

☎ 010/8872 4148

$ $

🚇 Metro: Line 1 to Pingguoyuan Subway Station, then taxi; Bus: 336, 396, 959, or 746 to Shougang Xiaoqu

The Temple of the Azure Clouds located in Fragrant Hills Park

Chinese temples

Three recognized and interlinked faiths belong to traditional China—the *sanjiao* or three teachings of Confucianism, Taoism, and Buddhism. Of these, the first two are purely indigenous while Buddhism traveled to China from India at least two millennia ago via the Silk Road. Although most Chinese temples are readily identifiable as being predominantly Confucian, Taoist, or Buddhist, the syncretic nature of sanjiao means that symbols and deities from all three interrelated faiths often appear in a single temple.

CONFUCIAN

Confucian temples, or *wenmiao*, are essentially dedicated to tradition, education, and filial piety. They commonly house stone steles mounted on the backs of stone tortoises recording the names of literary graduates, honoring the tradition of learning, which "hangs like perfume through the ages." Most contain a statue of the Great Sage, Kong Fuzi (Confucius, 551–479 B.C.), as well as images of his disciples, especially the Confucian philosopher Meng Zi (Mencius, 372–289 B.C.). There are relatively few Confucius temples, the most important being in the master's hometown of Qufu, in Beijing, appropriately called the Confucious Temple (see pp. 86–87).

TAOIST

Taoist temples, or *guan*, are dedicated to the teachings of Laozi (Sixth century B.C.), founder of the faith and author of the *Daodejing (Classic of the Way of Power).* Besides images of Laozi, Taoist guan generally contain images of the Eight Immortals, the Jade Emperor, and often the goddess charged with protecting seafarers, Tianhou (aka Mazu). Taoism teaches practicing harmony with *tao*, the Way, and is often described as naturist. Taoist monks, or *taoshi*, wind their long hair up in knots and wear jackets and trousers. Dongyue Temple (see pp. 150–151) and White Cloud Temple (see pp. 142–143) are among the most celebrated Taoist temples in Beijing.

BUDDHIST

Buddhist temples, or *simiao* (those dedicated to Zen Buddhism are called *chansi*), are distinguished by images of a laughing and jovial Buddha and by statues of Sakyamuni, also called Gautama (the Historic Buddha), Maitreya (the Future Buddha), and Amitabha (the infinite Buddha). Also enduringly popular is the goddess of mercy, Guanyin, who was somehow transformed into a female deity in her passage across the Himalaya, from her Indian male form Avalokitisevara. In addition, the east and west walls of the main hall of many Buddhist temples typically depict the 18 luohan (arhats). The temples are guarded by the Four Heavenly Kings, filled with incense smoke, and inhabited by shaven-

Boaters glide past the Pavilion of Buddhist Incense on Longevity Hill, Summer Palace.

headed, robe-wearing Buddhist monks. The most famous in the Beijing area include the Lama Temple (see pp. 90–91) and Tanzhe Temple (see pp. 232–234).

RELIGIOUS MINGLINGS

All sanjiao temples—Confucian, Taoist, or Buddhist—are arranged according to divine cosmological principles, and more especially to feng shui, the science of geomancy. Accordingly, temple axes run north–south, with doors and entranceways facing the auspicious south. Evil spirits can only travel in straight lines or across dry land, so walls blocking gateways, ponds, and reflective mirrors fend them off. Auspicious beasts like lions and dragons decorate the temples and intertwine across pillars and eaves. ∎

Wanfu Pavilion, part of the Lama Temple

Fahai Temple

Fahai Temple
- 211 C3
- 28 Moshikou, Shijingshan District
- 010/8871 3976
- Under renovation until mid-2008
- Metro: Line 1 to Pingguo Yuan, then taxi; or Bus: 331 to temple

A VISIT TO FAHAI TEMPLE (FAHAI SI) IS WORTHWHILE after a trip to the Tomb of Tianyi and the Eunuch Museum (see p. 223), which are just a short walk away. The temple's detailed and colorful Buddhist murals are considered to be the finest examples of mural art remaining in China today.

Located at the foot of Cuiwei Hill, to the south and west of Beijing, Fahai Temple was completed in about 1443 by Li Tong, a eunuch in the court of Emperor Zhengtong (*R*.1435–1449 and 1457–1464), with funds he collected from various officials, Buddhist leaders, and lay people.

ple's construction. Two master palace artists and 13 artisans spent four years completing the work. The artists' names are carved on a stone tablet outside.

Considered very important works in the history of Chinese art, the amazingly detailed frescoes depict the bodhisattvas Guanyin,

Portion of the centuries-old mural that adorns the walls of the Fahai Temple

The design of the temple is laid out on three levels.

The best works of art found here are the wonderful Ming-dynasty frescoes painted on the inner walls of the **Mahavira Hall** (Daxiong Baodian), which stands on the north side of the rear courtyard. This is the only original structure still standing; the others have all been replaced. The paintings were created at the time of the tem-

Puxian, and Wenshu. The latter two are considered to be the best paintings in the temple. Note the six-tusked elephant on the back wall. Each of the tusks represents a quality that will lead you to enlightenment. During the Cultural Revolution, rampaging Red Guards destroyed the statues that originally stood in the temple. Reproductions of the statues were erected in the temple in 1996. ∎

The Pagoda of the Buddha's Tooth has 13 levels.

Badachu

BADACHU, OR "EIGHT GREAT SITES," REFERS TO THE EIGHT
monasteries, nunneries, and temples nestled in the woods at the
southern foot of the Western Hills. Although many of the structures
in the area date from the Ming and Qing dynasties, most of these religious complexes were first built during the late Sui (581–618) and
early Tang (618–907) dynasties and renovated in the centuries that
followed. The wonderful local landscape makes for a worthwhile hike
between each of the eight old sites. Badachu is crowded on weekends,
however, so it is best to visit on a weekday.

Built in 1504, the **Temple of
Eternal Peace** (Chang'an Si), is
located outside the main gate of

Badachu on a plain at the foot of
Cuiwei Hill. This Ming-dynasty
temple is made up of two

Badachu

🅰 211 C3

✉ Badachu Lu,
Shijingshan District

☎ 010/8896 4661

💲 $

🚍 Bus: 972 from
Pingguo Yuan
Subway Station; 347
from Xinjiekou; or
389 from Yuquan Lu
Subway Station

courtyards. The first includes **Sakyamuni Hall,** which houses a bronze statue of Guan Yu, a hero of the Three Kingdoms period. In the south corner of the corridor in the rear part of the hall is a bronze bell cast in 1600. The second courtyard is home to **Niangniang Hall,** which is dedicated to a female deity.

The **Temple of Divine Light** (Lingguang Si), built during the Tang dynasty, is about a mile (1.6 km) up Cuiwei Hill from the Temple of Eternal Peace. The only one of the eight that still has monks as residents, this temple is the most worthwhile to visit in Badachu. The temple was destroyed by the Allied Forces in 1900, and the **Zhaoxian Pagoda**—built in the southeast corner of the temple grounds in 1071 during the Liao dynasty—was damaged by rifle fire. Monks later claim to have found Sakyamuni Buddha's real tooth in a wooden box in the ruins. A statue of Sakyamuni sits in the main hall.

The tooth now sits in the **Pagoda of the Buddha's Tooth** (Foya Sheli Ta), which was built in 1956. The new pagoda has 13 levels of eaves, similar to the original Zhaoxian Pagoda. And like the multi-eaved pagodas of the Liao and Jin dynasties, the structure sits on a huge Sumeru pedestal. The relic tooth is preserved in a small gold pagoda in the middle of the main hall. On the other levels are ceremonial articles, statues, and Buddhist scriptures written in Hah, Tibetan, Mongolian, and Dai.

To the northeast is the **Mahavira Hall,** which dates from 1920 and was not part of the original temple.

A short distance away is the **Three Hill Nunnery** (Sanshan An), which is so named because of its location between Cuiwei Hill, Pingpo Hill, and Lushi Hill. Built in 1151, the convent has just one courtyard but is still interesting.

From the nunnery, you can see the pine and cypress trees that cover the surrounding mountain area.

Walk up from the Three Hill Nunnery until you reach the **Temple of Great Mercy** (Dabei Si), built sometime before 1033. The 18 luohan in the first hall are said to have been made by Liu Yuan, a famous sculptor of the Yuan dynasty. The courtyard in front of **Daxiong Hall** has a rare species of bamboo—planted in the Ming dynasty—that stays green all winter. Two large ginkgo trees in the rear courtyard are said to be more than 800 years old.

To the northwest is the **Temple of the Dragon King** (Longwang Tang), which is also known as Dragon Spring Nunnery (Longquan An). A spring flows from the second courtyard to the first, where it exits from the mouth of a stone dragon head. There are two pavilions at the rear of the temple.

The **Temple of the Fragrant World** (Xiangjie Si) was built in 760 during the Tang dynasty; the other buildings in the complex date from the Ming and Qing dynasties. The largest temple in Badachu, it was once the summer getaway for China's emperors. The temple was rebuilt and renamed three times; it received its present name in 1748 from Emperor Qianlong, who built an imperial palace and scripture repository here. The temple also has many historic relics, as well as paintings and calligraphy by well-known artists. A Ming-dynasty princess named Cuiwei—for whom the hill was named—was buried here in the 15th century.

HIGHER TEMPLES

Take the steep row of steps up to the **Mahayana Gate,** the entrance to the temple. The main

building here is the **Scripture Repository,** which is flanked by drum and bell towers. The repository has statues of Randengfo, Sakyamuni, and Maitreya—the Past, Historic, and Future Buddhas. Polychrome statues of the 18 Luohan stand on either side. In the entrance hall of the **Imperial Palace** (Xing Gong) to the east is the **Study for Distant Viewing,** which offers nice vistas of the surrounding countryside.

Continue up the steep path from the Temple of the Fragrant World to the **Cave of the Precious Pearl** (Baozhu Dong), which dates from 1780. Seek out the memorial archway here inscribed with "Place of Happiness" on one side and "Forest of Solidity"

on the other. The hall standing behind the archway is the **Temple of Precious Pearls,** which is the highest of the eight temples here. On a clear day, you can see the city of Beijing: Kunming Lake to the east, the Yongding River to the south, and the city skyline in the center. The other seven temples are located right below the Temple of Precious Pearls. Its name comes from the cave behind the main hall and the stone near its entrance, which looks like a large pearl.

The large bell in **Zhengguo Temple** was cast during the Ming dynasty. Two tall steles stand on either side of the entrance. Built in either the Tang or Sui dynasty, the temple is believed to be the oldest in the complex. ■

Visitors enjoy Badachu, which dates back to the Sui dynasty.

The three tiers of the Ordination Altar contain 113 figures.

Temple of the Ordination Terrace

THE TEMPLE OF THE ORDINATION TERRACE (JIETAI SI) LIES in the Western Hills, about 16 miles (25 km) southwest of Beijing. There has been a temple on this mountain for 1,350 years. However, it was not until the Liao dynasty (916–1125) that a monk built an altar to be used in the ordination ceremony of Buddhist novices; monks have been coming here to take their vows ever since.

Chinese temples normally face south, but this temple was built according to Liao custom, facing east. Although the temple was laid out during the Liao dynasty, most of the structures that exist at the site today date from the Ming and Qing dynasties. Emperor Qianlong was a regular visitor to the temple during the 18th century, and many of the current buildings are the result of his largesse.

As one approaches the hillside temple, it appears like a fortress with tall, forbidding, red walls. On a clear day pause and note the Beijing skyline off to the distant northwest

INSIDE COURTYARDS

Statues of General Ha and General Heng stand watch over the **Hall of the Front Gate.** Pass through the first courtyard, and you'll see the traditional drum and bell towers. There are also four steles resting here on the backs of impressive stone tortoises.

The **Hall of Heavenly Kings** (Tianwang Dian) has a Maitreya Buddha, also known as the Bag Buddha because of the large cloth bag that he carries with him. The fierce-looking Four Heavenly Kings, with Weituo, the guardian of Buddhism, protect Maitreya's large rotund back.

As you stroll the courtyard take note of the old trees. The ancient trees found throughout the complex are renowned, the subject of song and poetry. In *Peking Picnic,* a 1932 novel, Ann Bridge, the wife of a former British diplomat, also gives an interesting account of the temple in the early 20th century. It tells of the adventures of some expats who camp out on the temple grounds.

Take the stairs up to the terrace and turn right. **Sleeping Dragon Pine** (Wolong Song), a pine tree with scale-shaped bark resembling a sleeping dragon, is said to be more than a thousand years old.

Another famous tree is **Nine Dragon Pine** (Jiulong Song), so named because of its nine large branches or trunks. Look over the wall and you'll see two ancient pagodas, where the remains and possessions of some monks are buried. Note the **stone column** that dates from 1075. Said to be the oldest and best preserved column around Beijing, the eight-sided column is beautifully inscribed with Buddhist scriptures and *zhou,* Chinese for "magic spell" or "charm."

Opposite lies the elaborate **Dragon Carved Niche** (Diaolong Fokan). Created during the Ming dynasty, the niche is elaborately decorated with slithering dragons that crawl all over—on the front, sides, back, and top. Next to this hall, another **stone column** from the Yuan dynasty (1369) records the life of Yuequan, a former abbot of the Jietai Temple. At the end of this section of the temple complex, the **Temple of the God of Wealth** (Caishen Shengdian) has a small shop selling Buddhist statues.

To the north of the Dragon Carved Niche awaits the **Hall of Ordination Altar** (Jietai Dian), also known as Xuanfo Chang. Four carved steles stand in its courtyard, along with a golden statue of Sakyamuni Buddha sitting inside on a lotus. The three tiers of the **Ordination Altar—** one of the three tallest ordination towers in China—are carved with 113 figures of the ordination god.

Once a year, at midnight, an initiation ceremony was conducted at the white marble altar. The novices, who had fasted all day, would light the incense sticks that were used to make burns on their freshly tonsured heads. The ancient pine trees add to the allure of the temple, whose grounds are also covered with beautiful cypress and ginkgo trees. ■

Temple of the Ordination Terrace

- △ 211 C3
- ✉ Ma'an Shan, Mentougou District
- ☎ 010/6980 6611
- 💲 $$
- 🚌 Bus: 931 from Pingguo Yuan Subway Station

Tanzhe Temple
nestles in the
Western Hills.

Tanzhe Temple

ACCORDING TO AN OLD SAYING, "FIRST THERE WAS Tanzhe, then came Youzhou" (one of Beijing's ancient names), hinting that Tanzhe Temple (Tanzhe Si) predates the old imperial capital. Built during the Jin dynasty (265–420), probably in 400, the temple—with its beautiful tree-covered grounds—may not really be older than Beijing, but it is one of the oldest temples in the Western Hills. And it still attracts Buddhist monks from around China.

Tanzhe Temple

- 211 C3
- At foot of
  Tanzhe Shan
  Mentougou District
- 010/6086 1699 or
  010/6086 2244
- $$
- Bus: 931 from
  Pingguo Yuan
  Subway Station

Tanzhe Temple was restored numerous times throughout the Jin, Yuan, Ming, and Qing dynasties, and most of the structures you see on the grounds today are from the Ming and Qing periods. The temple was particularly popular with Qing-dynasty emperors, including Kangxi, Yongzheng, Qianlong, and Jiaqing, all of whom were frequent visitors.

You will know you're getting close to the temple when you begin to spot people beside the road selling large sticks of incense. You'll also find villagers selling goods beside the parking lot. It's worthwhile to browse their wares, which usually include many natural products from the nearby countryside, such as raisins, almonds, walnuts, mushrooms, and dried fruit.

VISITING THE TEMPLE
Tanzhe Temple is divided into four sections, with the main attractions—the memorial archway, Hall of Heavenly Kings, Mahavira Hall, Pilu Pavilion, Dizang Hall, and Guanyin Hall—all situated along the central north–south axis.

Among the statues of six Buddhas in the **Hall of Heavenly Kings** (Tianwang Dian), the Maitreya Buddha, better known as the Laughing Buddha because he is always smiling, sits in the seat of honor. As usual, he is flanked by the Four Heavenly Kings. According to legend, the Maitreya Buddha walked on the streets preaching and begging for alms while carrying a cloth bag. As a result, people called him the Bag Buddha. He is the incarnation of the Future Buddha, Maitreya, or of the Amitabha Buddha.

Pilu Pavilion (Pilu Ge), constructed during the Yuan dynasty, occupies the highest point of the temple. It provides a wonderful vantage point for visitors who wish to look at the layout of the temple complex and enjoy the expansive view of the surrounding countryside. Each of the five gold Buddhist statues in the hall symbolizes one of the five wisdoms of the Buddha. The animals on the edge of the roof are interesting, a sort of cross between the mythical qilin and a lizard.

Visitors burn incense in the courtyard of Tanzhe Temple.

The second building is **Mahavira Hall** (Daxiongbao Dian), or the Great Hall of the Powerful Treasure. This hall is devoted to Sakyamuni, who is flanked by his two favorite disciples, Ananda and Kasyapa. Manjusri Bodhisattva, or Wenshu, is on the left, and Visvabhadra Bodhisattva, or Puxian, is on the right. On opposite sides of the hall stand the 18 gold luohan, 9 on each side. They are said to have been disciples of Sakyamuni, who entrusted them to spread Buddhism on Earth.

To the right of Pilu Pavilion, **Yanshou Pagoda** (Great Longevity Pagoda) stands 50 feet (15 m) tall. This tomb—which was built by a prince during the Ming dynasty—holds the remains of a Buddhist monk.

On the right-hand wall of **Dizang Hall** (Dizang Dian), grotesque depictions of the 18 levels of hell are highly reminiscent of Dante's *Inferno*. Sinners are shown being crushed by boulders, whipped, having stakes driven into their heads, their bodies either sawed or chopped in half, or their intestines pulled out. A group of people shown on the left-hand side drinks a concoction labeled "Forget Sadness Soup." Don't be surprised if you see fortune-tellers sitting in the hall's courtyard.

Follow the path behind Dizang Hall to **Guanyin Hall** (Guanyin Dian), which is the last hall in the complex. The hall is dedicated to Guanyin, the goddess of mercy, who has a thousand hands and

Elaborate detail from a temple roof

eyes. In front of the red-robed Guanyin stand Charitable Boy and Dragon Daughter. Large purple and yellow coils of incense are placed here, their smoke and sweet smell curling into the air.

Another popular attraction at Tanzhe Temple are the so-called **footprints of Princess Miaoyan,** the daughter of Kublai Khan, who shaved her head and became a nun here during the Yuan dynasty. A

devout Buddhist, she allegedly prayed so fervently to Guanyin that she left indentations of her footprints on the flagstone.

The temple's abbots lived in the **Hall of Patriarchs** (Zushi Dian), to the west, prior to the Ming dynasty. During the reign of Emperor Wanli (R.1573–1620), this building was changed into a memorial hall in honor of the abbots. Inside you'll find scroll paintings of the various patriarchs.

If you continue moving west, heading down a flight of stairs and then up another set of steps, you'll come to **Guanyin Cave,** a very quiet, tree-shaded courtyard filled with the sound of crickets chirping. Dozens of turtles sit on a bamboo raft in the small lotus pond. Several statues of Guanyin stand in a small cavelike temple built into the mountain, and in a hall on the right-hand side is a gold statue of the goddess pouring water from a vase. Behind her are several smaller representations of herself.

Retrace your steps back east, and take the first row of steps down, heading south toward the exit. If you have time, visit some of the side halls along the way, such as the **Hall of Medicine** (Yaoshi Dian).

Tanzhe Temple is also famous for its old and beautiful trees. The sal tree originated in northern India, and it is considered to be the "Precious Tree of Buddhism" since the Buddha died while sitting under one. Sal trees were planted in many Chinese temples in the years when Buddhism spread across China. There are also some very old and attractive ginkgo and magnolia trees on the temple grounds.

For those wishing to spend the night, Tanzhe Temple has a small hotel just outside the main gate. There are also several vegetarian restaurants in the area. ■

Cuandixia

CUANDIXIA, WHICH LITERALLY MEANS "UNDER THE EARTHEN cooking pot," is the village that time forgot. According to local legend, this small, out-of-the-way town dates back more than 600 years to the Ming dynasty (1368–1644). It was then that a man and a woman, fleeing floods in Shanxi Province, found their way to this haven, which has seen little change in the past few hundred years—a living fossil of the Qing dynasty.

Cuandixia
- ✉ 210 B3
- ☎ 010/6981 9333 (village office)
- 💲 $
- 🚌 Hiring a day taxi is best. Metro: Pingguo Yuan Subway Station, then Bus: 929 to Zhitang, then taxi

There are now just around 20 households left here, a sharp decline from the 108 families at the end of the Qing dynasty. Locals attribute the preservation of the village—and its impoverished economy—to poor local transportation and the exodus of villagers over the past century.

Situated in a valley, the small village of Cuandixia is surrounded by four rocky hills and is divided into two sections, upper and lower, which are separated by a curved stone wall. Stone steps provide access to each of the houses.

The houses were constructed in accordance with strict norms, which included arched gates, tiled roofs, and even hitching posts for horses outside the front gate. The wooden parts of the houses have been worn by time but are still intact, and you can still see the intricate carvings of bats (symbolizing fortune), magpies (happiness), peonies (splendor), and peaches (longevity).

Vertical couplets hang from the front door of one house, whose walls are covered with fading murals—dating back to the Qing

Life in the village of Cuandixia has changed little since it was first established some 600 years ago.

A woman dries vegetables the traditional way.

dynasty—that depict stories from the past. In another courtyard house, rabbit and squirrel skins hang from the walls. There are also several wooden boxes filled with honeycombs, as well as the sound of bees busy at work. A press used to extract the honey stands beside the front door. Grass grows out of the roof tiles, and the torn paper covering the windows blows in the wind, giving the house an eerie ghostlike atmosphere.

In the past, the huge stone wheel in the village shed was used to grind corn kernels into corn gruel; such grinding stones are common in rural areas outside Beijing. The villagers don't use it anymore, however, preferring to buy their ground products from local shops.

Especially interesting are the painted slogans from the Cultural Revolution that remain on the walls of some of the houses. "Long Live Chairman Mao," says one, paint peeling from the wall. "Arm Our

Minds with Mao Zedong Thought!" proclaims another. And finally, "Mao Zedong Thought is the Red Sun in Our Hearts." These days, sayings like these are increasingly difficult to find.

A winding stone path leads to a small, lonely looking temple situated on a hill; this site is a great vantage point for taking in the entire prospect of the village. The temple is very run-down, but there are some faded murals on the walls, and a stone tablet dating back to the reign of Kangxi lists the names of villagers who donated money for the construction of the temple.

There are several small "inns" in the village. The conditions are a bit rough; however, these are good places for you to enjoy a home-cooked meal. A typical lunch consists of mutton (one of the mainstays of the local economy, along with honey), wild vegetables picked from the nearby mountains, and corn bread. ■

Travelwise

Tasty morsels await.

PLANNING YOUR TRIP

WHEN TO GO

Summers are brutally hot and the winters are harsh, but Beijing can be visited any time of the year. The weather in Beijing is most pleasant during the spring and fall, and there are fewer people competing for space at the major tourist sites. As China's economy has expanded, both domestic and international tourism has grown by leaps and bounds, resulting in very crowded tourist sites, a trend that is especially noticeable between mid-July and the end of August, when Chinese students are on summer vacation. Although it does not snow often in Beijing, when it does, the peaceful, deserted grounds of the Forbidden City and temples take on a magical look, with their arched rooftops covered in a layer of snow.

Millions of Chinese and hordes of tourists are on the move during the three long national holidays—Chinese New Year/Spring Festival (late Jan.–early Feb.); Labor Day (May 1); National Day (Oct. 1)—making them the least desirable times to visit Beijing and the hardest to book transportation, tours, and hotels.

CLIMATE

September and October days are sunny, and the temperature is mild. Winters are cold and dry. Most hotels are well heated; restaurants, however, can be chilly, so it is wise to layer with a heavy sweater when eating out. April through June is most enjoyable, but July and August can be extremely hot and humid and come with the greatest chance of rain.

The average high temperatures are as follows:
January 54°F/12°C
February 64°F/17.8°C
March 82°F/27.8°C
April 90°F/32.2°C
May 99°F/37.2°C
June 104°F/40°C
July 104°F/40°F
August 107°F/41.7°C
September 92°F/33.3°C
October 84°F/28.9°C
November 75°F/23.9°C
December 66°F/18.9°C

WHAT TO BRING

The sun is strong in the summer months, so be prepared with sunblock, sunglasses, and a hat. In the winter you will want to have gloves, a hat, and a scarf. It is a good idea to layer, and you will need a good winter coat. A comfortable and sturdy pair of walking shoes or sneakers will also be good to have if you plan to do a lot of walking in the city.

Casual dress is suitable. However, how you dress can determine how you are treated. Clothes should always be clean and neat. Appropriate covering is needed for most temples.

ENTRY FORMALITIES

VISAS

All foreign passport holders require a visa in advance of travel to China—there is no visa-on-arrival provision except in extraordinary cases.

Nonetheless, acquiring the standard one-month tourist visa is not difficult. You should apply to the Chinese embassy or consulate closest to your home. Your passport must be valid for six months from your proposed date of entry and contain two blank visa pages when you hand in the visa application. Visas for longer periods, business visas, or multiple-entry visas are also available, with a commensurate increase in the fee.

The standard one-month tourist visa can be extended for an additional month at the offices of the Public Security Bureau throughout the country. The PSB office (gonganju) in Shanghai is located at 1500 Minsheng Lu, tel 010/6834 6205 or 010/2895 1900.

If you happen to be entering via the Hong Kong Special Administrative Region for which no visa is required except for those holding Middle Eastern or African passports, you can get most any length and type of visa using a local travel agent.

Some embassies and consulates accept applications by mail, while others require that you either submit the application in person or use a visa service—contact the embassy or consulate for specific details.

Selected Chinese embassies and consulates are listed below; for a complete list check the Chinese Ministry of Foreign Affairs website: www.fmprc.gov .cn/eng.

Australia
15 Coronation Dr.
Yarralumla, ACT 2600
Canberra
Tel 02/6273-4783
Fax 02/6273-5189
www.chinaembassy.org.au

39 Dunblane St.
Camperdown
NSW 2050
Tel 02/8595-8002
Fax 02/8595-8001

Canada
515 Patrick St.
Ottawa, ON K1N 5H3
Tel 613/789-3434
Fax 613/789-1911
www.chinaembassy
.canada.org

New Zealand
2–6 Glenmore St.
Wellington
Tel 04/472-1382
Fax 04/499-0419
www.chinaembassy.org.nz

United Kingdom
31 Portland Pl.
London W1N 3AG
Tel 020/7631-1430
Fax 020/7588-2500
www.chinese-embassy
.org.uk
or

Denison House
71 Denison Rd.
Rusholme
Manchester M14 5RX
Tel 161/224-7443
Fax 161/257-2672

United States
2201 Wisconsin Ave.
Room 110
Washington, DC 20007
Tel 202/338-6688
Fax 202/588-9760
www.china-embassy.org

443 Shatto Pl.
Los Angeles, CA 90020
Tel 213/807-8088
Fax 213/807-8091

100 West Erie St.
Chicago, IL 60610
Tel 312/803-0095
Fax 312/803-0110

CUSTOMS
Foreign visitors are allowed
to bring all personal effects,
such as cameras, video re-
corders, laptop computers,
GPS systems, etc., into China
without problem. The duty-
free allowance permits three
bottles of alcoholic beverages
and two cartons of cigarettes.
Foreign currency exceeding
the equivalent of $5,000 is
supposed to be declared, but
this stipulation is not strictly
followed.

Avoid carrying any books
on sensitive political subjects,
such as Tibet. Pornography and
religious materials in Chinese
are also unwelcome.

During periods of concern
about contagious diseases, such
as SARS or avian flu, arriving
passengers may have their temperatures taken using touch
sensors.

Upon departure, note that
Chinese law stipulates antiques
dating from 1795 to 1949 be
accompanied by an official cer-
tificate stating their provenance,
and that antiques dating prior
to 1795 may not be legally
exported.

HOW TO GET TO BEIJING

BY AIRPLANE

Beijing Capital International
Airport (PEK) is the only airport that serves international
flights in Beijing (Tel 010/6454
1100, www.en.bcia.com.cn).
The airport is about 30 to 40
minutes, or 16 miles (26 km),
northwest of the city. A taxi to
the center of Beijing will cost
about 80 to 100RMB ($11–
$13), including the 10RMB
($1.33) toll fee. There are two
taxi lines outside the arrival
area. Avoid taxi drivers who
approach you in arrivals as
more often then not you'll be
overcharged. There are also
buses running between the
airport and downtown Beijing,
with the ride taking about 40
to 90 minutes, depending on
the traffic and your origin and
destination—there are four
different routes. Bus tickets
cost 16RMB ($2.13). Airport
commuter bus telephone
hotline is 010/8788 9552 (no
English provided at this time).

The following airlines provide
frequent service to Beijing:

Air Canada
www.aircanada.com
Tel 888/247-2262
Tel 010/6468 2001 (in China)

Air China
www.airchina.com.cn
Tel 866/270-5897
Tel 010/400 810 0999 (in China)

Air France
www.airfrance.com
Tel 800/237-2747
Tel 010/400 880 8808 (in China)

Asiana
us.flyasiana.com
Tel 888/437-7718
Tel 010/6468 4000 (in China)

British Airways
www.britishairways.com
Tel 800/247-9297
Tel 010/400 650 0073 (in China)

Cathay Pacific
www.cathaypacific.com
Tel 800/233-2742
Tel 010/8486 8532 (in China)

China Southern
www.cs-air.com
Tel 888/338-8988
Tel 010/6459 0539 (in China)

Continental Airlines
www.continental.com
Tel 800/231-0856
Tel 010/8527 6686 (in China)

Dragon Air
www.dragonair.com
Tel 800/233-2742
Tel 010/400 881 0288 (in China)

Japan Airlines
www.jal.com
Tel 800/525-3663
Tel 010/400 888 0808 (in China)

KLM Royal Dutch Airlines
www.klm.com
Tel 800/477-4747
Tel 010/400 880 8222 (in China)

Lufthansa Airlines
www.lufthansa.com
Tel 800/399-5838
Tel 010/6468 8838 (in China)

Northwest
nwa.com
Tel 800/225-2525
Tel 010/6505 3505 (in China)

Qantas
www.qantas.com.au
Tel 800/227-4500
Tel 010/6567 9006 (in China)

Singapore Airlines
www.singaporeair.com
Tel 800/742-3333
Tel 010/6505 2233 (in China)

Thai Airways
www.thaiair.com
Tel 800/426-5204
Tel 010/8515 0088 (in China)

United
www.united.com
Tel 800/538-2929
Tel 010/800 810 8282 (in China)

BY BUS

You can take a long-distance bus to Beijing from either Hong Kong or Macao. There are six long-distance bus stations in Beijing and a new one under construction. Information on long-distance tour buses call 010/8353 1111.

BY TRAIN

Beijing can be reached by rail from Europe aboard the Trans-Mongolian or Trans-Siberian Railway, and from Hong Kong, North Korea, and Vietnam. Trains arrive and depart at the Beijing Train Station (tel 010/5101 9999) or the West Train Station (tel 010/5182 6273). Visit www.chinatripadvisor.com/english/ or www.china-train-ticket.com/ for schedule information and reservations.

GETTING AROUND

Beijing's public transportation system has improved a great deal since preparations for the 2008 Olympics began, with new highways and overpasses, new subway lines, and an expanded airport. A new rail line has also been constructed to carry people to and from the airport.

BY AUTOMOBILE

Only foreign residents with a valid Chinese driver's license, passport, and a Beijing Residence Permit may drive in China. Foreign and international driver's licenses are not recognized in China, so driving may not an option on your visit to Beijing. Moreover, driving is not recommended, since traffic is chaotic and road signs are not always in English. However, Avis does offer cars with drivers as part of the rental package. This can cost from around 740RMB ($98) per day (Avis tel 010/8406 3343).

BY BICYCLE

The bicycle is still considered an important mode of transportation for a lot of people in Beijing, and there are dedicated bicycle lanes on most avenues. The pollution and danger of collision with cars makes it less fun than it once was.

If you're an experienced cyclist, give it a try. A brand-new basic model bicycle costs around 300RMB ($40) and you can buy one at any department store. Be sure to get a lock and park in the guarded bicycle parking lots the locals use.

BY BUS

Buses are the cheapest way to get around town. Most city buses are priced at 1RMB (13 cents), while some buses are charged by mileage—1RMB for the first 7.5 miles (12 km), an extra 0.5RMB for every additional 3.1 miles (5 km.) Air-conditioned buses are priced from 2RMB (26 cents).

You may buy prepaid IC cards for public transport, at a 60 percent discount. Beijing Public Transport also issues three special passes for short-time visitors. A 3-day pass for 18 rides costs 10RMB ($1.33); a 42-ride/7-day pass is 20RMB ($2.66); or a 15-day pass is 40RMB ($5.33). Cards are sold at hotels and designated places; some short-time passes are sold at bus terminals.

Buses are often crowded and stops are not identified in English, so buses can be a challenge. Worse yet, you can get caught in Beijing's dense traffic jams. Limited English information is found at www.bjbus.com/english/default.htm.

BY SUBWAY

The subway system is clean, safe, efficient, and probably the fastest way to move around the city. Beijing has eight subway

lines in operation: lines 1, 2, 5, 13, the Batong Line, the new line 10, line 8 (Olympic Sub-Line), and the Airport Line.

Subway entrances are clearly marked with a blue capital "D" within a circle. Subway tickets are 3RMB (40 cents) while tickets for the light rail are 2RMB (26 cents). If you plan to transfer between the two systems, you can purchase a combination ticket for 5RMB (67 cents).

Stations are clearly marked in Chinese and pinyin, and the next station is announced in both Chinese and English. There are also maps inside each car listing the various stops and connections. The subway runs from 5 a.m. to 10:30 p.m. and the light rail from 6 a.m. to 11 p.m.

For detailed information check www.bjsubway.com/ens/index.html. Subway service hotlines are tel 010/6834 0565 (Mon.–Fri.) or tel 010/6834 0563 (evenings and weekends).

BY TAXI

In recent years, Beijing has introduced whole new fleets of modern and comfortable taxis, mainly bigger and roomier Hyundais and Volkswagens. Taxis are a reasonable and easy way to get around the city. The basic fare starts at 10RMB ($1.34) for the first 1.8 miles (3 km), and then rises by 2RMB (26 cents) for every additional 0.6 mile (1 km). A surcharge is added between 11 p.m. and 5 a.m. Few taxi drivers are fluent in English, so have your hotel write down the name of your destination in Chinese. And make sure to take a hotel card with you when you go out so you can find your way back.

PRACTICAL ADVICE

BARGAINING

Bargaining is essential, except in major department stores and high-end shops. Foreigners are often grossly overcharged (especially in heavily touristed areas), so feel free to haggle. Be friendly but firm, and have fun with it. Once you have settled on an item, walk around and see what other vendors are asking for the same thing—prices can differ sharply. Begin by cutting the starting offer in half. If you hit an impasse, pretend to walk away. If the seller is willing to meet your asking price, he or she will run after you.

COMMUNICATIONS

INTERNET
Most hotel rooms will offer an Internet connection for your laptop. Starbucks, SPR, and a number of other coffee shops and restaurants provide free Wi-fi. If you do not have a laptop, inexpensive Internet cafés are also scattered around the city. For up-to-date information on hot spots or cafés look at www.chinapulse.com.

POST OFFICES
Airmail letters to the United States, Britain, and Australia should take between four days and a week to reach their destinations. Mark envelopes "airmail/par avion." Stamps are sold at the post office counter; there are no machines. Envelopes are often gumless, but glue is available at the post office. (Some staff speak simple English.)

TELEPHONE
China's country code is 86 and the Beijing code is 010—eliminate the first 0 when dialing from overseas. When making calls from China first dial 00 followed by the international code and then your telephone number.
Phone cards can be purchased at the airport and in small shops and newspaper stands for use with public telephones. You will also see telephones in small shops and at newspaper stands that are for public use for a small fee. A three-minute city call usually costs 0.5RMB (7

cents). If you're going to be in Beijing for more than a few days, you may want to purchase a secondhand mobile phone for under $40. An unlocked U.S. triband (GSM 1900/1800/900) phone can be used in China when you buy a new SIM card.
Local directory assistance can be reached at 114. You'll be transferred to an English-speaking operator once they realize you're a foreigner.
Using the home country direct number, 108, it is possible to be connected with a local operator in your home country, from whom you can place a collect or credit card call. The following numbers are used:
Australia 108 610
Canada 108 186
Hong Kong 108 852
New Zealand 108 640
United Kingdom 108 440
United States 108 11
China Netcom issues Internet Protocol (IP) phone cards that can be used to call abroad at highly attractive rates, especially since the cards are sold at a discount from their face value.
Important: 800 numbers can not be accessed by cell phone. Some companies have toll-free numbers initiated with 400. You may either call a non-800 number with a cell phone or use a fixed line to call.

CONVERSIONS

Although a traditional measurement system exists, China now follows the metric system.

1 kilometer = 0.62 mile
1 meter = 1.09 yards
1 centimeter = 0.39 inch
1 kilogram = 2.2 pounds
1 gram = 0.035 ounce
1 liter = 0.76 pint
0°C = 32°F

DRUGS & NARCOTICS

No illegal drugs, including marijuana, may be carried into

or consumed in China. While foreigners will not usually be subjected to the penalties meted out to Chinese for such infractions, discovery of even small quantities of illegal drugs will doubtlessly lead to an unpleasant encounter with the judicial system, followed by deportation.
If you take medicine that has an abuse potential, such as painkillers, diet pills, or sleeping pills, be sure to keep them in the container bearing a prescription label, and if possible carry a letter from your doctor noting that they are prescribed for you.

ELECTRICITY

China uses a 220-volt electrical system. Although most electrical items intended for overseas travel (such as digital camera and laptop computer battery chargers) are automatically switched between 110 and 220 volts, be sure to check the manual or look for markings on the device itself before plugging it in. Hair dryers and electric shavers intended for use in the United States are usually 110 volt only. Transformers are available, but they are either heavy or can overheat and create a fire hazard. Plugs come in a variety of shapes (usually two or three flat or round pins), so a conversion plug is useful.

HOLIDAYS

On official holidays, banks, most companies, and government offices are closed.

New Year's Day—January 1
Chinese New Year, also called Spring Festival, follows the lunar calendar. Dates for the next few years are as follows:
January 25, 2009
February 14, 2010
February 3, 2011
This date marks the beginning of a weeklong period of travel when the Chinese visit their hometowns or just take a trip.

PRACTICAL ADVICE

Expect transportation and accommodations to be limited. **International Women's Day**—March 8 **Labor Day**—May 1, another weeklong travel binge **Youth Day**—May 4 **Children's Day**—June 1 **Anniversary of the Founding of the Chinese Communist Party**—July 1 **Anniversary of the Founding of the People's Liberation Army**—August 1 **Anniversary of the Founding of the People's Republic of China**—October 1. Like Chinese New Year and Labor Day, expect crowds and travel congestion. These are great fun to watch as long as you have a hotel and aren't trying to get anywhere.

INSURANCE & HEALTH

There are several foreign-run medical clinics in Beijing, but charges can be high, so health insurance is essential. Make sure that the medical coverage in your travel insurance is adequate and accepted in China.

If you plan an extended stay in China, take out internationally recognized medical insurance before going. Medical evacuation policies are also available.

Bring any medicines you might need as it may be difficult to obtain them in China. Most OTC and some prescription drugs can be purchased in branches of Watson's, which can be found around Beijing, or in any of the foreign clinics, but prices may be very high in the clinics.

LANGUAGE

Luxury hotels generally offer passable, but limited, standards of English. Few staff members at less expensive hotels will speak English. Patience is essential. Don't expect the staff to understand you, and expect to do a lot of pointing.

LOCAL CUSTOMS

BEGGARS

Chinese economic reforms have removed many safety nets for the impoverished. Rural hopefuls travel to large cities in search of work; some end up penniless and hungry. Foreigners are natural targets for beggars. Very young children frequently beg into the late hours of the evening, but any money they collect will only be taken away by nefarious adults claiming to be their "parents."

BUSINESS CARDS

It's well worth printing up some business cards with your name and company written in both English and Chinese. The process of exchanging cards is very much like a handshake and is more widespread than in the West. The Chinese respectfully deliver their cards with both hands; it is polite to accept with both hands.

FACE

The concept of saving face (*mianzi*) is often a stumbling block for foreigners. Although it exists in the West, it is more important in China. Causing someone to lose face—i.e., making them appear foolish—is to be avoided. Try to be sensitive to their feelings. It is advisable to remain respectful, making any complaints with decorum, peppered with firmness.

GUANXI

Guanxi, or connection, takes on a different meaning in Communist China. The code of guanxi is mutual assistance in procuring what you want and giving what others need. As a foreigner, you may have what some Chinese want (a useful contact abroad); the offer of a business card signals a desire for guanxi.

KARAOKE

The Chinese take karaoke very seriously. If you are entertained by the Chinese at a banquet, the karaoke equipment will inevitably be wheeled out and you will be urged to sing the one Western song on the menu. If you are staying in one of the less expensive hotels, inquire where the karaoke lounge is and ask for the room farthest from that point if you want any sleep.

LINES

The Chinese are slowly learning the patient art of standing in line, but be prepared to see a jostling mass with no beginning or end, all elbows and bellowing voices. Polite attempts at lining up are usually ignored. If you are waiting for an empty stall in the restroom, do not be alarmed if people walk right in front of you to stand in front of an individual stall. In this case, politely let them know (or gesture) that you are in fact waiting in line, and they will back up.

SMOKING

Nicotine addiction is widespread in China. Authorities have started to impose bans on smoking in certain public places; however, few restaurants have no-smoking zones. If you smoke, most Chinese cigarettes are cheap and have a strong, dry flavor. If you are allergic to smoke, you may find China a hard place to visit.

SPITTING

Fines are sporadically levied on offenders, but spitting carries on wholesale, even in crowded buses, trains, and sometimes even in restaurants. Do not take offense; it is acceptable behavior. But, apart from being unpleasant, this is a main transmission route for tuberculosis. As a part of the 2008 Olympics campaign, spitting is now being heavily discouraged.

STARING

Getting stared at by locals is still a common occurrence in Beijing. There is nothing threatening about it, as it is simply curiosity, but it can be annoying. You will have to learn to ignore it; overreacting will only magnify the intensity of the stare.

TABOOS

Most Chinese avoid frank political discussions with Westerners. They are not given to speaking openly about their concerns, and they may be sensitive to the implications of discussing such issues with you. It is recommended that you avoid all sensitive political topics.

MEDIA

NEWSPAPERS & MAGAZINES

English papers include the China Daily and Beijing Today. You can buy international newspapers and magazines at leading hotels and the Friendship Store on Jianguomenwai Dajie.

A number of magazines full of information on local restaurants and events also circulate around the city—Time Out Beijing (www.timeout.com/travel/beijing), The Beijinger (www.thebeijinger.com), and City Weekend Beijing (www.cityweekend.com.cn/beijing) are available for free in bars, cafés, restaurants, and some hotels. Each also sends out weekly e-mail updates.

TELEVISION & RADIO

Medium- and high-end hotels all offer a number of satellite stations such as CNN, BBC, HBO, Star TV, and other international channels. CCTV9 broadcasts in English. China Radio International broadcasts daily in English.

USEFUL WEBSITES

Beijing Municipal Administration of Cultural Heritage
english.bjww.gov.cn
This government-run website provides information about the history of Beijing and its cultural heritage sites.

The Beijing Page
www.beijingpage.com
This site provides links to a huge amount of information about tourism in Beijing.

The China Guide
www.thechinaguide.com
Run by an American, this interactive site offers restaurant reviews, details about tourist sites and tours, and other general information.

Cities Guide Beijing
www.economist.com/cities
This useful tourist website was set up by The Economist magazine, and it provides details about a limited number of tourist sites, restaurants, bars, hotels, and more. It also features up-to-date news reports related to Beijing.

Visit Beijing
http://english.visitbeijing.com.cn
This is the official website of the Beijing Tourism Administration.

MONEY MATTERS

The Chinese currency is known as renminbi (RMB), literally "the people's currency." The basic unit is the yuan, commonly referred to as kuai. The yuan is divided into 10 jiao, also called mao, and each jiao is further divided into 10 fen, but you'll only see these in banks. Paper notes come in denominations of 100, 50, 20, 10, 5, and 1 yuan. Smaller notes are 5, 2, and 1 jiao. Coins are circulated in 1 yuan and 1, 2, and 5 mao denominations.

Renminbi is not yet internationally convertible, so you will have to wait until you arrive in China to exchange your money. The best places to convert your dollars into yuan are at the front desk of your hotel or at a branch of a major bank, such as the Bank of China or CITIC. All of these operate with standardized government rates—anything cheaper is illegal and thus risky. You need to present your passport in order to change money. Save the receipts from your currency transaction. You will need to show this to

change renminbi back to your own currency when departing China. The rate may vary, but as of press time, it stands at 7.4 RMB to the dollar.

Carry a decent amount of cash with you at all times, and wear a money belt to thwart pickpockets (especially prevalent on crowded buses and in busy shops and tourist places).

ATM MACHINES

ATM cards are gaining ground in China, and it's now easy to find machines around the city that accept international cards. Maximum daily withdrawals differ, but are usually 5,000 to 6,000RMB ($675–$800). However, normally you can only withdraw 2,000 to 2500RMB ($267–$330) per transaction, so to withdraw 6,000RMB you will need to do three consecutive transactions. Be sure to look for stickers on the ATM machines that say MasterCard, Visa, Plus, or Cirrus. The best ATMs are at the Bank of China, the Industrial and Commercial Bank of China (ICBC), CITIC, and China Merchants. International banks such as Citibank, HSBC, and Standard Chartered are often more reliable—there are Citibank and HSBC ATMs in the Beijing Capital International Airport. As machines often have technical problems, or run out of cash, it's best not to allow yourself to run short of cash.

Debit cards or bank-issued cash cards are less likely to work in Chinese ATMs.

OPENING TIMES

Banks, businesses, and government offices are officially open weekdays from roughly 8:30 a.m. to 5:30 p.m., with some closed for an hour or two for lunch. Many banks have branches that are open on Saturdays and Sundays. Temples, museums, zoos, and other tourist sites are generally open daily, from 8 a.m. or 9 a.m. to

5 p.m. Parks generally open earlier and close later.

PASSPORTS & VISAS

You are technically required to have your passport with you at all times, but to prevent losing it, make a copy of the page with your photo and passport number and keep it in your wallet.

If you lose your passport, report it to the Foreign Affairs Section of the Beijing Public Security Bureau and your embassy or nearest consulate immediately. The PSB office (gonganju) in Beijing is located at No. 2, Andingmen Dong Dajie, tel 010/8402 0101, the nearest subway station is Yonghegong. You are requested to go to PSB yourself to fill in a declaration form

If you're planning an extended stay in China, it's advisable to register with your nearest embassy or consulate. Thirty-day tourist visas (type L) are usually issued, but longer periods may be granted. You can extend your L visa twice by going to the Public Security Bureau before it expires.

REST ROOMS

Public toilets can be quite dirty and offensive. Be sure to take toilet paper with you as it's often not available in the stalls. Most hotels, apart from the very cheapest, will provide a Western-style toilet. Beyond that, however, expect to acquaint yourself with the Chinese squat toilet.

TIME DIFFERENCES

Beijing is eight hours ahead of Greenwich Mean Time (GMT). Noon in Beijing is 11 p.m. in New York, 8 p.m. in Los Angeles, 5 a.m. in Paris, 4 a.m. in London, 2 p.m. in Melbourne, and 4 p.m. in Wellington.

TIPPING

Tipping is not common in China unless someone has gone out of his or her way. If you try to tip, the recipient may refuse, but try three times before giving up to make sure the person is not just being polite. If the person is willing to accept the tip, he or she will do so by the third offer. Otherwise politely drop the matter. Many tour guides and drivers survive on gratuities and will expect a tip. A 12 to 15 percent service charge is added to the bill in hotel dining rooms. A 15 percent service charge is usually added to your room bill, but bellboys will expect a tip for carrying your bags.

TOURIST OFFICE

China is beginning to see the benefits of tourism and the revenue it generates. There are no tourist centers like those you might find in other countries—replete with free maps and brochures, advice, and help—but some centers offering limited assistance opened their doors in the days leading up to the Olympics. There is also a 24-hour English-language Beijing Tourism Hotline, which is normally friendly and helpful. Tel: 010/6513 0828.

The China International Travel Service (CITS), a nationwide organization, deals unimaginatively with foreign guests and can be used as a last ditch measure to join a tour. It is often easier just to use the travel desk at your hotel, where you may find better English skills.

FOREIGN TOURISM OFFICES

The China National Tourism Administration (CNTA) has offices in many countries abroad. The information they provide is useful, including a list of specialized tour operators, but like the government-owned

newspapers, the idealized portrait of the country they offer can mislead travelers.

CNTA has 15 overseas tourist offices around the world including three in North America: New York, Los Angeles, and Toronto. For a complete list of overseas offices and contact details, visit www.cnto.org/aboutcnto.asp. You can also visit http://old.cnta.gov.cn/lyen/index.asp for tour information about China.

TRAVELERS WITH DISABILITIES

Disabled travelers will find China inadequately equipped to deal with them. Public transportation remains largely inaccessible, and only the best hotels and restaurants are prepared to host handicapped travelers. To make matters worse, there are no sidewalks in many places, and the only way to cross large streets is via an underground tunnel or an elevated stairway.

EMERGENCIES

CRIME

Most travelers feel very safe when visiting Beijing, although crime has been rising. Most serious crimes occur do not involve foreigners.

Pickpocketing is a problem, however. Spread your money between a number of pockets, and wear a money belt. Never change money on the street—it is likely that you'll be cheated or end up with counterfeit notes. When traveling on buses and subways or walking on busy streets, keep a close eye on your bag.

Not a crime as such, but one unfortunate racket involves English-language "students" who prey on good-natured foreigners, tricking them into going into a teahouse to chat. Impressing travelers with their

English and friendly manner, they manipulate them into paying for drinks and food. Foreigners are also often tricked into visiting art stores by young people who claim to be students wishing to show their original artwork. However, these stores typically sell nothing more than mass-produced paintings.

Always ask for your receipt when you exit a taxi so that you can locate the driver if you leave anything behind.

EMERGENCY PHONE NUMBERS

Ambulance 120 or 999
Fire 119
Police 110
Traffic accident 122

EMBASSIES & CONSULATES

Australian Embassy
21 Dongzhimenwai Dajie
Sanlitun
Tel 010/5140 4111
Fax 010/5140 4204
www.china.embassy.gov.au

British Embassy
11 Guanghua Lu
Jianguomenwai Dajie
Tel 010/5192 4000
Fax 010/6532 1937
www.uk.cn

Canadian Embassy
19 Dongzhimenwai Dajie
Sanlitun
Tel 010/6532 3536
Fax 010/6532 5544
www.china.gc.ca

New Zealand Embassy
1 Ritan Dongerjie
Chaoyang District
Tel 010/6532 2731
Fax 010/6532 4317
www.nzembassy.com

U.S. Embassy
3 Xiushui Beijie
Tel 010/6532 3831
beijing.usembassy-china.org.cn

For detailed information about diplomatic missions in Beijing, you may refer to www.fmprc.gov.cn/chn/lbfw/namelist/embassy%20list/default.htm

HEALTH

The most common ailments to afflict travelers are either digestive (diarrhea or stomach cramps) caused by unfamiliar or unclean foods, or respiratory, either from infections such as the common cold or air pollution. Either, while not usually serious, make traveling difficult and are best prevented rather than treated. Drink only bottled water and avoid street food. Don't overexert yourself and be careful of rapid temperature changes.

More serious conditions should be guarded against by immunization injections prior to travel. See your doctor three months in advance of your trip, since some injections must be given separately.

A good source of current information is a governmental travel health website.

United States
www.cdc.gov/travel
Australia
www.smarttraveller.gov.au
Canada
www.hc-sc.gc.ca
New Zealand
www.safetravel.govt.nz
United Kingdom
www.dh.gov.uk

News about avian influenza (bird flu) has frightened many travelers, but the medical evidence shows little cause for alarm. The virus is passed from migratory birds to domestic fowl, such as chickens. Transmission to humans requires close contact with an infected bird. Common sense precautions include avoiding live poultry markets and not eating raw or undercooked chicken or eggs. Wash your hands frequently and see a doctor if you develop a fever

LOST CREDIT CARDS

American Express
852/2277 71010

MasterCard
852/8009 66677

Visa
852/8009 00782

MEDICAL EMERGENCIES

Asia Emergency Assistance Center
2-1-1 Tayuan Diplomatic Office Building
14 Liangmahe Nan Lu
Chaoyang District
Tel 010/6462 9112 or 010/6462 9100 (after hours)

Beijing United Family Health Center
2 Jiangtai Lu
(near the Lido Hotel)
Chaoyang District
Tel 010/6433 3960 or 010/6433 2345 for emergencies
www.unitedfamily hospitals.com

SOS International
Building C
BITIC Leasing Center
1 North Rd.
Xing Fu San Cun
Chaoyang District
Tel 010/6462 9112
www.internationalsos.com

HOTELS & RESTAURANTS

The combination of China's economic boom and the 2008 Beijing Olympics has fueled a rapid expansion in the number of hotels and restaurants in the city, providing visitors with an unprecedented variety of places to stay and eat. Choosing the right one can turn a good visit into a great one.

HOTELS

As Beijing readied for the 2008 Olympics, many older hotels carried out extensive renovations while the number of new hotels surged—from top-of-the-line five-star hotels and quaint courtyard inns set up in ancient *hutongs* to comfortable and inexpensive budget hotels. This array of choices is a far cry from the late 1970s, when the old Beijing Hotel was really the only place for foreign guests to stay; plush hotels were simply not a part of old communist China. It was big news, then, when the Jianguo Hotel threw open its doors in 1983 as the first and only joint-venture hotel in the entire city.

The Ritz-Carlton and the Intercontinental are among the new high-end arrivals in Beijing's fast-rising Financial District, while the newly emerging Central Business District is home to the Regent and the posh Park Hyatt.

New boutique hotels include Hotel Kapok, a comfortable and stylish Western-style hotel, and Côté Cour SL, a nicely renovated courtyard hotel. And then there are the small and simple hotels located within Buddhist temple grounds and along the Great Wall.

Those traveling on a tight budget now have more and better options, such as Super 8, Home Inns, and Comfort Inns, which offer rooms for under $40 (including free Internet) and convenient locations throughout the city. There's also a growing number of backpacker inns.

The busiest times of the year—and therefore the most expensive—are spring and fall, when the weather is at its best. If time is not an issue, consider visiting Beijing off-season, when the tourist sites are less crowded. Ctrip (http://english.ctrip.com) is a great place to see what's available and compare prices. But no matter what, always ask for a discount.

RESTAURANTS

Over the past decade, a culinary renaissance in Beijing has revived the city's centuries-old reputation for food. Young entrepreneurs brought cuisines from all over China and opened new restaurants around the city, ranging from sleek, modern dining rooms in shiny new high-rises on Beijing's grand boulevards to small store fronts hidden in Beijing's old hutongs. Now you can dine on earthy Hakka cooking from southern China, specialities from the Yunnan Province, lamb and yak dishes from Tibet, spicy foods from Sichuan, thick noodles from Shaanxi, and even imperial cuisine from the past. Discovering places to eat that are off the beaten track is part of the fun of any visit to Beijing.

What a change from just a decade ago, when diners had limited choices, often eating on plastic tablecloths under plastic grapes hanging from the ceiling. Today's situation is even more remarkable when one considers that 20 years ago Beijing was a virtual culinary desert. In the 1950s, Mao Zedong decided to cut off China's capitalist tails, a move that led private restaurants to shut their doors, including brand-name favorites (known as *laozihao* in Chinese), and to the disappearance of a generation of good chefs.

In 1980, Yuebin Fanzhuang opened in a tiny hutong, becoming the first getihu, or private, restaurant to reopen in Beijing, ending the long drought and offering markedly better food and service than state-run restaurants. Thousands of simple restaurants followed, providing Beijing with a plethora of new eateries.

Some vegetarian restaurant options are noted in the menu reader. Although Buddhist temples and restaurants are the best places for meat-free food, most restaurants will have a sufficient amount of vegetables on their menus. But be careful. Many dishes are prepared with meat-based cooking oils, and some waiters and waitresses will consider a dish vegetarian even if it has a small bit of diced meat in it. When ordering, be clear that you do not want any meat. Sometimes you will get what you ask for, but frequently you will find bits of dried shrimp or meat in your tofu or vegetables.

PRICES

HOTELS
The $ signs indicate the maximum high-season cost of a double room with breakfast.

$$$$$	Over $400 Over 3,092RMB
$$$$	$300–$400 2,320–3,092RMB
$$$	$200–$300 1,546–2,320RMB
$$	$100–$200 773–1,546RMB
$	Under $100 Under 773RMB

RESTAURANTS
The $ signs indicate the cost of a three-course dinner without drinks.

$$$$$	Over $100 Over 773RMB
$$$$	$70–$100 541–773RMB
$$$	$40–$70 309–541RMB
$$	$20–$40 154–309RMB
$	Under $20 Under 154RMB

LISTINGS

The hotels and restaurants listed here have been grouped first according to their district or area (as organized in the main guide), then listed alphabetically in descending order of price. For disabled access, it is recommended that you check with the establishments to verify the extent of their facilities.

CREDIT CARDS

Abbreviations used are: AE (American Express), DC (Diners Club), MC (Mastercard), V (Visa)

DONGCHENG DISTRICT

HOTELS

🏨 PENINSULA BEIJING
🍴 (WANGFU FANDIAN)
$$$$$
8 JINYU HUTONG
WANGFUJING DAJIE
TEL 010/8516 2888
FAX 010/6510 6311
http://beijing.peninsula.com
E-MAIL pbj@peninsula.com
Formerly the Palace Hotel, this hotel, one of the nicest in Beijing, is just a short stroll from Tiananmen Square and the Forbidden City. Guest rooms and suites boast teak and rosewood flooring and 42-inch (106 cm) flat-screen televisions. The Peninsula Academy offers tours as well as expert guidance on antiques, Chinese medicine, and tea. The **Huang Ting** restaurant (see p. 249) serves acclaimed cantonese cuisine.
ⓘ 525 rooms, including 59 suites 🚇 Wangfujing 🔁 🅲 🔁 🌊 🎾 💺 All major cards

🏨 RAFFLES BEIJING
🍴 HOTEL
(BEIJING FANDIAN LAIFOSHI)
$$$$$
33 DONGCHANG'AN JIE
TEL 010/6526 3388
FAX 010/6527 3838
http://beijing.raffles.com
E-MAIL beijing@raffles.com
The luxurious Raffles Beijing Hotel is conveniently located just minutes from the Forbidden City and Wangfujing. The hotel's rooms combine Asian accents with French elegance. **Jaan** offers modern French cuisine, while **East 33 Raffles** has Asian and Western food—these are among the city's priciest hotel eateries.
ⓘ 171 rooms, including 24 suites 🚇 Wangfujing 🔁 🅲 🌊 🎾 💺 All major cards

🏨 GRAND HOTEL
🍴 BEIJING
$$$$
35 DONGCHANG'AN JIE
TEL 010/6513 7788
FAX 010/6513 0048
www.grandhotelbeijing.com/
english/index.asp
This five-star hotel faces Chang'an Avenue, providing expansive views of Beijing's grand boulevard. The Grand Hotel has a wide range of restaurants. In the warmer months, stop by for a drink on the open-air terrace as the sun sets over the rooftops of the Forbidden City.
ⓘ 227 rooms, including 57 suites 🚇 Wangfujing 🔁 🅲 🅲 🌊 🎾 💺 All major cards

🏨 GRAND HYATT BEIJING
🍴 (DONGFANG JUNYUE DAJIUDIAN)
$$$$
1 DONGCHANG'AN JIE
TEL 010/8518 1234
FAX 010/8518 0000
http://beijing.grand.hyatt.com
E-MAIL reservation.beigh@
hyattintl.com
The stylish Grand Hyatt is one of the best places to stay in Beijing. The rooms are state of the art, many with floor-to-ceiling windows overlooking one of the city's historic districts. Just a ten-minute walk from the Forbidden City and Tiananmen Square, the hotel stands above one of Beijing's newest landmarks, Oriental Plaza, an upscale shopping mall. The trendy **Made in China** restaurant (see p. 249) has received high marks for its innovative cuise.
ⓘ 825 rooms, including 155 suites 🚇 Wangfujing 🔁 🅲 🅲 🌊 🎾 💺 All major cards

🏨 HOTEL CÔTÉ COUR SL
$$$$
70 YANYUE HUTONG
DONGSI NAN DAJIE
TEL 010/6512 8020
FAX 010/6512 7295
www.hotelcotecoursl.com
E-MAIL reserve@hotelcote
coursl.com
Located in a historic lane that was home to dancers, musicians, and opera singers of the Ming-dynasty imperial court, this hotel features rooms situated around a quiet courtyard. Each is fitted with elegant furniture, goose-down duvets, and beautiful silk from southern China. In addition to the touches of Old Peking, the rooms include modern luxuries like Wi-fi and satellite TV.
ⓘ 14 🚇 Dengshi Dongkou 🅲 🅲 💺 All major cards

🏨 BEIJING HOTEL
(BEIJING FANDIAN)
$$$
33 DONGCHANG'AN JIE
TEL 010/6513 7766
www.chinabeijinghotel.com
.cn/en/main.asp
Established in 1900 as the Grand Hôtel de Pékin, this hotel is a short walk from the Forbidden City and Wangfujing, one of Beijing's busiest shopping areas. For decades, it was the center of foreign social life in the capital, and it is said that Mao Zedong once twirled his way around the ballroom's dance floor. On a clear day, head to the roof for panoramic views of the city.
ⓘ 800 🚇 Wangfujing 🔁 🅲 🌊 🎾 💺 All major cards

🏨 HOLIDAY INN
CROWNE PLAZA
(GUOJI YIYUAN HUANGGUAN FANDIAN)
$$$
48 WANGFUJING DAJIE

TEL 010/5911 9999
A much needed renovation in 2005 turned this hotel into something sleek. Redone in warm tones, the guest rooms are decorated with black-and-white photographs of old Beijing and feature marble-floored bathrooms. For extra space, opt for one of the rooms on the executive floor.
🛏 360 rooms, including 27 suites 🚇 Wangfujing/Dengshi Xikou ⬆ 🚭 🚭 🚭 📺 🚭 ❄️ 📺
🃏 All major cards

🏨 PARK PLAZA BEIJING
$$$
97 JINBAO JIE
TEL 010/8235 6699
www.parkplaza.com/beijingcn
E-MAIL beijing@parkplaza.com
The Park Plaza Beijing is located directly behind its sister hotel, the Regent. One of Beijing's newest hotels, the Plaza will appeal to those looking for a smaller, cozier, and more professional hotel that won't be too hard on the wallet.
🛏 394 🚇 Dongdan ⬆ 🚭
🚭 📺 🃏 All major cards

🏨 RED CAPITAL RESIDENCE
(XINHONGZI KEZHAN)
$$$
9 DONGSI LIUTIAO
TEL 010/8403 5308
FAX 010/8403 5303
One of Beijing's few authentic courtyard hotels, the Red Capital Residence offers just five rooms, each furnished with period pieces. You can choose from the Chairman's Suite, one of the Concubines' Private Courtyards, or an Author's Suite (one inspired by Edgar Snow, an American writer, the other by Han Suyin, a Eurasian novelist).
🛏 5 🚇 Qianliang Hutong
🚭 🃏 All major cards

🏨 REGENT HOTEL
🍴 (BEIJING LIJING JIUDIAN)
$$$
99 JINBAO JIE
TEL 010/8522 1888

E-MAIL beijing@regenthotels .com
The Regent has a great location: one block from the Wangfujing shopping street and a short walk to the Forbidden City. Rooms have natural light and king-size beds, plus large desks for a pleasant working environment. The hotel has several restaurants, including **Daccapo**, an Italian dining room, and **Li Jing Xuan**, a good Cantonese and dim-sum restaurant.
🛏 500 🚇 Dongdan ⬆ 🚭
🚭 📺 🃏 All major cards

🏨 BEIJING GUXIANG 20
🍴 CLUB
(GUXIANG SHANGWU HUISUO)
$$
20 NAN LUOGU XIANG
TEL 010/6400 5566
This small club with hotel rooms is a recent arrival on Nan Luogu Xiang, one of Beijing's oldest streets. It has a very good restaurant, where sepia photographs of Old Peking hang on the walls beside stone carvings. The rooms are simple but stylish, with Chinese furnishings and motifs. Internet connection.
🛏 80 🚇 Luogu Xiang
🚭 🃏 All major cards

🏨 DAYS INN FORBIDDEN CITY BEIJING
$$
1 NANWANZI HUTONG
NANHEYAN DAJIE
TEL 010/6512 7788
www.daysinn.com
Days Inn Forbidden City is a gem. This inexpensive but nicely designed hotel is just a few minutes from the Forbidden City. The design is a contemporary take on courtyard houses, with brick walls inlaid with stone carvings.
🛏 172 🚇 Tiananmen East, Exit B ⬆ 🚭 🚭 🃏 All major cards

🏨 HOTEL KAPOK
$$
16 DONGHUAMEN JIE

TEL 010/6525 9988
FAX 010/6528 9512
www.hotelkapok.com
E-MAIL reservation@hotel kapok.com
One of a handful of boutique hotels, Hotel Kapok is the creation of Beijing architect, Pei Zhu. The New York Times praised the hotel's "spartanly stylish rooms in a five-story minimalist box wrapped in a diaphanous fiberglass grid." The design includes a bamboo-and-pebble garden in front of every room. The hotel is within walking distance of the Forbidden City.
🛏 89 🚇 Wangfujing 🚭
🚭 🃏 All major cards

🏨 LUSONGYUAN
(LUSONGYUAN BINGUAN)
$
22 BANCHANG HUTONG
KUANJIE

TEL 010/6401 1116
Lusongyuan, set in a traditional courtyard, is said to have been built by a Mongolian general during the Qing dynasty. It still retains much of its old charm.
🛏 57 🚇 Kuanjie 🅰 🚫 All major cards

RESTAURANTS

🍴 HUANG TING
$$$$
PENINSULA BEIJING
8 JINYU HUTONG
WANGFUJING DAJIE
TEL 010/8516 2888 ext. 6707
Huang Ting is a Cantonese restaurant operated by the Peninsula Beijing. The stunning decor is made up of bricks from dismantled courtyard houses and antiquated screens and panels from an old mansion in Suzhou. Equally exquisite are Huang Ting's dim sum, which should be enjoyed with a pot of oolong, pu'er, or jasmine tea.
🍴 100 🚇 Dongdan 🚫 All major cards

🍴 MADE IN CHINA
$$$$
GRAND HYATT BEIJING
1 DONGCHANG'AN JIE
TEL 010/6510 9608
Made in China's open-style kitchen provides diners with front row seats to watch all the action. Flames shoot up from beneath giant woks as chefs stir-fry Sichuan-style green beans, while others are left the less hazardous, but deft, task of stuffing and folding dumplings. You can also get a peek at your own Peking duck as it roasts in a brick oven just steps away.
🍴 100 🚇 Wangfujing 🚫 All major cards

🍴 TIANDI YIJIA
$$$$
140 NACHIZI DAJIE
(CLOSE TO CHANGPU RIVER PARK)
TEL 010/8511 5556
This place is nestled in the

shadows of the Forbidden City. Mythological qilins stare from the traditional stone screen wall as you enter. The yellow parasols overhead and the calligraphy carefully positioned around the restaurant lend the place a harmonious feeling. The menu is pan-Chinese cuisine and runs the gamut from home-style dishes to shark's fin, abalone, bird's nest, and sea cucumber. Whet your appetite with the goose liver marinated in sake and served on a bed of crispy French beans (qingjiu e'gan).
🍴 200 🚇 Tiananmen East, Exit B, 3-min. walk 🚫 All major cards

🍴 CAFÉ DE LA POSTE
$$$
58 YONGHEGONG DAJIE
TEL 010/6416 8802
This small French café serves up marinated beefsteak a multitude of ways: with a lemon herb vinaigrette, with pepper, l'entrecôte, and raw steak tartare. Call ahead to reserve the popular Best Steak topped with a delicious shallot sauce. All the wines come from southern France, but the vin au vevre, house wine, is highly recommended and among the cheapest in town.
🍴 40 🚇 Yonghegong 🕐 Closed Mon.

🍴 GUOYAO XIAOJU
$$$
58 BEI SANTIAO
JIAODAOKOU
ANDINGMENNEI DAJIE
TEL 010/6403 1940
Guoyao Xiaoju is a family restaurant that specializes in Tan cuisine (tanjia cai). Tan, a high-ranking official serving the Qing court, was passionate about good food and delicacies. Guests invited to dine with him were impressed with the refined, delicate food he prepared. Tan cuisine includes cold and hot dishes, soups, desserts, and fruits. Reservations recommended.
🍴 22 🚇 Andingmen/

Jiaodaokou 🚫 No credit cards

🍴 LAIJIN YUXUAN
$$$
INSIDE ZHONGSHAN PARK, NEAR WEST GATE
TEL 010/6605 6676
Laijin Yuxuan is the only place in Beijing that serves the Red Mansion banquet, a lavish 20-course meal based on a feast described in the 18th-century Chinese novel The Dream of the Red Mansion. Advance reservations are required to enjoy the full banquet. However, Sichuan-style dishes are available throughout the day.
🍴 300 🚇 Tiananmen East, 20-min. walk

🍴 LEI GARDEN
(LI YUAN)
$$$
3/F JINBAO TOWER
89 JINBAO JIE
TEL 010/8522 1212
FAX 010/8522 1360
www.leigarden.com.hk
Lei Garden is the Beijing branch of the upscale Hong Kong-based Cantonese chain. Famous for its baked soft shell crabs, Lei Garden also offers beef fillet sautéed with sacha sauce, spareribs in black-bean sauce, and stir-fried rice noodles—all traditionally prepared.
🍴 400 🚇 Mishi Dajie 🚫 All major cards

🍴 MOREL'S
$$$
(MOLAO XICANTING)
1ST FLOOR, BLDG. 5
XINZHONG JIE (OPPOSITE WORKERS' GYMNASIUM)
TEL 010/6416 8802
Lively and packed with "local" residents of all nationalities, Morel's is remarkable not only for its pot mussels and superb locally bred steak, but also for its ambience. It offers an extensive list of Belgian beers, and the Belgian waffle topped with strawberries makes a perfect end to any meal. Reservations recommended.

🏨 80 🚇 Dongsishitiao
🕐 Closed Mon. 💳 All major cards

SOMETHING SPECIAL

🍴 RED CAPITAL CLUB
(XINHONGZI JULEBU)

Dining outdoors in the courtyard of the Red Capital Club, a beautifully restored, 200-year-old courtyard house, you feel like you are miles away from the city and decades earlier. The restaurant features what owner Laurence Brahm calls "Zhong-nanhai" cuisine, based on the favorite dishes of past Communist officials. South of the Clouds, a filleted fish covered with scallions and spices and baked between pieces of bamboo netting, was the favorite of one official who sampled it during the epic Long March. Guests are welcome to squeeze down the narrow steps in the courtyard for a look at the wine cellar.

$$$
66 DONGSI JIUTIAO
TEL 010/8401 6152
FAX 010/6402 7153
www.redcapitalclub.com.cn
🏨 65 🚇 Qianliang Hutong
🕐 dinner only 💳 All major cards

🍴 CAFÉ VINEYARD
$$
31 WUDAOYING HUTONG
(NEAR LAMA TEMPLE)
TEL 6402 7961

Hidden in small hutong not far from the Lama Temple, this café offers simple Western food. There is a grapevine-adorned courtyard that doubles as a lounge area. Café Vineyard serves a hearty British brunch on the weekends—eggs, bangers, sautéed mushrooms, fried potatoes and baked beans, fresh-squeezed orange juice.
🏨 60 🚇 Yonghegong 💳 All major cards

🍴 CARIBOU CAFE
$$

32 QIANLIANG HUTONG
TEL 010/8402 1529

Caribou, with its walls covered with cartoons drawn courtesy of its somewhat young clientele, is one of the cutest restaurants in Beijing. The menu provides variety: French onion soup, pasta with home-made pesto or sun-dried tomatoes, and salmon steak. One of the best dishes is duck served with a raspberry sauce. The desserts range from lava cake to brownies to crème brûlée, and they're all excellent. The owner is the cook—a former Hong Kong photojournalist who traded his camera for a skillet while living in Paris.
🏨 25 🕐 Closed Mon. 💳 No credit cards

🍴 NO. 28 COURTYARD
$$
1 XILOU HUTONG (JUST SOUTH OF LAMA TEMPLE)
TEL 010/8401 6788

This small and casual restaurant sits in an old courtyard house with a date tree and a little pond where fish are kept until the kitchen calls. No. 28 serves exotic minority specialties from the Guangxi Zhuang Autonomous Region. Dishes paired with bamboo shoots are the Zhuang's signature dish. The taro is also good.
🏨 50 🚇 Yonghegong 💳 No credit cards

🍴 JINGSI SU SHIFANG
$
18A DAFOSI DONGJIE
TEL 010/6400 8941

Although it seems a bit of a contradiction, much of the food prepared in this vegetarian locale is prepared to look and taste like meat. Try the crispy Peking "duck" complete with thin pancakes for rolling the duck, or sample the "ham," Zaisu jinshen. The soft sound of Buddhist chants play quietly in the background and the bookshelves are full.
🏨 50 💳 All major cards

🍴 KEJIA XIAOZHEN
$
103 NANHEYAN DAJIE (NEAR GRAND HOTEL)
TEL 010/6522 8993

This rustic restaurant, furnished with simple wooden tables and chairs serves special dishes of the Hakkas, or Guest People—a group living in southern China and made famous by Amy Tan's *One Hundred Secret Senses*. Kejia Village, features traditional dishes—stuffed bean curd, three-cup duck, salt-baked chicken, and fish in sweet and pungent sauce.
🏨 60 🚇 Wangfujing 💳 No credit cards

🍴 LIU ZHAI SHIFU
$
8 MEISHUGUAN DONGJIE
TEL 010/6400 5912

The House of Liu is tucked away in a quiet alleyway but brims with color and movement inside. The century-old house has been transformed into a venue serving traditional Beijing foods at very reasonable prices: Peking duck, thick, hand-pulled noodles, chewy chive pancakes, and braised meat, all downed with cold Yanjing draft beer.
🏨 70 💳 No credit cards

🍴 SHUDU BINGUAN
$
30 SHATAN HOU JIE
TEL 010/6403 5281 2214

This restaurant serves up the best and most authentic Sichuan fare. Hongyou chaoshou—delicious wontons served in an amazing red chili sauce—is a must. End your meal with chilled bingfen, a jello-like dessert drizzled with brown sugar, or tangyuan, glutinous rice balls filled with black sesame, peanut, or red bean paste and served in rice wine.
🏨 60 🚇 Shatan 💳 No credit cards

🍴 WANWAN YUELIANG
$
DONGSI LIUTIAO

DONGSI BEI DAJIE
LIUTIAO HUTONG
TEL 010/6400 5281
This eatery is one of the best Uighur restaurants in town, known for its lamb and breads, from a brick barrel oven. The roasted leg of lamb is exceptionally delicious; equally impressive are the lamb skewers, seasoned with cumin, ground chili, and salt. Stir-fried noodles with peppers, onions, tomatoes, or rice pilaf with shaved carrots are distinctive.
🚹 60 🚇 Dongsi Liutiao
🚫 No credit cards

🍴 XIAO NANGUO
$
2/F JINBAO TOWER
89 JINBAO JIE
TEL 010/8522 1717
Xiao Nanguo cuts the oil and soy sauce in its recipes to create healthier and lighter dishes. Try the spareribs in sweet-and-sour sauce, or *malan xianggan*, a fennel-like vegetable mixed with bean curd and tossed in sesame oil. Deep-fried snake and stewed turtle are available for those with adventurous taste buds.
🚹 150 🚇 Mishi Dajie 🚫 All major cards

XICHENG DISTRICT

HOTELS

🏨 RITZ-CARLTON
🍴 BEIJING
(LISI KA'ERDUN JIUDIAN)
$$$$$
18 FINANCIAL ST.
TEL 010/6601 6666
FAX 010/6601 6029
www.ritzcarlton.com
New and old Chinese art brightens up the walls in the lobby of this smart new hotel, while in the **Tea Apothecary** waitresses clad in yellow silk *qipao* (the typical Chinese dress for women) serve tea and coffee. In the rooms, which are among the largest in any of Beijing's hotels, you will find state-of-the-art amenities

such as Wi-fi and LCD televisions, as well as Tang-dynasty wood-block reproductions on the walls. The restaurant **Cepe** (see below) serves up creative italian cuisine.
🛏 253 🚇 Fuxingmen, 15-min. walk 🔄 🚫 🔄 🚇 🚹 🚫 All major cards

🏨 INTERCONTINENTAL
(JINRONGJIE ZHOUJI JIUDIAN)
$$$$
11 FINANCIAL ST.
TEL 010/5852 5888
FAX 010/5852 5999
The Chinese flagship of the InterContinental chain, this was the first international luxury hotel to open on Beijing's fast-rising Financial Street in the city's northwest corner. The hotel has a 24-hour business center.
🛏 330 🚇 Fuxingmen 🔄 🚫 🔄 🚇 🚹 🚫 All major cards

🏨 BAMBOO GARDEN
HOTEL
(ZHUYUAN BINGUAN)
$$
24 XIAOSHIQIAO HUTONG
JIU GULOU DAJIE
TEL 010/5852 0088
FAX 010/5852 0066
www.bbgh.com.cn
E-MAIL bbgh@bbgh.com.cn
One of Beijing's courtyard-style hotels, the Bamboo Garden occupies a building believed to date from the late 1800s. The rooms, some furnished with Ming-style furniture, overlook three courtyards, each featuring a rock garden, bamboo, and covered corridors. The location makes a great jumping-off point for exploring old Beijing.
🛏 48 🚇 Gulou Dajie 🔄 🚫 All major cards

RESTAURANTS

🍴 CEPE
(YIWEI XUAN)
$$$$
1/F RITZ-CARLTON HOTEL
18 FINANCIAL ST.
TEL 010/6601 6666
FAX 010/6601 6029

Chef Giovanni Terracciano, a native of Naples, Italy, is the brains behind Cepe, whose specialties include roasted pork tenderloin filled with black truffles and pasta served with fungi sauce. The highlight is Terracciano's homemade limoncello. The fresh lemon drink, with a little kick of vodka, is a pleasure.
🚹 60 🚇 Fuxingmen, 15-min. walk 🚫 🚫 All major cards

🍴 FANGSHAN
$$$
1 WENJIN JIE
(INSIDE BEIHAI PARK)
TEL 010/6401 1879
Imperial court cuisine is a style of cooking based on the foods served to the emperor and his court. The Man-Han banquet consists of 134 imperial dishes, served over six days. With a minimum of ten people, the cost is 10,800RMB ($1,438) each. The cheaper version starts at 200RMB ($27). This restaurant started as a teahouse with several former imperial chefs. In 1956, the place was reborn serving a full Man-Han imperial banquet in Beihai Park. Dining in this imperial structure, and being served by waitresses decked out in elaborate Qing-dynasty Manchu outfits, is a treat.
🚹 500 🚫 All major cards

SOMETHING SPECIAL

🍴 ZHANGQUN'S HOME
(ZHANGQUN JIA)
This single-table restaurant was originally used as a meeting place for friends but was soon converted into an exclusive place to eat. The dining area is small, but the natural light penetrating through the skylight creates a warm and welcoming feeling.
$$$
5 YANDAI XIEJIE
TEL 010/8404 6662
🚹 4–10 🚇 Di'anmen Wai
🚫 No credit cards

HOTELS & RESTAURANTS

🍴 DALI
$$

67 XIAO JINGCHANG HUTONG
GULOU DONG DAJIE
TEL 010/8404 1430

This lovely restaurant was once a courtyard house. There are no menus; you are served the dish of the day, which includes a cold appetizer, soup, vegetables, and meat or fish. Each meal is a specialty of the ethnic Bai who reside in Dali, a quaint town in Yunnan Province.

🔧 50 🚇 Jiaodaokou 🚭 No credit cards

🍴 DA SAN YUAN
$$

50 JINGSHAN XIJIE
TEL 010/6401 8184

Located not too far from Jingshan Park, and a convenient luncheon spot near the Forbidden City, Da San Yuan was the first Cantonese restaurant in Beijing. It opens as early as 7:30 a.m., serving dim sum until 10:00 a.m. The roasted pork is fantastic and comes with a fermented wheat dipping sauce.

🔧 200 🚇 Gugong (Forbidden City) 🚭 All major cards

🍴 HAN CANG HAKKA RESTAURANT
(KEJIA JIULOU)
$$

SHICHAHAI DONG'AN
ON EAST BANK OF SHICHA-HAI LAKE, NEAR GATE OF LOTUS MARKET
TEL 010/6404 2259

Han Cang owes much of its success to the hearty cuisine of the Hakka people—three-cup duck, baked chicken in salt, fatty pork turned over, sweet-and-sour fish, and steamed stuffed bean curd. The rustic decor, featuring rice-papered walls with random calligraphy, makes the place feel like home.

🔧 300 🚇 Beihai Beimen (North Gate Beihai) 🚭 All major cards

🍴 HOUYAN
$$

NO. 5, LANE 3, GONGJIAN HUTONG,
PING'AN, DADAO
TEL 010/6402 3055

Dining at the Houyan (Backyard) is like having a meal at a friend's home. The five-room courtyard house has been converted into a small eatery serving simple but delicious food. "Three Ways of Eating Fish" is an absolute must—braised fish slightly spicy; stir-fried fish; and lastly fish soup. The tossed salad is delicious; it consists of small cubes of beef mixed with a variety of veggies. The place is filled with warmth, birds happily reside in their cages, and gourds serve as a sort of hotel for *ququ*, Chinese crickets.

🔧 25 🚭 No credit cards

🍴 JING WEI LOU
$$

181A DI'ANMEN XI DAJIE
TEL 010/6617 6514

Always packed with locals, Jing Wei Lou, or House of Beijing Flavors, specializes in traditional Beijing snacks. Peking cuisine is miles apart from traditional Chinese fare. Popular dishes include *madoufu* (sautéed mung bean pulp), *miancha* (a millet-flour gruel), *zhagezha* (french fries made with mung bean flour), *douzhi* (fermented mung bean juice), and many mutton dishes, part of the city's Muslim heritage.

🔧 200 🚭 All major cards

🍴 SHAGUO JU
$$

60 XISI NAN DAJIE
TEL 010/6602 1126

Shaguo Ju prepares the simple Manchu favorite *bairou*, or white meat (pork)—first popular 300 years ago, when paper-thin strips of lean and fatty pork were lined up row by row concealing the bok choy and glass noodles below, and served with a dipping sauce which consists of fermented bean curd, rice wine, chili oil, and sesame seeds. Shaguo Ju came about as a result of the need for meat for court celebrations in the mid-1700s.

🔧 200 🚭 All major cards

🍴 HUTONG PIZZA
$

YINDING QIAO
(SILVER INGOT BRIDGE)
HOUHAI
TEL 010/6617 5916 or 6657 0741
www.hutongpizza.com

The best pizza and calzones in Beijing are surprisingly served in this traditional courtyard house, just a few minutes' walk from Silver Ingot Bridge.

🔧 50 🚇 Beihai Beimen (North Gate Beihai)

PRICES

HOTELS
The $ signs indicate the maximum high-season cost of a double room with breakfast.

$$$$$	Over $400	Over 3,092RMB
$$$$	$300–$400	2,320–3,092RMB
$$$	$200–$300	1,546–2,320RMB
$$	$100–$200	773–1,546RMB
$	Under $100	Under 773RMB

RESTAURANTS
The $ signs indicate the cost of a three-course dinner without drinks.

$$$$$	Over $100	Over 773RMB
$$$$	$70–$100	541–773RMB
$$$	$40–$70	309–541RMB
$$	$20–$40	154–309RMB
$	Under $20	Under 154RMB

🍴 KONGYIJI RESTAURANT

$

A2 DONGMING HUTONG
DESHENGMENNEI DAJIE
(SOUTH SHORE OF
SHICHAHAI)
TEL 010/6618 4915

This restaurant is named after the protagonist from a short story by China's Lu Xun, a native of Zhejiang Province (famous for its stinky bean curd). Anise-star-flavored broad bean and Shaoxing wine are popular. The fatty pork, slow cooked in a casserole, is sinfully delicious.
🪑 300 🚇 Jishuitan 💳 All major cards

🍴 XIXIANGZI

$

36 DINGFU JIE
DENEI DAJIE
TEL 010/139 0136 8036

A small dining venue opened by a French and Hunanese couple, this restaurant serves dishes from Hunan Province, the hometown of the Chinese leader Mao Zedong. Braised fatty pork is Hunan's trademark dish. Strips of smoked bean curd, stir-fried with celery or smoked bacon and accented with fresh chili, is a memorable dish.
🪑 25 🚇 Changqiao 💳 All major cards

CHONGWEN DISTRICT

HOTELS

🏨 NEW WORLD COURTYARD BEIJING HOTEL

(XINSHIJIE WANYI FANDIAN)
$$

3–18 CHONGWENMENWAI
DAJIE
TEL 010/6708 1188
FAX 010/6708 1808
www.marriott.com

This hotel, managed by Marriott Courtyard, is not far from major sites. It is adjacent to a big department store operated by New World

Group. Traffic may be a problem during rush hour.
🛏 299 🚇 Chongwenmen, 3-min. walk 🅰 🏊 🏋 💳 All major cards

🏨 NOVOTEL XINQIAO 🍴 BEIJING

(XINQIAO FANDIAN)
$$

2 DONGJIAOMINXIANG
TEL 010/6513 3366
FAX 010/6512 5126
E-MAIL rsvn@novotelxin qiaobj.com

This hotel enjoys an excellent location with convenient transportation; both Tiananmen Square and the Temple of Heaven are within a ten-minute drive. **Tang Palace,** famous for its Hong Kong-style dim sum, is also a good place to taste Cantonese cuisine.
🛏 700 🚇 Chongwenmen 🅰 🏊 🏋 💳 All major cards

RESTAURANT

SOMETHING SPECIAL

🍴 LI QUN ROAST DUCK

(LIQUN KAOYA DIAN)

Despite the run-down neighborhood, Li Qun Roast Duck is always full. The entrance has been turned into a furnace for roasting ducks and the rooms made suitable for dining. Li Qun may not have the orderliness of other restaurants, but its appealing roast duck, with little fat between the crispy skin and tender meat, is arguably among the best.
$

11 BEIXIANGFENG
ZHENGYI LU
TEL 010/6705 5578
🪑 60 💳 All major cards

XUANWU

HOTELS

🏨 ST. REGIS BEIJING

(GUOJI JULEBU FANDIAN)

$$$$

21 JIANGUOMENWAI DAJIE
TEL 010/6460 6688
FAX 010/6460 3299
www.stregis.com
E-MAIL stregis.beijing@stregis.com

The St. Regis Beijing is one of the most luxurious hotels in the city and has counted George Bush and other heads of state among its guests. Its health club is probably the best in Beijing, boasting a striking, glass-enclosed pool, a state-of-the-art gym, spa services, and natural hot-spring water from a source deep beneath the hotel.
🛏 273 🚇 Jianguomen 🅰 🏊 🏋 💳 All major cards

🏨 CHINA WORLD HOTEL

(ZHONGGUO DAFANDIAN)
$$$

I JIANGUOMENWAI DAJIE
TEL 010/6505 2266
FAX 010/6505 0828
www.shangri-la.com
E-MAIL cwh@shangri-la.com

The China World Hotel is located in the heart of Beijing's diplomatic and business district. As well as offering guests free Internet access, the hotel is also home to one of Beijing's largest conference and meetings facilities. Its location inside the China World Trade Center complex offers easy access to upscale restaurants and shops selling luxury goods.
🛏 716 rooms, including 26 suites 🚇 Guomao/Dabeiyao 🅰 🏊 🏋 💳 All major cards

🏨 HILTON BEIJING

🍴 (XI'ERDUN JIUDIAN)
$$

I DONGFANG LU
DONG SANHUAN BEI LU
TEL 010/5865 5000
FAX 010/5865 5800
www.hilton.com

The elegant Hilton is a good choice for those who want easy access to Beijing's airport (which is about 20 minutes away). Its rooms were refurbished in 2005, and new bars and restaurants in 2006. The **Zeta Bar,** with its Warhol-esque design, has become one of the most popular spots in the city. **Elements** restaurant serves specialties from around China, Japan, and Southeast Asia, with a wonderful dim-sum brunch on weekends.

ⓘ 375 rooms, including 12 suites 🚇 Sanyuanqiao 🔁 🚭 🅿 🛗 🅿 All major cards

RESTAURANTS

🍴 YOTSUBA

(SI YE)
$$$$
2 XINYUAN XILI ZHONGJIE
TEL 010/6467 1837
The seafood served at Yotsuba is flown in from Tokyo daily. It is best to park yourself at the sushi counter, where your meal is prepared directly in front of you. Choose *otoro* (fatty tuna), *chutoro* (medium fat), or *akami* (no fat). The grilled eel, brushed with home-brewed soy, is slightly sweet and tasty and best enjoyed with several glasses of warmed sake.

🪑 19 🚇 Dongsi Shitiao 🚭 All major cards

🍴 AI JIANG SHAN

$$$
9–7 JIANGTAI XILU
(NORTH GATE, SIDE PARK)
TEL 010/8456 9336
Ai Jiang Shan offers an excellent Korean barbeque in a smoke-free environment. There is a wide selection of beef, including sirloin, filet, marble meat, short rib, and fatty pork. Each order is com-plemented with side dishes such as kimchee, delectable cellophane noodles, assorted raw vegetables, and a variety of dipping sauces.

🪑 300 🚇 Fangyuan Xilu 🚭 All major cards

🍴 HATSUNE

(YINQUAN)
$$$
2/F HEQIAO BLDG. C

8A GUANGHUA LU
TEL 010/6581 3939
Hatsune is popular for its California-style sushi, which mixes avocado with crab meat. Beef on hot iron plate is outstanding with a black peppery sauce. Frequented by foreign expatriates working nearby, this restaurant is located in the downtown district not far from the embassies and offices of multinational companies.

🪑 130 🚇 Guanghua Zhonglu 🚭 All major cards

🍴 LAN

Designed by famed French designer Philippe Starck, Lan's decor is wild, bizarre, and seductive. The vast dining room is divided into private "cubicles" enclosed by canvas curtains. The seafood counter offers an array of raw oysters and sea creatures, while delicacies like shark's fin, bird's nest, fish maw, and abalone are on display. Avoid ordering anything that is not Sichuanese.

$$$
4/F LG TWIN TOWERS
12B JIANGUOMENWAI DAJIE
TEL 010/5109 6012
🪑 800 🚭 All major cards

🍴 MARE

$$$
14 XINDONG LU
TEL 010/6417 1459
FAX 010/6417 1459
E-MAIL marebeijing@hotmail.com
A suitable spot for a business lunch, Mare serves up New Spanish Cuisine, offering dozens of wonderful tapas selections, an assorted cheese platter, as well as a good collection of wine. The almond cake is fantastic; the freshly baked chocolate lava cake is served with hazelnut and vanilla ice cream.

🪑 80 🚇 Gongren Tiyuchang 🚭 All major cards

🍴 PEOPLE 8

(RENJIAN XUANBA)
$$$
18 JIANGUOMENWAI DAJIE
TEL 010/6515 8585
The interior of People 8, which offers both Japanese and Chinese cuisine, is nearly pitch-black, illuminated only by sparse ceiling spotlights. Served in a stylized and beautiful ceramic bowl, an assorted sashimi plate makes a good appetizer. Spareribs with plum sauce and spicy bean curd in a paper cup are highly recommended.

🪑 246 🚇 Jianguomen 🚭 All major cards

🍴 BELLAGIO

(LU GANG XIAO ZHEN)
$$
6 GONGTI XILU
TEL 010/6551 3533
Bellagio serves up delectable Taiwanese fare, from oyster omelets to *dandan* noodles and turnips with puffy scram-bled eggs. The impressive drink and dessert selection includes peanut smoothies, papaya milkshakes, and shaved ice with red beans, lotus seeds, red dates, and silver fungi slow cooked with crystal rock sugar.

🪑 100 🚇 Gongren Tiyu-guan 🚭 MC, V

🍴 KONG YIJI

$$
8 CHAOYANG PARK LU
(NEAR WEST GATE CHAO-YANG PARK)
TEL 010/6508 2228
Professional nutritionist Chen Qing, aka Michael, has given a new image to the humble Kong Yiji by holding on to traditional cooking styles and tastes and relying on basic ingredients like salt, sugar, and sesame oil. Kumquat with shrimp and Jiaxing crispy duck are two of the innovative dishes that Michael has introduced. Expect more to come every month.

🪑 200 🚇 Chaoyang Gongyuan 🚭 MC, V

🍴 LA MAISON DE MARGUERITE

$$

7 SANLITUN BEILU
(BEHIND 3.3 MALL)
TEL 010/6417 3822

Named after famed French writer Marguerite Duras, La Maison de Marguerite serves up the excellent cuisines of both France and Vietnam. The heavenly spring rolls are wrapped with homemade rice paper and served with lettuce, mint leaves, and fish sauce. The caramelized pork and chicken, and shrimp in coconut milk are impressive. And the marvelous coconut flan is not to be missed.

🔲 130 🗝 All major cards

🍴 XIAO WANGFU

$$

RITAN PARK
(BY NORTH GATE ENTRANCE)
TEL 010/8561 5985

Xiao Wangfu, or Little Wang's Residence, is popular among the expat community for its Peking duck and home-style Sichuan cooking. The restaurant overlooks a serene section of Ritan Park, ideal for alfresco dining in summer. Plenty of light pours through the skylights of the interior dining room.

🔲 200 🚇 Jianguomen; 20-min. walk 🗝 All major cards

🍴 GUILIN REN SIJIACAI

$

2 QISHENG XIANG
WANMING LU
TEL 010/6304 5269

Opened by a native of Guilin, this memorable hole-in-the-wall eatery offers traditional Guilin fare like sour bamboo shoots and taro. Another unforgettable dish is the char-grilled streaky pork, which is incredibly delicious when paired with duck and simmered in beer.

🔲 50 🚇 Tianqiao 🗝 No credit cards

🍴 KIOSK

$

NALI MALL
SANLITUN BEIJIE
TEL 6413 2461

The only large item that the Kiosk kitchen has is the deep fryer that turns out hand-cut, thick-wedge golden fries. Owned by a Serbian native, this outdoor venue is the place to come for sandwiches made with ground beef, chicken, and sausage, and livened up with pickled paprika—the red one is spicy and the green is mild.

🔲 12 outdoor 🚇 Sanlitun 🕐 Closed Mon. 🗝 No credit cards

🍴 LAI LAI XUAN

$

8 XINYUAN XI LI ZHONG JIE
TEL 010/6467 8719

Simply decorated with solid wooden tables and chairs, Lai Lai Xuan is frequented by the Japanese community for its delicious ramen cooked al dente in a rich miso-based broth. The wonderful mixed salad is tossed in a dressing with toasted sesame seeds and combined with Japanese condiments, creating an unusually unique and savory dressing.

🔲 50 🚇 Xinyuanli 🗝 All major cards

CHAOYANG DISTRICT

HOTELS

🏨 GLORIA PLAZA HOTEL

🍴 **$$$$$**

83 JIANGUO LU
TEL 010/6515 8855
FAX 010/6515 8533
www.gphbeijing.com

The Gloria Plaza is one of Beijing's oldest hotels, located in the Jianguomenwai embassy district. It's also a short taxi ride to the Forbidden City and other nearby historical sites. The **Sampan Cantonese** restaurant offers excel-

lent dim sum.

ℹ️ 420 🚇 Dawang Lu, Exit A
❄️ 🗝 ♨️ 🏊 💪 🗝 All major cards

🏨 PARK HYATT BEIJING

$$$$$

2 JIANGUOMENWAI DAJIE
TEL 010/8567 1234
FAX 010/8567 1000
http://beijing.park.hyatt.com
E-MAIL: parkhyattbeijing@hyattintl.com

The Park Hyatt located in the impressive Beijing Yintai Center is a boutique hotel. It combines Asian aesthetics with sleek, contemporary design. Rooms are situated on floors 37 to 49. The hotel's rooftop bar, designed to resemble a Chinese lantern, has dramatic views of the city.

ℹ️ 219 rooms, including 18 suites 🚇 Guomao ❄️ 🗝 ♨️ 🏊 💪 🗝 All major cards

🏨 TRADERS HOTEL

🍴 **$$$$$**

1 JIANGUOMENWAI DAJIE
TEL 010/6505 2277
FAX 010/6505 0838
www.shangri-la.com/en/property/beijing/traders

The Traders Hotel is a convenient and reasonably priced option to the more expensive Shangri-la-run China World Hotel and the Beijing Kerry Centre, sister establishments. **The Oriental** (see p. 257) is an excellent Cantonese restaurant with reasonably priced dishes. The hotel is linked to the China World Trade Center via an underground shopping mall passageway.

ℹ️ 305 🚇 Dawang Lu, Exit A
❄️ 🗝 ♨️ 🏊 💪 🗝 All major cards

🏨 SOFITEL WANDA BEIJING

🍴 **$$$$**

93 JIANGUO LU
TEL 010/8599 6666
FAX 010/8599 6686
www.sofitel.com
E-MAIL sofitel@sofitelwandabj.com

The Sofitel Wanda Beijing opened its doors in the summer of 2007 to rave reviews about its classic design, a blend of Tang-dynasty China with contemporary French style. The rooms feature warm beiges and Chinese motifs. Le Spa offers beauty treatments blending local plant life and traditional Chinese techniques. Sofitel is also known for its excellent French and Cantonese restaurants, notably **Le Pre Lenotre** (see below).

ⓘ 417 rooms, including 63 suites 🚇 Dawang Lu, Exit A 🚌 🚭 🏊 🛎 📺 🚭 All major cards

🏨 KEMPINSKI HOTEL
🍴 (KAIBIN SIJI FANDIAN)
$$$
50 LIANGMAQIAO LU
TEL 010/6465 3388
FAX 010/6465 1202
www.kempinski-beijing.com

The opulent Kempinski Hotel is located in the busy Lufthansa Center, an impressive complex of offices, shops, and apartments in Beijing's new diplomatic and business district. All the guest rooms are spacious and comfortable. The **Paulaner Brauhaus** is considered the best German restaurant in the city, and the **Kempi Deli**, with its small wooden stools and tables, is an excellent bakery.

ⓘ 526 rooms, including 114 suites 🚇 Liangmaqiao 🚌 🚭 🏊 📺 🚭 All major cards

🏨 BEIJING KERRY CENTRE
(JIALI ZHONGXIN FANDIAN)
$$
1 GUANGHUA LU
TEL 010/6561 8833
www.beijingkerrycentre.com

The Beijing Kerry Centre is located in the Chaoyang diplomatic and commercial district, just a short drive from the city's popular historic sites, including the Forbidden City and Tiananmen Square. It is

filled with contemporary touches: The trendy lobby is bright and cheerful, and the rooms are decorated in fashionably neutral tones. The hotel also has an impressive sports center.

ⓘ 487 rooms, including 23 suites 🚇 Guomao/Guang-huaqiao 🚌 🏊 🛎 📺 🚭 All major cards

🏨 HOLIDAY INN LIDO
$$
6 JIANGTAI LU
TEL 010/6437 6688
FAX 010/6437 6237

China's first Holiday Inn Lido continues to attract business travelers looking for comfort and familiarity, but the location —20 minutes by taxi from the airport—makes it difficult for tourists visiting historic sites. The 400-odd rooms are what you'd expect from this plain but reliable chain, but the hotel's restaurants (Chinese, Tex-Mex, Thai, Indonesian, among others) inject a bit of color.

ⓘ 433 rooms, including 24 suites 🚌 🚭 🏊 📺 🚭 All major cards

RESTAURANTS

🍴 LE PRE LENOTRE
$$$$
6/F SOFITEL WANDA BEIJING
93 JIANGUO LU
TEL 010/8599 6666

Le Pre Lenotre, the sister of notable Le Pre Catelan, has brought authentic French cuisine to Beijing, adding to the excitement of the city's increasingly mixed-bag culinary scene. The cod studded with bits of smoked salmon served with eggplant marmalade is wonderful. The restaurant serves small brioche, reminiscent of Parisian baguettes. Elegant and romantic the Lenotre provides the perfect locale for an intimate dinner.

🪑 100 🚇 Dawang Lu, Exit A 🚭 All major cards

PRICES

HOTELS
The **$** signs indicate the maximum high-season cost of a double room with breakfast.

$$$$$	Over $400
	Over 3,092RMB
$$$$	$300–$400
	2,320–3,092RMB
$$$	$200–$300
	1,546–2,320RMB
$$	$100–$200
	773–1,546RMB
$	Under $100
	Under 773RMB

RESTAURANTS
The **$** signs indicate the cost of a three-course dinner without drinks.

$$$$$	Over $100
	Over 773RMB
$$$$	$70–$100
	541–773RMB
$$$	$40–$70
	309–541RMB
$$	$20–$40
	154–309RMB
$	Under $20
	Under 154RMB

🍴 AWANA
$$$
32 TIANZE LU
TEL 010/6462 0004

The chef here is a native Malaysian chef from Seremban, south of Kuala Lumpur. His specialties for openers include *roti channay*, thin crispy bread, and grapefruit seafood salad. Beef *rendang* or *kapitan ayam*, a type of curry with nice lemongrass flavor are the main dishes. Awana *mamak* fish—sweet and sour with a hint of shrimp taste—is an all-time Malaysia favorite. End your meal with cold *bubur chacha*, a creamy coconut milk with tapioca pearls, small chunks of taro and sweet potatoes; or try a frothy cup of *teh tarik* to rinse the spices away.

🪑 150 🚭 MC, V

JIU YUAN
$$$
6 DONG SANHUAN BEILU
RAINBOW PLAZA
TEL 010/6595 1199
Zhang Ziyi, China's most popular actress, owns this place, so expect to see the glitterati and maybe Zhang herself here. Jiu Yuan serves Japanese food and the sushi rolled in five grains is interesting and delicious. The tempura and teppanyaki are also excellent. Expect to see a large ice Buddha statue in a meditative position, which glows alternately in red, blue, green, purple. and milky white.
🏠 150 🚇 Guomao 💳 MC, V

LA DOLCE VITA
$$$
8 XINDONG LU
TEL 010/6468 2894
La Dolce Vita's soft lighting, arches and alcoves, and yellow walls put you in a Mediterranean mood. The wood-burning brick oven bakes wonderful pizzas and breads. Pastas are served with classic bolognese, pomodoro, or carbonara sauces. A wide selection of Italian wines are available by the glass.
🏠 80 💳 MC, V

MAKYE AME
$$$
11A XIUSHUI NANJIE,
JIANGUOMENWAI DAJIE
TEL 010/6506 9696
Step under the fluttering prayer flags hanging outside and walk past the brass prayer wheel inside, and here the scent of yak butter tea permeates. You'll feel transported to some remote Tibetan village. The best dishes are the grilled mushrooms, curried potatoes, leg of lamb, and stir-fried beef with pickled carrots. Wash it down with a cold Tibetan beer or local Tibetan wine served in an intricately designed metal pot. The Tibetan performance starts at 8 p.m. nightly, ending with the staff and guests doing a

Tibetan rumba around the room—this is not the place to go if you want to talk, but the atmosphere is exciting.
🏠 150 🚇 Gianguomen 💳 MC, V

MY HUMBLE HOUSE
$$$
CHINA CENTRAL PLACE
LEVEL 2 CLUB HOUSE
89 JIANGUO LU
TEL 010/6530 7770
This is one of the few Chinese restaurants that have succeeded in the Chinese fusion experiment. Andrew Tjioe, the Indonesian-Chinese owner, eschews the term "fusion," preferring to call it "contemporary Chinese." The food served is incredibly tongue pleasing, using carefully picked spices and ingredients that marry well. This sleekly designed restaurant is the place to go when you want to make a good impression.
🏠 80 🚇 Dawang Lu, Exit A 💳 MC, V

SAHARA
$$$
SANLITUN NANJIE
(BEHIND COMFORT INN)
TEL 010/6507 3521
Sahara bears a resemblance to a typical Chinese opera house, with balcony seats going around the second floor while the middle empty space is a stage for live music and dancing. The restaurant specializes in fine Middle Eastern cuisine. Two master chefs run the kitchen, creating a wide selection of pita-bread dipping sauces—the classic purée, chickpeas, eggplant purée, diced tomato, cilantro, and a creamy cinnamon spread. For meat lovers, the lamb, roasted until the meat falls off the bone, is tender and juicy. All food served at Sahara is halal; alcohol is not served.
🏠 150 💳 MC, V

THE ORIENTAL
$$$
TRADERS HOTEL
1 JIANGUOMENWAI DAJIE
TEL 010/ 6505 2277
The Oriental is known for its dim sum and Cantonese cuisine, but it frequently invites master chefs from around China to showcase other regional Chinese cuisine, often lesser known cooking styles, such as Anhui. The quality of the food is excellent.
🏠 100 🚇 Guomao & Dawang Lu, Exit A 💳 All major cards

TIM'S TEXAS BAR-B-Q
$$$
14 DONG DAQIAO LU
TEL 010/6591 9161
The restaurant's unvarnished wooden walls accented with worn cowboy boots, old farm tools, Texas license plates, and a bunch of other items give Tim's Texas Bar-B-Q the look of a simple restaurant in America's South circa 1950. Diners can get old-fashioned beef brisket, smoked slowly to enable the flavors of the meat to seep through, fish kebabs, shrimp creole, and ratatouille. Fried mushrooms and nachos go great with a beer, and the authentic Mexican tacos are cooked every Wednesday and Friday.
🏠 80 🚇 Yong'anli 💳 MC, V

YUAN YUAN
$$$
16 TUANJIEHU PARK
(WEST GATE)
DONG SANHUAN
TEL 010/6508 2202
Yuan Yuan was the winner of the Golden Chopstick award for its braised pork (hongshao rou) in the 2006 Shanghai New Cuisine competition. The caramelized belly pork, which melts in your mouth, is a Shanghainese signature dish, and an all-time favorite. Other well-known dishes not to be missed are stir-fried glutinous rice cake, bean-curd thread in

chicken consommé, scrumptious wild vegetables in sesame oil, and peanuts mixed with bean curd tossed in light soy dressing.

🔳 150 🅂 MC, V

🍴 NOODLE LOFT
$$
20 XIDAWANG LU
TEL 010/6774 9950
The freshly hand-pulled noodles here are second to none. The noodles are cooked al dente and have a chewy texture. The varieties of noodles are endless. Try knife-shaved noodles, one strand noodle, cat's ears, or *kao laolao*, a honeycomb-like noodle served with the sauce of your choice: minced meat sauce, tomato and eggs, or a vinegar and soy sauce combination.

🔳 150 🅂 MC, V

HAIDIAN DISTRICT

HOTELS

🏨 FRAGRANT HILL HOTEL
(XIANGSHAN FANDIAN)
$$
INSIDE XIANGSHAN PARK
TEL 010/6259 1166
FAX 010/6259 1762
This hotel, designed by Chinese-American architect I. M. Pei, opened with much fanfare but soon fell into neglect and disrepair. Still, it's an ideal place to stay if you're visiting sites in western Beijing.

🛈 286 ⬛ 🅂 🈺 📺 🅂 All major cards

🏨 SHANGRI-LA HOTEL
(XIANGGE LILA FANDIAN)
$$
29 ZIZHUYUAN LU
TEL 010/6841 2211
FAX 010/6841 8002 or
010/6841 8003
www.shangri-la.com
E-MAIL slb@shangri-la.com
Located in Beijing's new financial district, the Shangri-La is surrounded by charming

landscaped gardens. From its western location, guests can easily access the nearby exhibition centers and high-tech zone (Beijing's Silicon Valley). Of greater interest to tourists is its proximity to major attractions in northwest Beijing, including the Summer Palace.

🛈 670 🚇 Wanshousi ⬛ 🅂 🈺 📺 🅂 All major cards

RESTAURANTS

🍴 BAIJIA DAZHAIMEN
$$
29 SUZHOU JIE
TEL 010/6265 4186
To eat at Baijia Dazhaimen is to travel back to the Qing dynasty. A waitress dressed in a colorful Manchu costume will escort you into the huge garden-style dining room, where the staff will welcome you with *Nin jixiang*, an ancient greeting that has long since vanished. The cuisine served is imperial Beijing, Cantonese, and Sichuanese.

🔳 200 🚇 Beijing Dizhenju 🅂 All major cards

🍴 BAOQIN DAIWEI RESTAURANT
$
4 MINZU DAXUE BEILU
WEIGONGCUN
TEL 010/6848 3189
The Baoqin Daiwei Restaurant serves the food of the Dai people, an ethnic group living in Yunnan Province in southwest China. Always packed with students and regular customers who miss their hometown cooking, it's best to make a reservation or arrive early. Savory potato balls, pineapple rice, salad with Dai dressing, and fish fried in lemongrass are all superb.

🔳 40 🚇 Minzu Daxue 🅂 No credit cards

🍴 GOLDEN PEACOCK
(JIN KONGQUE)
$
16 MINZU DAXUE BEILU

WEIGONGCUN
TEL 010/6893 2030
Golden Peacock is only a few doors away from Baoqin and offers a similar menu. The owners of both restaurants come from villages that are only several miles apart. Like Baoqin, Golden Peacock is always packed, with people lining up for tables. Interestingly, those who frequent one of the restaurants rarely patronize the other.

🔳 60 🚇 Minzu Daxue 🅂 No credit cards

EXCURSIONS NORTH TO THE GREAT WALL

🏨🍴 COMMUNE BY THE WALL KEMPINSKI
$$$$$
EXIT AT SHUIGUAN,
BADALING HWY.
TEL 010/8118 1888
www.communebythegreat
wall.com/en/
This boutique hotel cum semi-architectural museum is the brainchild of Zhang Xin and Pan Shiyi. Set amid the peaceful green mountains near the Shuiguan of the Great Wall, the place is a collection of contemporary architecture designed by 12 Asian architects. There are 42 villas with unique designs spread out across the steep valley with views of the nearby Great Wall. The Club House includes the **Courtyard Restaurant** (worth the trip alone).

🛈 46 ⬛ 🅂 📺 🅂 All major cards

🏨 GRANDMA'S PLACE
$$$$
12 MUTIANYU VILLAGE
HUAIROU COUNTY
TEL 010/6162 6282
A rustic hotel built of stones and bricks from Ming- and Qing-dynasty structures and huge beams from old village houses, Grandma's Place is furnished with peasant pieces.

The bedrooms use *kangs*—heated sleeping areas made of bricks. Enjoy views of the Great Wall from the garden.
🛏 10 ❄ 🅰 All major cards

RED CAPITAL RANCH
(WANSHOU GONG)
$$$$
28 XIAGUANDI VILLAGE
YANXI TOWNSHIP
HUAIROU COUNTY
TEL 010/8401 8886
www.redcapitalclub.com.cn
/ranch.html
Nestled between a small river and a wild section of the Great Wall, the ranch is made up of individual houses, equipped with modern facilities. The dining room serves Manchu dishes and locally picked wild vegetables. The bar has colorful furniture and rugs, and overlooks the stream. The hotel offers spa services, including Tibetan massage. Transportation from Beijing is included in price.
🛏 10 ❄ ceiling fans 🅰 All major cards

LONGEVITY PALACE
$
HEXI VILLAGE
GUBEIKOU TOWNSHIP
MIYUN COUNTY
TEL 010/8105 1166
This rustic guesthouse is located at the foot of Tiger Mountain, a serene and peaceful courtyard residence with easy access to a nice hiking trail that winds beneath and along a section of the Great Wall. The hotel rooms are simple but clean; they face a nice courtyard with colorful flowers and plants and a pond. There's a good restaurant offering home-style Chinese cooking.
🛏 28 🚉 Gubeikou by train ❄ 🅰 All major cards

RESTAURANT

XIAOLUMIAN
$
130 YINGBEIGOU CUN
HUAIROU DISTRICT
TEL 010/6162 6506
Xiaolumian focuses on noodles, with a selection of buckwheat and veggie noodles flavored with spinach, carrot, or wormwood Artemisia. Set in a weathered stone farmhouse surrounded by a walled orchard in the shadow of the Great Wall, this is an ideal place for lunch during your hike on the wall.
🍴 20 inside plus 60 terrace
🕐 Open Sat.–Sun. 🅰 All major cards

EXCURSIONS SOUTH

TIANJIN

HYATT REGENCY
(KAIYUE FANDIAN)
$$$
219 JIEFANG BEILU
TEL 022/2330-1234
FAX 022/2331-1234
www.hyatt.com
The four-star Hyatt is an elegantly styled hotel benefiting from an excellent position on Tianjin's historic Jiefang Lu near the Hai River. This may not be Tianjin's most lavish hotel, but service is welcoming, the location convenient.
🛏 450 🚹 ❄ 🅰 All major cards

ASTOR HOTEL
(LISHUNDE DAFANDIAN)
$$
33 TAI'ERZHUANG LU
TEL 022/2331-1688
FAX 022/2331-6282
One of Tianjin's most historic hotels, the Astor was built in 1863. Puyi (the last emperor), Sun Yat-sen, and Yuan Shikai have stayed here. Situated near the Hai River, it was the first to use electric lights in Tianjin during the Qing dynasty. Fragments of history remain inside: The original American Otis elevators are there, mid-19th-century furniture remains, and you can find the radio used by Puyi. A new building, constructed in 1987, was added to the existing hotel. If you can afford it, you can stay in the Sun Zhongshan (Yat-sen) Presidential Suite and eat in the vast Buckingham Palace banqueting hall (*baijinhangong guoyanting*).
🛏 223 🅰 All credit cards

GOUBULI
$
77 SHANDONG LU
TEL 022/2730-2540
The famous Goubuli, located just off the shopping drag of Binjiang Dadao, has been serving up its trademark specialty steamed buns (*baozi*) for over a hundred years. The appetizing buns come in almost one hundred varieties (pork, chicken, shrimp, vegetable, and more) and a selection of tasty and good value set meals is also available. There are other branches dotted around town, Beijing, and beyond.
🍴 300 ❄ 🅰 No credit cards

LITTLE SHEEP
(XIAOFEIYANG)
$
RONGYE DAJIE
TEL 022/2730-8318
Warm up cold Tianjin winter days with a steaming Mongolian lamb hot pot at this branch of the successful nationwide chain.
🍴 500 ❄ 🅰 Cash only

XIANG WEI ZHAI
$
HYATT HOTEL TIANJIN
219 JIEFANG BEILU
TEL 022/2331-8888
This pleasantly designed dumpling restaurant is a joy. The name means "countryside flavor," pointing to its emphasis on traditional simplicity. Try the crab and chive dumpling or the seafood and noodle soup, and wash it down with Chinese tea. Inexpensive and all very worthwhile. Service charge included. English menu.
🍴 44 ❄ 🅰 All major cards

SHOPPING

Beijing is a treasure trove for shoppers. From antiques to silk, knock-offs to designers, the new economy has brough a multitude of consumer goods. The most interesting items may be found as you walk the lanes of the hutongs and the side streets away from other tourists. Do beware, however, that in the smaller places most shop keepers will not be able to converse in English; prices are usually shown on calculators, and bargaining is expected.

ANTIQUES SHOPS

Beijing Curio City (Beijing Guwan Cheng)
 21 Dongsanhuan Nanlu
 (Exit Third Ring Rd. at
 Panjiayuan Bridge)
 Chaoyang District
 Tel 010/6774 7711
 Bus: Shilihe
 Open 9:30 a.m.–6:30 p.m.
An indoor market, Beijing Curio City boasts four floors of everything from Chinese kitsch to factory-fresh antiques. You can buy jewelry, porcelain, teapots, Buddhist statues, furniture, and more. It's a bit more formal than the outdoor Panjiayuan (see Flea Markets p. 261), but still worth a visit.

C. L. Ma Furniture (Kele Ma Jiaju)
 Room 109–110, Bldg. 4
 Park Avenue, No. 6
 Chaoyang Gongyuan Nanlu
 Chaoyang District
 Tel 010/6530 6475 or
 010/6466 7040
 www.clmafurniture.com
 Open 10 a.m.–6:30 p.m.
 Or
 803 Longzhaoshu
 Xiaohongmen
 Chaoyang District
 Tel 010/8769 9084
 Open 9 a.m.–5:30 p.m.
A well-respected dealer and expert, C. L. Ma is the author of several glossy books on traditional Chinese furniture. He also sells antiques and nicely reproduced tables, chairs, cabinets, and screens. He has his own restoration workshop and several showrooms stocked with restored and unrestored pieces.

Gold Barn
 A52 Sanlitun Nanjie
 Chaoyang District
 Tel 010/6463 7389
 Open 11 a.m.–midnight
This high-end antiques shop sells furniture and antique reproductions. This store provides a comfortable atmosphere with new age music. Along with furniture, Gold Barn also serves extravagant teas, wine, and snacks.

Liangma Antique Market
 27 Liangmaqiao Lu
 Open 9:30 a.m–6:30 p.m.
A market made for the cost-conscious individual, Liangma has an array of goods such as bird-cages, scroll paintings, and an extensive carpet selection. Less crowded than other markets.

BOOKSTORES

Beijing Foreign Languages Bookstore (Beijing Waiwen Shudian)
 235 Wangfujing Dajie
 Dongcheng District
 Tel 010/6512 6903
 Metro: Wangfujing
 Open 9 a.m.–9 p.m.
It may have a limited selection, but this longtime seller of foreign-language books is strong in locally published books on Chinese history, culture, and language. It also offers a wide variety of dictionaries. Imported publications are on the third floor.

Bookworm (Shu Chong)
 Behind Bldg. 4
 Nan Sanlitun Lu
 Chaoyang District
 Tel 010/6586 9507
 Bus: Sanlitun
 Open 9 a.m.–2 a.m.
Offering free Wi-fi and plenty of space to work, the Bookworm is a bookstore, lending library, restaurant, and coffee shop rolled into one. The book selection is small but includes some latest best sellers and a good collection of books on China. It also frequently hosts talks by local writers and authors passing through Beijing.

Charterhouse Bookstore
 107 The Place
 9 Guanghua Lu
 Chaoyang District
 Tel 010/6587 1328
 Bus: Dongdaqiao/Fangcaodi
 Open 10 a.m.–10 p.m.
Charterhouse Bookstore was the first bookshop in Beijing dedicated solely to works in English. It has a small but interesting collection.

Friendship Store (Youyi Shangdian)
 17 Jianguomenwai Dajie
 Chaoyang District
 Tel 010/6500 3311
 Metro: Jianguomen
 Bus: Ritan Lu
 Open 9:30 a.m.–8:30 p.m.
The Friendship Store has the biggest collection of books and maps dealing with travel in China, as well as many books on Chinese arts. It also has a good selection of international magazines and newspapers, including *The Economist, Time, Newsweek,* and the *Asian Wall Street Journal.*

Wangfujing Bookstore (Wangfujing Xinhua Shudian)
 218 Wangfujing Dajie
 Dongcheng District
 Tel 010/6525 1816 or
 010/6513 2842
 Metro: Wangfujing
 Open 9 a.m.–9 p.m.
Wangfujing Bookstore offers an eclectic array of airport novels, best sellers, books about China, and very cheap classics, from Mark Twain and Charles Dickens to Jack London. It also has a good collection of DVDs in the basement.

FLEA MARKETS

Baoguo Temple Cultural Market (Baoguo Si Wenhua Shichang)
1 Baoguo Si
Guang'anmennei
Xuanwu District
Tel 010/6303 0976
Bus: Niujie/Baiguanglu Beikou
Founded in 1466 as a Buddhist complex, the Baoguo Temple became a metal-smelting factory after liberation in 1949. Today it is a busy flea market, where friendly hawkers display their goods on the ground, in bicycle carts, and in small makeshift rooms. Items for sale include Cultural Revolution kitsch, old coins and stamps, jade, old books, and antiques.

Hongqiao Market
Tiantan Donglu
Chongwen District
Tel 010/6713 3354
Metro: Chongwenmen, then Bus 610
Open 8:30 a.m.–7 p.m.
This market sells a variety of items such as T-shirts, silk pajamas, beads, shoes, some electronics, and fish at the fish market in the basement. It is well known for its pearls; there is a wide range of prices and quality. As this is a tourist market, everything is on the pricey side. The Fifth-floor balcony offers an amazing view of the Temple of Heaven so don't forget to bring your camera.

Panjiayuan Market (Panjiayuan Jiuhuo Shichang)
18 Huaweili
West of Panjiayuan Bridge
East Third Ring Rd.
Chaoyang District
Bus: Panjiayuan Qiao/Jiuhuo Shichang
Tel 010/6775 2405
Open Mon.–Fri. 8:30 a.m.–6 p.m., Sat.–Sun. 4:30 a.m.–6 p.m.
The Panjiayuan Market, located on what looks like an abandoned building site, is Beijing's premier flea market, with some 3,000 sellers. In addition to the snuff bottles, porcelain, and traditional paintings that are sold in other places around the city, here you can find odd and interesting pieces—much of it apparently gathered from all over China. On any given day you may stumble across stone temple lions, Chinese bows, a leather Qing-dynasty saddle with fine metal trim, or wooden grain boxes, worn smooth from generations of use. The market also has a large collection of memorabilia from the Cultural Revolution.

HANDMADE & DESIGNER ITEMS

Botao Haute Couture
Bldg. 18 Dongzhimenwai
Chaoyang District
Tel 010/6417 2472
Open 9:30 a.m.–9 p.m.
One of China's most well-known boutiques for brand names and high-end professional clothing. Features dresses tailored by local designers.

Pi'erman Maoyi
37 Gulou Dongdajie (west of Jiaodaokou)
Dongcheng District
Tel 010/6404 1406
Open 9:30 a.m.–9 p.m.
Bring in a photo of your dream shoe, and this man will manufacture a comfortable pair of shoes or boots in about three weeks. Prices for shoes and boots start at about 360RMB ($49) and 800RMB ($108), respectively.

Red Hero
191 Haidian Lu
Haidian District
Tel 010/6256 1148
Open 9:30 a.m.–9:30 p.m.
Clothes created by Beijing designer and heavily influenced by hippy-chic. Customers can find A-line peasant skirts, Mandarin-collar tops, and wide-leg trousers that are simple and feminine. Most of the clothing and bags are 100 percent cotton and very affordable.

SHOPPING STREETS

Liulichang Xijie
Xuanwu District
Metro: Hepingmen
The place to go for souvenirs. The antiques stores and art galleries combine to demonstrate the flavor of China's pre-communist era. Here you'll find: old books, faux imperial porcelain, Cultural Revolution mementoes, silk, and carvings.

Dazhalan Jie
Off Qianmen Dajie
Metro: Qianmen
A chaotic lane stuffed full of silk shops, herbal medicine stores, and theaters. Also has an abundance of food and clothing specialists.

Silk Street
Corner of Jianguomen Dajie & Dongdaqiao Lu
Metro: Yonganli
Floor after floor of silk, clothing, shoes, jewelry, and more. All run by garrulous vendors who enjoy haggling.

Wangfujing Dajie
Dongcheng District
Metro: Wangfujing
This north–south walking street is found east of the Forbidden City, west of the Grand Hyatt. It is the home of designer and upscale shops.

ENTERTAINMENT
(sidebar: ENTERTAINMENT)

Even before the Olympics were granted to Beijing, the city was developing as the hottest art scene in Asia, and with money came international recognition. While the Beijing Opera and acrobatics have been around for generations, the clubs and music scene are recent arrivals. For specific information on performances and times check out *Beijing Talk, That's Beijing,* and *Time Out Beijing,* available free in many hotel lobbies, or visit www.thebeijinger.com.

BARS & NIGHTCLUBS

After decades of stringent Marxism and Maoism, Beijing is barging into the 21st century, and the bustling music scene—hip-hop, jazz, R&B, house, and techno—is just an indication of the dramatic changes taking place around the city. Sample the new China at one of the many bars and clubs opening up all over the city.

For the latest news about happenings on the Beijing bar and club scene, visit Beijing Boyce (www.beijingboyce.com), a blog written by one of Beijing's most knowledgeable bar hounds.

Bar Blu
4/F Tongli Studio
Sanlitun Beilu
Chaoyang District
Tel 010/6416 7567
Bus: Sanlitun
Bar Blu has a very nice outdoor terrace.

Bed Tapas & Bar (Chuang Ba)
17 Zhangwang Hutong
Jiu Gulou Dajie
Dongcheng District
Tel 010/8400 1554
Metro: Gulou Dajie
At the minimalist but chic Bed Bar, take your drinks lying down on one of the Qing-style opium beds scattered around the place. The simple menu includes tapas and Asian snacks. House DJs play underground techno and house music on the weekends.

Centro
1/F Beijing Kerry Centre
1 Guanghua Lu
Xuanwu District
Tel 010/6561 8833 ext. 42
Metro: Guomao
Bus: Guanghua Lu
Who says hotel lobby bars are boring? Sleek and chic Centro is one the best and most polished bars in Beijing. The place is large, well designed, and comfortable, but don't plan on having a business meeting here; the live jazz music may be too loud.

China Doll (Zhongguo Wawa)
2/F Tongli Studio
Sanlitun Beilu
Chaoyang District
Tel 010/6416 7968
Bus: Sanlitun
Spread over three floors of hip warehouse space, the sensually designed China Doll is a good place for late night drinking and dancing to music played by live DJs.

Face
26 Dongcao Yuan
Gongti Nanlu
Chaoyang District (behind Cervantes Institute)
Tel 010/ 6551 6788
Bus: Chaoyang Yiyuan/Shenlu Jie
A pricey but fun place for a drink before dinner, this bar stirs up memories of author Rudyard Kipling's Asia, with Chinese, Indian, and Southeast Asian art juxtaposed with colonial furniture. Enjoy your drinks along with a game of pool, or head onto the serene and intimate patio.

Lan
4/F LG Twin Towers
B12 Jianguomenwai Dajie
Chaoyang District
Tel 010/5109 6012
Metro: Yong'anli
Designed by trendy French designer Philippe Starck, Beijing's hippest bar will make you feel like you've fallen down the rabbit hole. Lan offers a good selection of wines and an oyster bar, as well as DJs and live entertainment in the evenings. Try the Sichuan Mary cocktail.

Mix
Inside the Workers' Stadium North Gate
Chaoyang District
Tel 010/6530 2889
Bus: Gongren Tiyuchang
If you want to mingle with Chinese bargoers, then the newly redesigned Mix—with its red glowing exterior—is the place to go. There are couches upstairs, while downstairs international DJs spin the latest hip-hop and R&B. On weekends you may have to squeeze your way onto the dance floor. The entrance fee Sunday through Thursday is 30RMB ($4); Friday and Saturday it's 50RMB ($7).

Pass By Bar (Guoke)
108 Nan Luogu Xiang
Dongcheng District
Tel 010/8403 8004
Bus: Di'anmen/Nan Luogu Xiang
Popular with the expat crowd, this rustic courtyard venue made Nan Luogu Xiang famous and spearheaded the transformation of this once sleepy street into Beijing's hippest (see p. 92). A great place for meeting friends, the laid-back Pass By Bar is decorated with Tibetan handicrafts and photographs taken by the owner.

Q Bar
Top Floor, Eastern Inn Hotel
6 Baijiazhuang Lu
Chaoyang District
Tel 010/6595 9239
Bus: Zhongfangjie
Q Bar is especially famous for its mixed drinks, which are poured by two of Sanlitun's most experienced bartenders and said to be the best in Beijing. Try a martini or margarita. In the warmer

months, relax on the rooftop patio.

The Rickshaw
Corner of Sanlitun Nanlu & Gongti Beilu
Tel 010/6500 4330
Bus: Sanlitun
The Rickshaw offers pizza, burritos, great wings, and cheap beer. Popular with all ages, it draws a younger crowd on weekends.

Souk
West Gate of Chaoyang Park (Opposite Kingda International Apartment)
Chaoyang District
Tel 010/6506 7309
This laid-back eatery cum bar offers inexpensive drinks as well as Mediterranean and Middle Eastern snacks. On Fridays enjoy cool acoustic sets by local bands.

Stone Boat Café
SE corner of Ritan Park
Tel 010/6501 9986
Bus: Ritan Lu
Once a teahouse, this Qing-dynasty stone boat has been reincarnated as a lakefront bar and café. Sit under the shade of the trees and contemplate the world. On weekends enjoy an interesting range of live music, including blues, jazz, R&B, and exotic Chinese folk.

Vics
Inside the Workers' Stadium North Gate,
Chaoyang District
Tel 010/6593 6215
Bus: Gongren Tiyuchang
Popular with 20- and 30-some-things, Vics is the place to dance in Beijing. It has two entrances, one leading to the very busy hip-hop and R&B area and the other to the techno and electronica space. Dance around the large circular bar, book a couch downstairs, or just sit upstairs and watch the goings-on down below.

The World of Suzie Wong
1A Nongzhanguan Nanlu
West Gate of Chaoyang Park
Chaoyang District
Tel 010/6500 3377
Named after the 1960 cinematic love story starring William Holden and Nancy Kuan, this is one of the few bars in Beijing with staying power. Suzie Wong's still attracts a loyal clientele with its 1930s atmosphere, antique decorations, opium beds, and outdoor patio. Entrance fee ($) on Wednesday (Ladies' Night) and ($$) on Friday and Saturday nights.

MUSIC

CD Jazz Café
16 Nongzhanguan Lu
Beside Agricultural Exhibition Center
Dong Sanhuan Beilu
Chaoyang District
Tel 010/6506 8288
Bus: Nongzhanguan
The small and intimate CD Jazz Café, one of the first jazz establishments in Beijing, is decorated with portraits of famous jazz musicians. Local bands play live jazz on weekends.

Concert Hall of Central Conservatory of Music (Zhongyang Yinyue Xueyuan Yinyue Ting)
43 Baojia Jie
Xicheng District
Tel 010/6642 5702
This simple and little-known music venue in the Central Conservatory of Music features international musicians, students and faculty, and the best local talent playing both Chinese and Western music.

D-22
242 Chengfu Lu
Haidian District
Tel 010/6265 3177
Bus: Lanqiying
If you're serious about music, head to D-22, a bar/club in the university district. Dedicated to identifying and supporting talented young musicians and

artists in Beijing, the club also invites leading experimental musicians from the United States, Japan, Europe, and elsewhere to perform and collaborate with local musicians.

East Shore Jazz Café
2/F Bldg. 2
Qianhai Nanyan
Di'anmenwai Dajie
Houhai
Xicheng District
Tel 010/8403 2131
Bus: Beihai Beimen
Located on the idyllic east shore of the Rear Lakes, this jazz club was established by Liu Yuan, the well-known local trumpeter who started the CD Jazz Café in the 1990s. Enjoy the panoramic views of the water just outside.

Forbidden City Concert Hall (Zhongshan Yinyue Tang)
Xi Chang'anjie
Inside Zhongshan Park
Dongcheng District
Tel 010/6559 8285
Metro: Tiananmen Xi
The Forbidden City Concert Hall features some of the best acoustics in China, and musicians who have played there include some of the biggest names in classical and traditional Chinese music. The hall, which has comfortable plush seating for 1,400 people, also has a good summer concert program.

CINEMAS

Beijing Wanda International Cinema Mall (Wanda Guoji Dianyingcheng)
Tower B
3/F 93 Jianguo Lu
Chaoyang District
Tel 010/5960 3399
Metro: Dawang Lu
Beijing's newest and most modern movie theater, the Wanda International shows the latest Chinese and Western blockbusters.

ENTERTAINMENT

Cherry Lane Movies
Inside Kent Centre
Anjialou
Chaoyang District
Tel 010/1350 1251 303
www.cherrylanemovies.com.cn

Every Saturday evening, Cherry Lane Movies shows classic Chinese films with English subtitles, with directors and actors occasionally taking questions from the audience after the show. Movies ($$) run at 8 p.m. on Fridays and Saturdays.

Star City (Xinshiji Yingyuan)
B1, Oriental Plaza
1 Dongchang'an Jie
Dongcheng District
Tel 010/8518 6778
Metro: Wangfujing

Star City, one of Beijing's plushest cinemas, shows popular Chinese and foreign commercial releases in their native languages. It also hosts occasional foreign film festivals.

SHOWS

Check out *The China Guide* (www.thechinaguide.com) for more details about the following shows, as well as discount tickets.

BEIJING OPERA
Performances of classic opera tales occur almost nightly. Frequently incomprehensible, but fun.

Chang'an Grand Theater (Chang'an Daxiyuan)
7 Jianguomen Neidajie
Dongcheng District
Tel 010/6510 1310
Metro: Jianguomen

This modern and comfortable opera theater stages colorful performances of Beijing opera, with English subtitles appearing to the side of the stage.

Huguang Guildhall (Huguang Huiguan Xilou)
3 Hufang Lu
Xuanwu District
Tel 010/6351 8284
www.beijinghuguang.com
Bus: Hufang Qiao

Recently restored to its original appearance, the Huguang Guildhall, which first opened its doors in 1807, is Beijing's oldest opera venue.

Lao She Teahouse (Lao She Chaguan)
3 Qianmen Xi Dajie
West of Qianmen
(South side of street)
Tel 010/6303 6830
Metro: Qianmen

This teahouse stages mini-performances of opera, martial arts, acrobatics, and comedy. Performances are held every day at 2:30 p.m. and 7:40 p.m. ($$–$$$$). The hall is named after the late Lao She, one of China's most popular contemporary authors, who often wrote about Beijing.

Liyuan
1/F Qianmen Jianguo Hotel
175 Yong'an Lu
Xuanwu District
Tel 010/6301 6688 ext. 8860
Bus: Hufang Qiao

Get to Liyuan early if you want to watch the actors put on their heavy makeup before the show. Snacks and tea are available during the performance, just as they were in the old days. English subtitles are flashed on the sides of the stage, and colorful brochures are also available in English.

Tianqiao Happy Teahouse (Tianqiao Le Chaguan)
1A Beiwei Lu
Xuanwu District
Tel 010/6304 0617

An old Beijing theater, Tianqiao Happy Teahouse puts on Beijing opera performances and acts by acrobats, jugglers, and contortionists.

ACROBATICS
The Chinese art of acrobatics dates back more than 2,500 years, making it one of China's oldest performance folk arts. This form of entertainment flourished during the Qing dynasty in the Tianqiao area of Beijing.

Chaoyang Theater (Chaoyang Juchang)
36 Dongsanhuan Beilu
Chaoyang District
Tel 010/6507 2421
Bus: Baijiazhuang

The Chaoyang Theater features traditional Chinese acrobatics and magic shows. There are two shows every night (at 5:15 p.m. and 7:15 p.m., $$$$–$$$$$).

The Red Theatre (Hong Juchang)
44 Xingfu Dajie
Chongwen District
Tel 010/6710 3671
Bus: Beijing Tiyuguan

The "Legend of Kung Fu" tells the story of a young boy and his dream of becoming a martial arts master. Rather than dialogue, this spectacular show uses a combination of martial arts, acrobatics, and dance. Supertext in English is projected about the stage; it will help you follow the plot. Daily shows at 5:15 p.m. and 7:30 p.m.

Tianqiao Acrobatic Theatre (Tianqiao Zaji Juchang)
95 Tianqiao Shichang Lu
East end of Beiwei Lu
Xuanwu District
Tel 010/6303 7449
Bus: Tianqiao

More than a hundred years old, this small theater gives the audience a chance to watch the acrobatics up close. Shows begin at 7:15 p.m. every day.

LANGUAGE GUIDE

USEFUL WORDS & PHRASES

PRONOUNS
I, me *wo*
He/she *ta*
We *women*
You *ni*
You (plural) *nimen*

CHITCHAT
Hello *ni hao*
Please *qing ni*
Thank-you *xie xie*
You're welcome *bukeqi*
Good-bye *zaijian*
Good night *zan'an*
Yes *shi*
No *bushi*
Excuse me *laojia*
Sorry *duibuqi*
OK *hao*
Where is...? *zai naili...?*
Here *zai zheli*
There *zai nali*
Open *kai*
Closed *guan*
What is your name? *Ni jiao shenme mingzi?/Nin guixing?*
My name is ... *Wo jiao...*
Do you speak English? *Ni hui shuo yingyu ma?*
I'm American *Wo shi Meiguo ren*
Canadian *Jia'nada ren*
British *Yingguo ren*
Australian *Audaliya ren*
I don't understand *Wo bu mingbai*
I don't know *Wo bu zhidao*
Please speak more slowly *Qing nin shuo man yi dian/Qing nin mandian jiang*
Can you help me? *Ni neng bangzhu wo ma?*
No problem *mei wenti*
That's it *Jiu shi zhe ge*
That's right *Dui le*
That's not right *Bu dui*
Let's go *Zou ba*
Where is the toilet? *Cesuo zai nar?*

DIRECTIONS
North *bei*
South *nan*
East *dong*
West *xi*
Avenue *dadao*

Road *lu*
Street *jie*
Temple *simiao/si/guan*
Main street *dajie*
Inside *limian*
Outside *waimian*
I want to go to... *Wo yao qu...*
Turn left *zuo guai*
Turn right *you guai*
Go straight *yizhi zou*
Stop here *Ting che*
How far is it? *Duo yuan?*

SHOPPING
Do you have...? *Ni you mei you...?*
I'd like/I want... *Wo yao/Wo xiang....*
How much is it? *Duoshao qian?*
It's too big *Tai da le*
It's too small *Tai xiao le*
Do you take credit cards? *Shou bu shou xinyongka?*

TIME
At what time? *shenme shihou?*
When? *senme shihou?*
What time is it? *Ji dian le?*
Today *jintian*
Yesterday *zuotian*
Tomorrow *mingtian*
This morning *jintian zaoshang*
This afternoon *jintian xiawu*
This evening *jintian wanshang*
Now *xianzai*
Later *yihui'r/shao hou*
Right away *mashang*

NUMBERS
zero *ling*
one *yi*
two *er*
two (when followed by a noun) *liang*
three *san*
four *si*
five *wu*
six *liu*
seven *qi*
eight *ba*
nine *jiu*
ten *shi*
11 *shiyi*
20 *ershi*
21 *ershiyi*
30 *sanshi*
100 *yi bai*
200 *liang bai*
1,000 *yi qian*

10,000 *yi wan*
1,000,000 *yi bai wan*

HOTEL
Do you have any rooms? *you mei you kong fangjian?*
Bed *chuangwei*
Check out *tuifang*
Deluxe room *haohuafang*
Double room *shuangrenfang*
Passport *huzhao*
Standard room *biaozhunfang*
Suite *taofang*
Toilet paper *weishengzhi*

GETTING AROUND
Airplane *feiji*
Airplane ticket *jipiao*
Airport *jichang*
Bicycle *zixingche*
Boarding card *dengjika*
Bus *gonggong qiche/bashi*
Car *qiche*
Map *ditu*
Seat *zuowei*
Subway *ditie*
Taxi *chuzu qiche*
Ticket *piao*
Train *huoche*
Give me a receipt, please. *Gei wo yi ge shoutiao, hao bu hao.*

EMERGENCY
Ambulance *jiuhuche*
Antibiotics *kangjunsu*
Doctor *yisheng*
Fire! *zhao huo le!*
Help! *jiuming a!*
Hospital *yiyuan*
Police *jingcha*
Public Security Bureau (PSB) *gonganju*
I feel ill *wo bu shufu*

POST OFFICE
Envelope *xinfeng*
Letter *xin*
Post office *youju*
Telephone *dianhua*

SIGHTSEEING
Lake *hu*
Mountain *shan*
River *he, jiang*

MENU READER

DINING OUT

Do you have ...? *Ni you mei you ...?*
Menu, please *qing gei wo caidan*
Do you have an English menu? *You mei you yingwen caidan?*
Bill, please *maidan/jiezhang*
I would like a receipt *Wo yao fapiao*
Do you take credit cards? *Shou bu shou xinyong ka?*
I want a cold beer *Wo yao liang de pijiu*
One more bowl of rice, please *Qing zai lai yiwan mifan*
I am a vegetarian *Wo chi su*
I only want vegetables *Wo zhi yao sucai*

MEAT, FOWL & FISH

Beef *niurou*
Chicken *jirou*
Crab *pangxie*
Duck *yarou*
Fish *yu*
Lobster *longxia*
Pork *zhurou*
Prawn *mingxia*
Shrimp *xia*

VEGETABLES

Broccoli *xilanhua*
Eggplant *qiezi*
Green peppers *qingjiao*
Mushrooms *xianggu*
Potatoes *tudou*
Spinach *bocai*
Tomatoes *xihongshi*

STAPLE ITEMS

Baked bread *shaobing*
Boiled dumplings *shuijiao*
Flat bread *laobing*
Fried noodles *chaomian*
Fried rice *chaofan*
Noodle soup *tangmian*
Scallion pancake *congyoubing*
Steamed bread *mantou*
Steamed rice *mifan*

FRUIT

Apple *pingguo*
Banana *xiangjiao*
Grape *putao*
Mango *mangguo*
Orange *chengzi*
Peach *taozi*
Pear *li*
Plum *lizi*

DRINKS

Beer *pijiu*
Tea *cha*
Water *shui*
Wine *putaojiu*

REGIONAL DISHES

BEIJING & NORTHEASTERN DISHES

Braised beef *jiang niurou*
Dumplings *shuijiao*
Earth's three fairies (consists of potato, eggplant, and green pepper) *di san xian*
Mung bean dredge *ma doufu*
Mustard *napa*
Nine twisted intestines *jiuzhuan dachang*
Noodles with sweet bean sauce *zhajiang mian*
Peking duck *Beijing kaoya*
Pot stickers *dalian huoshao*
Rinsed mutton hot pot *shuan yangrou*
Stewed pork with noodles *zhurou dun fentiao*
Turnover *jiemuo dun*

CANTONESE & CHAOZHOU DISHES

Beef in black pepper sauce *heijiao niuliu*
Poached Chinese kale *baizhuo jielan*
Spareribs in black bean sauce *chi zhi zheng paigu*
Steamed fish *qingzheng yu*
Sweet-and-sour pork *gulao rou*

DIM SUM DIANXIN

Barbecued pork buns *chashao bao*
Chicken feet in black bean sauce *fengzhua*
Pan-fried turnip *luobo gao*
Rice noodle rolls *changfen*
Steamed shrimp dumplings *xiajiao*
Steamed pork dumplings *shaomai*
Sticky rice and meat wrapped in lotus leaves *nuomi ji*
Taro croquette *yujiao*

HUNAN DISHES

Braised pork *hongshao rou*
Dried bean curd with celery *xianggan chao xiqin*
Farmer's pork with spicy chilies *nongjia xiaochao*
Smoked bean curd fried with cured bacon *xianggan chao larou*

SICHUAN DISHES

Boiled fish in fiery chilies *shuizhu yu*
Cellophane noodles with minced pork (ants crawling on the tree) *mayi shangshu*
Chicken with chilies *lazi ji*
Dry-fried stringbeans *ganbian sijidou*
Fish-fragrant eggplant *yuxiang qiezi*
Husband-and-wife meat platter *fuqi feipian*
Kung Pao chicken *gongbao jiding*
Pock-marked Chen's bean curd *mapo doufu*
Tea-smoked duck *zhangcha ya*
Twice-cooked pork *huiguo rou*

SHANGHAI, JIANGSU, & ZHEJIANG DISHES

Bean curd and crab casserole *xiefen doufu*
Beggar's chicken *jiaohua ji*
Braised bamboo shoots *youmen sun*
Braised gluten with shitake mushrooms *kaofu*
Dongpo's pork *dongpo rou*
Drunken chicken *zui ji*
Steamed buns *xiaolong bao*
Stuffed lotus root with glutinous rice *nuomi ou*

ILLUSTRATIONS CREDITS

All photographs are by Catherine Karnow unless otherwise noted below.

Cover: left, Gilles Sabrié; center, Visions of America/Joe Sohm/Getty Images; right, Peter Gridley/Getty Images; 28, Asian Art and Archeology Inc./CORBIS; 29, Archivio Iconografico, SA/CORBIS; 33, Topical Press Agency/Getty Images; 34, NGS Archives; 35, New China Pictures/Magnum Photos; 36, Underwood & Underwood/CORBIS; 38-39, Rene Burr/Magnum Photos; 48-49, Chang W. Lee/New York Times; 57 (up), Robert Eric/CORBIS SYGMA; 57 (low), Bai Xiao Yan/Sony Pictures Classics/Bureau L.A. Collection/ CORBIS; 60, Frederic J. Brown/AFP/Getty Images; 61, Cancan Chu/Getty Images; 106, Teresa Mooney; 119, Maltings Partnership; 121, Michael Yamashita; 150-151, Frederic J. Brown/AFP/Getty Images; 156, Liu Liqun/CORBIS; 160, Andy Nelson/The Christian Science Monitor/Getty Images; 161, China Photos/Getty Images; 171, Michael Reynolds/epa/CORBIS; 173, Guang Niu/Getty Images; 180, Liu Liqun/ChinaStock; 181, Teh Eng Koon/AFP/Getty Images; 187, Guang Niu/Getty Images; 195, Feng Li/Getty Images; 196, Reuters/CORBIS; 197, Courtesy of Commune by the Great Wall; 203, Andrew Gough/Planet Wide Photo/photographersdirect.com; 208, Elisabeth Rosenthal/New York Times; 219, Nathan McMahon/drr.net; 220, Michael Yamashita; 221, Wilson Chu/Reuters/ CORBIS; 222, DK Limited/CORBIS; 223, Teresa Mooney; 226, Panorama Media (Beijing) Ltd./Alamy Ltd; 227, Teresa Mooney; 229, Teresa Mooney; 230, Pixtal/age footstock.

Founded in 1888, the National Geographic Society is one of the largest nonprofit scientific and educational organizations in the world. It reaches more than 285 million people world-wide each month through its official journal, NATIONAL GEOGRAPHIC, and its four other magazines; the National Geographic Channel; television documentaries; radio programs; films; books; videos and DVDs; maps; and interactive media. National Geographic has funded more than 8,000 scientific research projects and supports an education program combating geographic illiteracy.

For more information, please call 1-800-NGS LINE (647-5463) or write to the following address: National Geographic Society 1145 17th Street N.W. Washington, D.C. 20036-4688 U.S.A.

For information about special discounts for bulk purchases, please contact National Geographic Books Special Sales: ngspecsales@ngs.org.

For rights or permissions inquiries, please contact National Geographic Books Subsidiary Rights: ngbookrights@ngs.org.

Order *Traveler* today, the magazine that travelers trust. In the U.S. and Canada call 1-800-NGS-LINE; 813-979-6845 for international. Or visit online at www.national geographic.com/traveler and click on SUBSCRIBE.

Travel the world with National Geographic Experts: www.national geographic.com/ngexpeditions

Printed in Spain

National Geographic Traveler: Beijing
by Paul Mooney

Published by the National Geographic Society

John M. Fahey, Jr., *President and Chief Executive Officer*
Gilbert M. Grosvenor, *Chairman of the Board*
Tim T. Kelly, *President, Global Media Group*
Nina D. Hoffman, *Executive Vice President;*
  President, Book Publishing Group

Prepared by the Book Division
Kevin Mulroy, *Senior Vice President and Publisher*
Leah Bendavid-Val, *Director of Photography Publishing and Illustrations*
Marianne R. Koszorus, *Director of Design*
Elizabeth Newhouse, *Director of Travel Publishing*
Carl Mehler, *Director of Maps*
Cinda Rose, *Art Director*
Barbara A. Noe, *Series Editor*

Staff for this book
Caroline Hickey, *Project Manager*
Kay Kobor Hankins, *Designer*
Jane Menyawi, *Illustrations Editor*
Mary Stephanos, *Text Editor*
Chaoyang Man, *Researcher*
Lise Sajewski, Jane Sunderland *Editorial Consultants*
Steven D. Gardner, Michael McNey, and Mapping Specialists,
  Map Edit, Research, and Production
Richard S. Wain, *Production Manager*
Marshall Kiker, *Illustrations Specialist*
Connie D. Binder, *Indexer*
Tim Stoutzenberger, Kara Walker *Contributors*

Jennifer A. Thornton, *Managing Editor*
R. Gary Colbert, *Production Director*

Artwork by Maltings Partnership, Derby, England (pp. 68–69 & 119).

National Geographic Traveler: Beijing

ISBN: 978-1-4262-0231-5

Printed and Bound by Mondadori Printing, Toledo, Spain. Color separations by Quad Graphics, Alexandria, VA.

The information in this book has been carefully checked and to the best of our knowledge is accurate. However, details are subject to change, and the National Geographic Society cannot be responsible for such changes, or for errors or omissions. Assessments of sites, hotels, and restaurants are based on the author's subjective opinions, which do not necessarily reflect the publisher's opinion. The publisher cannot be responsible for any consequences arising from the use of this book.

Visit us online at www.nationalgeographic.com/books.

NATIONAL GEOGRAPHIC
TRAVELER
A Century of Travel Expertise in Every Guide

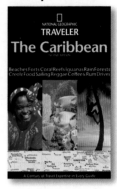

AVAILABLE WHEREVER BOOKS ARE SOLD